English L2 Reading

Getting to the Bottom

Second Edition

ESL & Applied Linguistics Professional Series

Eli Hinkel, Series Editor

For a complete list of titles in LEA's ESL & Applied Linguistics Professional Series, please contact Lawrence Erlbaum Associates, Publishers, at www.erlbaum.com

English L2 Reading

Getting to the Bottom

Second Edition

Barbara M. Birch
California State University-Fresno

Routledge
Taylor & Francis Group
New York   London

First published by Lawrence Erlbaum Associates, Inc., Publishers
10 Industrial Avenue
Mahwah, New Jersey 07430
www.erlbaum.com

Reprinted 2008 by Routledge

Routledge
Taylor & Francis Group
270 Madison Avenue
New York, NY 10016

Routledge
Taylor & Francis Group
2 Park Square
Milton Park, Abingdon
Oxon OX14 4RN

Cover design by Tomai Maridou

Library of Congress Cataloging-in-Publication Data

Birch, Barbara M. English L2 reading : getting to the bottom /
    Barbara M. Birch.—2nd ed.
        p.   cm. — (ESL and applied linguistics professional series)
        Includes bibliographical references and index.
ISBN 0-8058-5929-2 (pbk. : alk. paper)
ISBN 1-4106-1493-X (e book)
1. English language—Study and teaching—Foreign speakers.
    2. Second language acquisition. 3. Reading comprehen-
    sion. I. Title. II. Series.
PE1128.A2B497   2006
428.0071—dc22   2006007163
                                                     CIP

Printed in the United States of America
10   9   8   7   6   5

To Jim, Elena, Susan, and Hannah

Contents

Preface

CHANGES IN THE SECOND EDITION

This edition is intended to be a more reader-friendly version of the first edition. The content of each chapter is much the same, but the organization is made clearer for the student and the few errors are corrected. Specific changes in this edition include:

- Expansion in chapter 2 on alphabets, writing systems, and a brief history of written English and spelling;
- Extended discussion in chapter 3 of the cognition of written language and reading transfer;
- Addition of phonemic, vocal, subvocal, and articulatory development and L2 reading processing in chapter 4, as well as instructional activities and strategies for teaching these skills to L2 readers;
- Elaboration of graphs and graphemes in chapter 5, including discussion of developing graphemic knowledge, processing strategies and their instructional application, and new sections on reading speed, pattern recognition, and word recognition;
- Development of the probabilistic section in chapter 6, particularly the probabilities in context of L2 reading;
- Updated information the topic of brain activation studies, which raise a lot of questions; and
- New treatment of the topic of reading fluency, added in response to requests from many readers of the first edition. Good silent and oral reading fluency depends on well-elaborated cognitive and linguistic knowledge structures and well-functioning high-level and low-level processing strategies. Fluency is the goal we would most want our ESL and EFL learners to achieve.

OVERVIEW

An ideology is more than just a theory or a practice. It is a complex body of interrelated concepts, opinions, and assumptions about an area of culture. Different ideologies are the foundations for different social positions. Nowhere is this truer than in education and, in education, nowhere is this truer than in the area of reading research and methodology. One ideology has dominated second language reading for quite a while. This ideology, usually called whole language, has many ideas and practices that have stood the test of time in research and in the classroom. Many English as a Second Language (ESL) and English as a Foreign Language (EFL) readers benefit greatly from this instruction, which generally takes a top-down view of reading, because students learn to take full advantage of their cognitive abilities to comprehend the text.

This book strongly supports the whole language ideology in general. The materials are exciting and interesting, and the methods are inviting and creative. In the hands of an expert teacher, students learn useful reading and vocabulary acquisition strategies. They learn about the importance of cultural knowledge and the characteristics of textual discourse, such as coherence and cohesion. Students learn to enjoy and appreciate reading and writing.

But in recent years, whole language has been characterized as incomplete, in that it seems to deemphasize certain aspects of reading. A complete, balanced reading ideology (a "truly whole" language ideology) should be big enough to embrace all reading theories and practices. In particular, it should be able to accommodate those researchers and teachers who find that attention to the details of language can also help students learn to read better. This book takes the position that supplementing whole language with a bottom-up focus can strengthen our approach, making it truly holistic.

In fact, research into native English reading processes has, in recent decades, included both the top and the bottom of the reading process; that is, higher level cognitive knowledge and abilities have been examined, but so have low-level linguistic knowledge and abilities. This is producing a more accurate and well-rounded view of reading and how English-speaking children become successful readers. High level reading and general learning strategies have fortunately been topics of research in the English as a second/foreign language field as well, to the benefit of teachers and learners alike. We now know more about English L2 reading than ever before. However, research interest in low-level linguistic knowledge and processing strategies has lagged somewhat behind interest in the top-level strategies. It is hoped that this book will stimulate more ESL/EFL reading researchers to join those who are exploring this relatively uncharted "ocean" with vigor, persistence, and imagination.

In general terms, this book is intended for all ESL and EFL practitioners interested in or involved in teaching reading. It is relevant to those who are teaching illiterate people to read in English or to those whose students already know how to read in their native language. Taking a fairly theory-neutral information-processing perspective for the sake of the organization and presentation of complex material, the book is relevant to reading researchers, curriculum designers, and materials writers. It is for teachers-in-training as well.

Chapter 1 introduces several of the organizing threads to be followed throughout the book. The metaphor of the psycholinguistic guessing game has been a common one since the 1970s, but in this chapter, reading is described as an interactive (top-down and bottom-up) process; this model is expanded on in each subsequent chapter. The psycholinguistic guessing game metaphor is critiqued and a new metaphor is suggested: that the reading process is an expert decision-making system based on a knowledge base (world and language) and high- and low-level processing strategies. Early developmental stages of native English reading are described in this chapter that will be applied to ESL and EFL learners in later chapters.

In chapter 2, after a discussion of various common writing systems in the world and their differences, I make a case that the second language reading literature generally disregards the importance of the L1 writing system. Chapter 3 questions the idea that low-level reading processes in L1 and L2 are the same and begins another organizing thread: that knowledge and processing strategies develop in response to L1, that they might transfer negatively to L2, and that strategies optimal for reading English may not develop without direct instruction. This point is further illustrated by four sample case histories that are followed throughout the remaining chapters: MariCarmen, a Spanish reader; Despina, a Greek reader; Mohammed, an Arabic reader, and Ho, a Chinese reader.

Chapter 4 asks about the relationship between pronunciation and reading, starting with a look at English consonant and vowel sounds and some contrasts with other languages and a discussion of some important concepts in linguistics. The idea that accurate pronunciation and reading are directly related is discarded in favor of the idea that accurate listening comprehension is more directly related to reading. From this chapter on, each chapter contains a section titled "Spotlight on Teaching," which gives some ideas about how the main concepts can be presented to ESL and EFL students and practiced. In this chapter, perception and discrimination activities that lead to phonemic awareness are the focus.

Chapter 5 argues in favor of a re-understanding of the common idea that readers just sample the text. This chapter begins with a look at the concept of the grapheme (as opposed to "letter") and a discussion of English graphemes. Summarizing research that shows that readers read fairly carefully and don't just sample the text, the chapter goes on to discuss expert graphic identification strategies in English and, in the "Spotlight on Teaching," suggest that teachers use direct instruction in grapheme-to-phoneme correspondences to help ESL and EFL learners.

Chapter 6 disputes an idea that is pervasive within the whole of the English-speaking culture throughout the world: that English spelling is chaotic. When carried to the classroom, this idea often means that teachers don't teach about our writing system because they believe that the system is so complex students cannot grasp it or take advantage of it. If they do teach it, it is often with the negative idea that it doesn't make any sense. In fact, our English writing does have a system.

Chapter 7 describes several approaches to phonics instruction in English L1 after outlining the strategies that native English-speaking readers develop to handle English vowels, because the correspondence between grapheme and phoneme is very predictable. Recent research from L1 English reading shows that children run through different processing strategies until they ultimately settle on the best strategies for English: the use of onsets and rimes and analogy to known spelling patterns. This is an example of cognitive restructuring of knowledge and suggests methodologies that are quite different from traditional views of "phonics," which should be discarded once and for all.

Chapter 8 revisits the theme that English spelling is systematic if you know what to look for. The chapter examines morphological processes in English, morphology in other languages, phonological processes in English words triggered by derivational changes (as in sane, sanity), and spelling difficulties that stem from them. English writing again is shown to follow fairly consistent morphophonemic spelling rules. There is evidence that readers use different processing strategies to deal with morphological information in reading L1 and L2. Implications for ESL and EFL pedagogy are presented in "Spotlight on Teaching."

Chapter 9 addresses an assumption that teachers sometimes take for granted: that skipping words you don't know is a good strategy for the ESL and EFL reader. This chapter is an exploration of word learning and word recognition, suggesting that the only way that readers can build up an ample mental lexicon in L2 is if they take responsibility for their learning and habitually use the best vocabulary acquisition strategies we know. This is the only way for the mental lexicon and semantic memory to grow and for the reader to improve in automaticity. Chapter 10 is an epilogue that summarizes the book.

In general, this book fits within the growing emphasis on accuracy of form (along with meaning and use) as an important component of communication. In writing this book, I hope to empower teachers to become better able to address specific student needs while maintaining their whole language methodology. I hope to stimulate interest among reading researchers in the study of low-level reading strategies. Although this book is focused exclusively on English reading instruction for the nonnative speaker, it can be of interest to anyone interested in second language reading instruction.

ACKNOWLEDGMENTS

I acknowledge the plucky and intrepid reviewers, including Patrick Kennell of Florida State University and Bertha Perez of The University of Texas at San Antonio, whose perceptive comments have made this manuscript what it is today. I am grateful for the very helpful suggestions made by Naomi Silverman of Lawrence Erlbaum Associates and Eli Hinkel, Series Editor for the ESL & Applied Linguistics series, and for the assistance of LEA Associate Editor, Erica Kica. I would like to remember Dr. David Eskey, who was the inspiration for this book.

I am also indebted to all of my colleagues in the Department of Linguistics at California State University-Fresno for their encouragement and help and for providing me with the opportunity to teach Linguistics and Reading, which was where this manuscript began 10 years ago. I must also thank those students of Linguistics 132 and graduate students who read earlier versions, gave insightful feedback, and helped me pilot materials. I am grateful for a sabbatical in 1998, during which I edited an earlier draft of this book and began the process of finding a publisher. Any mistakes are, of course, my own.

1

The Expert Decision Maker

Prereading Questions. Before you read, think about and discuss the following:

1. How do people read? What happens in your mind when you are reading?
2. Do you remember learning to read as a child? Was it a positive or negative experience?
3. Do you enjoy reading now? Why or why not?
4. What do you have to read? What do you like to read? How are these reading experiences different for you?
5. If you are a nonnative speaker of English, do you like to read English as well as your native language? Why or why not?
6. What problems do you have with reading? What is the cause of the problems?

Study Guide Questions: Answer these questions while or after reading the chapter:

1. What are the various metaphors that help us understand the reading process?
2. Explain the components of Figure 1.1.
3. Explain the components of Figure 1.2.
4. What are the developmental stages in reading?
5. What special considerations make English reading difficult for English as a second language (ESL) and English as a foreign language (EFL) learners?

1

For many of us, when we sit down to read something, our eyes move across and down the page, understanding the message that the text contains without apparent effort. Such an unconscious process seems simple, but in fact, like many of the other mental activities we do, reading is complex when examined in all its detail. It is complicated because it involves a great deal of precise knowledge that must be acquired or learned and many processing strategies that must be practiced until they are automatic.

This chapter deals with two introductory topics so that we can begin to understand the reading process. First, we usually use metaphors to think about the reading process because a complex process like reading seems simpler if it is compared to something we already have some knowledge of. Metaphors (or models, as they are sometimes called) become pedagogical tools, convenient fictions, mere analogies that permit explanation of some of the complexities of reading in a systematic way. Some metaphors provide a coherent framework on which to arrange the linguistic information that expert readers need to acquire and that teachers need to know. This chapter discusses the pros and cons of three such metaphors; two will serve as the organizational infrastructure of this book, and one will be discarded.

Second, we explore the stages that English-speaking children go through as they learn to read. This is a starting point for examining English L2 (English as a second or foreign language) reading. English L2 readers face some special circumstances when they learn to read English: interference from their first language, incomplete knowledge of English, and missing processing strategies for English.

THREE METAPHORS OF THE READING PROCESS

A complex process like reading is often understood by comparing it to something else that we know more about or that we can describe better. Metaphors/models are simply ways to organize and present graphically all the information we know about the process. However, some metaphors are more helpful than others. It is useful to think of reading first as a kind of information processor and second as a kind of expert decision maker, because those concepts capture some essential characteristics of the reading process. It is less helpful to think of reading as a psycholinguistic guessing game, for reasons we show very soon.

The Interactive Information Processing Metaphor

For instance, we can create a model of a hypothetical information processor in which the different parts and procedures illustrate the different skills of reading and their interaction. There are two basic parts to the processor, a knowledge storage area and a more dynamic processing component that uses strategies to cope with the text. Such a model might look like Figure 1.1.

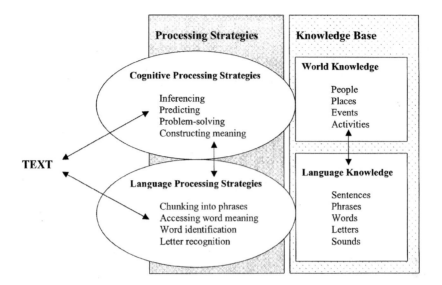

Figure 1.1   A hypothetical model of the reading process with some sample processing strategies and types of knowledge.

A Knowledge Base and Processing Strategies.

A very simplified model of the reading process (Adams, 1990; Crowder & Wagner, 1992; Perfetti, Liu, & Tan, 2002; Underwood & Batt, 1996) would include storage for general and specific knowledge in long-term memory. The knowledge is organized into memory structures like images, networks, schemas, and frames, which are discussed in later chapters. The knowledge base is not sufficient for reading by itself, because it cannot interact directly with the text without some kind of processing mechanism. The processing component consists of a variety of strategies that the reader has acquired or learned. The strategies allow the reader to take the text as a source of information and, drawing on the knowledge base as another source, make sense of what is on the printed page. The processing strategies can be optionally consciously or unconsciously applied; that is, they can operate automatically beneath the level of our awareness or they can kick in selectively because of our attention to something we perceive.

The Top and the Bottom of the Model.   The processor uses cultural and world knowledge and generalized cognitive processing strategies at the "top" to construct a meaning for big pieces of text, like sentences, paragraphs, or stories. Using these high-level processing strategies the reader makes predictions about what the text is going to be like, inferences about the motivations of the characters, decisions about how certain events are related in the reading, and the like. The bottom of the model contains precise bits of knowledge about language and writing and processing strategies that permit our minds to turn squiggles on the page into meaningful symbols.

In this model of the reading process, the processing strategies work together in parallel, that is, at the same time, with access to the knowledge base to permit the reader to construct ideas and meaning from the printed text. When someone is reading, they need both the information flowing upward from the bottom to the top and the information flowing downward from the top to the bottom in order to understand the meaning successfully. For example, our perception and recognition of letters leads to our recognition of words, from which we construct meanings. In the other direction, contextual information, inferences, and world knowledge can influence the processing strategies at lower levels. World knowledge can affect our expectations about words and meaning, which can allow us to recognize some words faster than others or understand some meanings faster than others (see Aebersold & Field, 1997, Day & Bamford, 1998, Urquhart & Weir, 1998, and other recent reading theory texts for similar views).

Although researchers now know that information flows in both directions while we are reading, there is still some debate among teachers and teacher-trainers about which is the most important in successful reading. Some emphasize the top-down flow of information, sometimes to the neglect of the bottom levels of processing. For example, Coady (1979, p. 11) said, "The teacher should always put primary emphasis in reading instruction on comprehension strategies...too much emphasis on concrete processing strategies such as letter–sound correspondences can leave the student with a poor priority of strategies." This point of view is generally associated with an approach called whole language instruction. Others place more importance on bottom-up flow of information, to the detriment of comprehension of meaning and world knowledge. This is most often called the phonics approach to reading.

A Balanced Approach.   In this book, a balanced or integrated approach is adopted. Here, we take the perspective that neither direction of information flow is more important than the other because the successful reader must be adept at both bottom-up and top-down processing (Nunes, 1999). Instead of focusing on bottom-up processing to the exclusion of top-down or vice versa, an approach that emphasizes the interactive nature of reading is chosen. Indeed, reading is interactive in three ways:

- The different processing strategies, both top and bottom, along with the knowledge base, interact with each other to accomplish the reading.
- The reader's mind interacts with the written text so that the reader can understand the message.

- The reader interacts indirectly with the writer of the text across time and space because it is the writer who is communicating information to the reader, but it is the reader who must grasp the information from the writer.

After describing an interactive approach to reading (much like the one advocated here) in Eskey (1988), Eskey said, "Despite the emergence of interactive models, I am concerned that much of the second language reading literature continues to exhibit a strongly top-down bias." In a footnote, he noted the preponderance of research into top-down reading, concluding, "This research has resulted in many useful insights, but the lack of attention to decoding problems has, I think, produced a somewhat distorted picture of the true range of problems second language readers face." (p. 95). He went on to say the following:

> In practical terms, my concern is thus to keep the language in the teaching of second language reading. That may not sound very controversial, but I think that in promoting higher-level strategies—like predicting from context or the use of schemata and other kinds of background knowledge—some researchers have been sending a message to teachers that the teaching of reading to second language readers is mostly just a matter of providing them with the right background knowledge for any texts they must read, and encouraging them to make full use of that knowledge in decoding those texts. Though that is certainly important, it is also, I think, potentially misleading as a total approach....We must not, I believe, lose sight of the fact that language is a major problem in second language reading, and that even educated guessing at meaning is not a substitute for accurate decoding. (p. 97)

Eskey's observation is still true today. Many recent texts on second-language reading recognize the importance of the bottom of the reading processing model, but their attention remains firmly on the top (Aebersold & Field, 1997; Day & Bamford, 1998; and others). Wallace (1992), for example, after a very brief discussion of bottom-up processing in reading, said the following:

> Eskey (1988) for instance, claims that second language readers need to attend more to "bottom-up" features than do first language readers. Eskey's view is based on the incontrovertible fact that the former will have weaker linguistic competence than the latter and will therefore have less ability to draw on the range of cues—both within and external to the text—which are available to readers in a first language. One response to this situation would be, not to encourage different reader strategies for second language readers, but to ensure that text, context, and reading task give maximum support to the second language learner's current linguistic and schematic knowledge. (pp. 42–43)

Wallace is correct in advocating maximum support for ESL and EFL readers' higher level processing to supplement deficiencies at the lower level
with language. This has been the foundation of second-language reading
instruction for many years, and should not be discarded. But teachers can,
in addition, help students acquire different, more efficient, bottom-up
reading strategies, if they know what to do. That's why, in this book, we focus on the bottom part of the reading model, which we might imagine to
look like Figure 1.2.

    Bottom-Level Strategies.   *Phonological strategies* allow us to recognize
the sounds of our language as we hear speech. As we show later, phonological
information is used in some word recognition strategies, especially in lan-

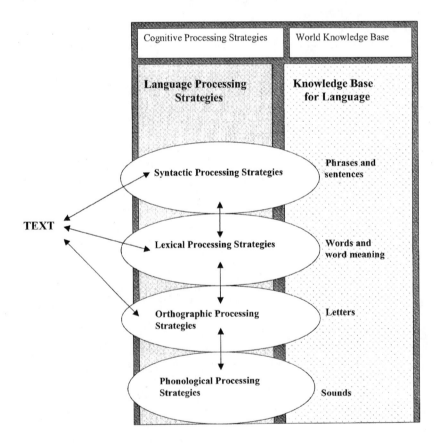

Figure 1.2 A hypothetical model of the bottom of the reading processor,
showing how processing strategies mediate between language knowledge and
the text to create a basic understanding of the text.

guages which use an alphabet for writing. *Orthographic strategies* allow us to recognize the letter shapes of our alphabet (often called *decoding*), and match them with the sounds of our language, forming a visual/auditory image of a word (often called *recoding*) in our mind. *Lexical strategies* are the processing strategies we use to recognize words and access word meaning. For frequent words, it is possible that we use a decoded visual image with a direct connection to meaning. For less frequent words we may use a recoded visual/auditory image to recognize the word through sound first and then access the meaning secondarily. Lexical strategies also help us to deal with unknown words. *Syntactic strategies* help us to unconsciously arrange the recognized words accurately and quickly into phrases and sentences, so that the meaning can be constructed at the top of the reading process. The different strategies each do their own specialized work in coordination with the others so that we can read successfully. Each of these sections of the model (except for syntactic strategies, which are omitted from this treatment due to space limitations) is discussed in detail in later chapters.

The Psycholinguistic Guessing Game Metaphor

The interactive model described earlier is complex and somewhat different from another metaphor that has helped us to understand reading in the past: Reading is a "psycholinguistic guessing game." The metaphor rests on the notion that readers use a small numbers of textual cues and their own knowledge to "guess" what the text message is. This metaphor (Eskey, 1979, p. 69) has become commonplace for describing second language reading since Goodman coined it in 1967, and it is still in use today (Underwood & Batt, 1996, pp. 78–79). Bernhardt (1991) put it the following way:

> One of the major findings in this examination of the literature is the dominance of the psycholinguistic model exemplified by the writings of Goodman (1968) and Smith (1971). It is remarkable that an area of disciplined inquiry such as reading in a second language could be so dominated by one conceptual framework. There may be two explanations for this phenomenon. It may be that academicians in this field have agreed that the psycholinguistic framework provides the most viable explanation of reading as a second language. Another is that there is a basic lack of awareness and perception of the capabilities of models other than those of Goodman (1968) and Smith (1971) to explain second language reading phenomena. Since unanimity is rare in any academic area, the latter explanation is more convincing. (p. 22)

In spite of its longevity, the "psycholinguistic guessing game" metaphor has certain limitations. One problem with it is that it oversimplifies many people's idea of the reading process, something that Goodman never intended. Guessing is a complex cognitive process of weighing the importance of different information to come up with the best answer; it is not like flipping a coin. Although much of this processing is unconscious, it is not easy, and correct guessing relies on having reasonably correct information to work with. Another consequence of the metaphor is that instruction about sounds and letters is sometimes neglected because, as teachers have been overheard to say, "Readers are just guessing anyway."

Goodbye to Guessing Games. There are two reasons why it's time to discard the "reading-as-a-psycholinguistic-guessing-game" metaphor, especially for ESL and EFL learners. Many learners learn to read English without much direct instruction in decoding or recoding the letters. They learn unconsciously by themselves the relationship between letters and sounds and can successfully generalize this information to apply it to new words they are confronted with. However, not all ESL and EFL learners become expert readers; they don't seem to catch on to the relationship between letters and sounds, or they are unable to extend their knowledge to words that they haven't seen before. Some ESL and EFL readers seem to get stuck in an early stage of reading development and they need direct intervention in order to move on. Some readers advance as far as they can with top-down reading strategies and then can go no further.

At the same time that teachers have noticed that not all ESL and EFL learners learn to read without direct instruction in decoding/recoding, researchers have become aware of the great complexity of the reading process, even at the lowest levels. They have learned that phonological knowledge is crucial for fluent alphabetic reading with comprehension, even though we are not consciously aware of it. They have learned that processing strategies are language dependent; that is, they differ from writing system to writing system. They have learned that such processing strategies can transfer from first language (L1) to second language (L2), and thus have positive or negative consequences for readers.

It is past time to discard this metaphor of the reading process as inaccurate for ESL and EFL readers. I suggest another metaphor for understanding reading, building on the interactive information processing model discussed earlier. Our model of the reading process is actually an expert decision-making system, a highly sophisticated computing system that allows good readers to make split-second decisions about what they are reading in such an effortless and unconscious way that they don't even realize they are doing anything special. It is only in this extremely specialized sense that reading is a guessing game.

The Expert Decision Maker Metaphor

Teachers and teacher-trainers should begin to think of reading as an expert decision-making system such as Medsker and Liebowitz (1994) describe. An expert system is an artificial intelligence application that takes information processing one step further to emulate the abilities of a human expert. (I appreciate the irony of using a computer model that is designed to emulate human processing as a metaphor for understanding human processing.) An *expert system* is a computer program that uses both symbolic processing strategies and a large number of facts and several hundred rules or heuristics stored in the knowledge base to make quick decisions about something that is perceived. *Heuristics* are rules of thumb learned either directly (i.e., through instruction) or indirectly (i.e., through experience) that guide the expert decision maker to its decisions. Expert systems are appropriate when there is consensus on the proper solution or decision, when decisions sometimes need to be based on incomplete or uncertain information, and when incorrect or nonoptimal results can be tolerated.

In other words, in reading, decoding/recoding is the processing of written symbols with strategies based on facts, patterns, and heuristics. There is consensus about the proper outcome in low-level processing because we agree (barring dialect differences) on the relationship between the written symbols and what they represent: letters and sounds, sequences of letters and sequences of sounds, written words and spoken words, and so on. In higher level processing of texts, there is also general consensus on what specific passages are supposed to mean, but they can be subject to individual interpretation at times. For example, in poetry, we may agree that certain words have a particular meaning or we may think that the words are being used in an individual way. The overall meaning of the poem may be accepted by many, but individual readers may also find different meanings.

In addition, in reading, incorrect outcomes, like misread letters or misinterpreted words, can be tolerated in specific tasks because there is quite a bit of redundancy in reading. Words and meanings are repeated several times, so the reader has ample chance to correct an incorrect outcome. Also, in reading, the reader's eye can travel backward on the page, going back to check earlier outcomes if there is some conflicting information that the reader detects. The information that the reader has is often incomplete or uncertain; certainly this is true in reading a stranger's handwriting, but it is also true in reading anything that might have errors, incompleteness, or ambiguities.

In accepting the metaphor of the reader as an expert decision maker, we are fine-tuning the information-processing model. We are saying that good readers effectively use their high- and low-level knowledge and processing strategies to assign meaning to letters, words, sentences, paragraphs, and so on by making informed decisions at strategic points. How does a reader become an expert decision maker?

THE DEVELOPMENT OF LOW-LEVEL READING

Both the interactive information-processing and the expert decision-making metaphors suggest that there are important bits of linguistic knowledge and different strategies that must be developed in order for a reader to become expert at reading an alphabetic system. Booth and Burman (2005) report experiments that show that as English-speaking children progress in reading they rely less on meaning for word recognition and more on the interaction of orthography and phonology. This recent evidence confirms earlier, more impressionistic, ideas of the development of reading.

Stages in English L1 Reading Development

Chall (1983) is still the best (and the original) source for a description of the five general developmental steps in learning to read English.

Stage 0.   Chall's first stage of reading is numbered as 0 because it is actually a prereading stage. It describes the optimal prereaders who can name and recognize the letters of the alphabet and write their own names. They can hold a book right side up and pretend to read it by remembering the words and looking at the pictures. They can use clues in the pictures to "guess" what the story is. If prereaders pretend to read a book without knowing how to read, they are relying on top-level abilities to get the information from the book: memory, guessing from context, and knowledge of the world. For this reason, Chall suggests that optimal prereaders seem to be using a top-down reading style.

Stage 1.   This is the beginning of reading, when readers begin to learn to decode/recode the written marks on the page and associate them with sounds, syllables, and words. Stage 1 readers learn the alphabetic principle: that the letters on the page "mean" the sounds of the language. They become preoccupied with learning the lower level skills of orthographic and phonological processing, and this preoccupation is seen in beginning readers' preference for reading out loud. They are linking the written symbols (letters) with the spoken symbols (sounds), and this linkage must become automatic in order for fluent silent reading to develop. As orthographic and phonological processing strategies become more automatic, they do not become less important, but they do become less perceptible. The strategies become so inaccessible to perception that we don't always realize that we are doing them while we are reading.

Stage 2.   In this stage, successful readers' abilities to decode/recode the written medium improve substantially. Automatic, fluent, and mainly unconscious bottom-up processing gives these readers the needed time to do more and better top-down processing of the written material, using context and world knowledge to make inferences about the reading material and to improve comprehension. We are beginning to understand how this automaticity and fluency is achieved in successful readers, and this is a topic for later chapters.

In Stage 2, however, some readers begin to lose momentum; they must be motivated to read extensively and abundantly with texts at their independent reading level. If for some reason this does not take place (e.g., if they are forced to read texts that are too difficult or unmotivating), readers often cease to improve their reading skill because they stop practicing. At this stage and the next, top-down comprehension processes can supplement deficient bottom-up decoding/recoding processes, but readers who cannot process English text automatically will face a handicap if they need to do extensive reading. A vicious cycle can develop. Poor readers avoid reading, and lack of reading practice means they do not improve.

Stages 3, 4 and 5. During stage 3, reading joins other learning methods: tasting, touching, listening, and watching. Readers begin to be able to use reading as a tool to acquire knowledge. Stage 3 readers are occupied with learning new vocabulary that encodes the information they are learning, so it is vital that reading material at this stage begin with the knowledge that learners have already acquired to establish a supportive framework for further learning. Vocabulary enrichment strategies are important for the reader at this stage. Top-down processing becomes especially important because readers must learn to look for facts, concepts, and points of view. Readers begin to use critical analysis while reading, but this ability becomes even more crucial in stages 4 and 5, when reading becomes a primary method of learning. Stage 4 reading takes place in high school and stage 5 reading develops in those readers who go to college. These advanced readers must read ever more complex texts and they must comprehend subtle nuances of meaning. They must be skillful at analysis, criticism, synthesis, and detecting secondary meanings. Throughout their lives people continue to improve their abilities to read as long as they read challenging and thought-provoking materials.

English L2 Reading Development

If these stages are normal for English speakers learning their alphabetic writing, we might wonder how many of our ESL and EFL students go through the early developmental stages that lead to later expert reading. We might ask what factors complicate the acquisition of the knowledge and processing strategies needed for effective reading in English.

Incomplete Knowledge of English. English L2 learners have knowledge of speech and listening in their first language. They can understand and use sounds, words, and typical sentences that are common in their L1 speech. However, their English L2 speech and listening skills may vary in completeness and fluency. They may not recognize all of the sounds they hear and they may not be able to produce them accurately in speech. They may not have sufficient vocabulary knowledge to understand English and they may not be sufficiently familiar with English grammatical structures. Also, the culture and world knowledge necessary for comprehension may be lacking. This means that the knowledge base that they have may simply not be adequate for English.

In addition, English L2 learners may or may not be literate in their first language. If they are not literate in their native language, learners start at "square one" in reading English. If they are literate in their first language, there may be other pitfalls in learning to read English because they would have learned processing strategies to read their L1. That means that in addition to a lack of English sounds, vocabulary, and grammar, they may face interference from existing L1 knowledge and processing strategies.

Interference.   Learning to read in English may in fact be harder for L2 learners than for English L1 prereaders because of interference from their L1. The languages of the world have different writing systems and each reader's knowledge base contains, at first, only that knowledge that is relevant to his or her own language and writing system. It is logical to think that exposure to any given writing system will cause L1 readers to develop different low-level reading strategies to deal with the exigencies of their writing systems. These L1 strategies, when the reader begins to learn to read English, may transfer to the L2. It is true that transfer may facilitate reading in the L2, but it is equally true that it might interfere.

Missing English Processing Strategies.   Besides problems associated with incomplete knowledge and interference, L2 readers may not develop the low-level processing strategies that native English speakers develop, so that they may not read English in the most efficient way. They may not be able to progress from the early developmental stages to later, more advanced stages. In order for students to advance in reading abilities, some may need direct instruction in the low-level processing strategies for English. Even students in advanced ESL and EFL reading classes may benefit from remediation so that their expert low-level decision-making capacity becomes automatic and fast. For English teachers to provide instructional support and remediation, they must know about how expert readers read in English, what linguistic knowledge they have, and what processing strategies work best. They must know something about what linguistic knowledge and processing strategies ESL and EFL students have developed for their L1. In the next chapter, we begin with a look at the different L1 writing systems of the world.

DISCUSSION QUESTIONS

1. Go over the model of the top and bottom of the reading processor in Figure 1.1. In your opinion, what specific problems might ESL and EFL readers face in each area (cognitive processing, world knowledge, language processing, and language knowledge) when they are dealing with English texts? For instance, how might

"inferencing" be a problem? What aspects of "letter recognition" might be problematic?

2. Moats (1995) argued that many reading teachers lack enough knowledge to teach English grammar, word structure, and writing explicitly. Do you know what these words mean? Take this quiz now and also when you finish reading the book to see if your answers have changed.

- Logogram.
- Transparent orthography.
- Phoneme.
- Phone.
- Grapheme.
- Morphology.
- Derivation.
- Inflection.
- Onset.
- Rime.
- Tense vowel.
- Morphophonemic writing.

Chapter 2

Writing Systems

Prereading questions. Before you read, think about and discuss the following:

1. What other writing systems do you know about?
2. Which of these representations of a number is more efficient to use in solving math problems: **one** or **1**? Why?
3. If you were to devise a writing system for a language used in a science fiction movie (like Klingon), which characteristics would it have?

Study Guide Questions. Answer these questions while and after reading the chapter.

1. How did writing develop in general?
2. What are the three main types of writing in the world today? Define them.
3. Is Chinese writing purely logographic? Is Japanese writing purely syllabic? Is English writing purely alphabetic?
4. What is the difference between transparent and opaque writing systems?
5. How has English writing become opaque? What are the chances of spelling reform?
6. For whom is opacity a problem? Why?

A hundred thousand years ago humans were communicating with spoken language, but true writing only began sometime within the last 10,000 years. Nearly everyone acquires speech and listening because people interact with each other in social networks. However, not everyone becomes literate because literacy usually requires that people receive some specific instruction in a culturally dependent writing system. Thus, while language itself is a universal characteristic of humans, reading and writing are less uniformly acquired.

Our prehistoric ancestors drew pictures of hunting activities on the walls and ceilings of the caves they inhabited. When modern humans find these pictures, they have a fairly good idea what they depict because they represent an object or event directly and not symbolically. Because they represent their meaning directly, cave drawings cannot be considered true writing. In a similar fashion, airports and train stations use standardized signs precisely because they are independent of specific languages. The stick figures used to symbolize restrooms or the crossed knife and fork for restaurants can be understood by those travelers who have acquired a certain global culture, no matter what language they speak. Similarly, on the Internet, a shorthand logogram :-) is used to express an emotion directly because words cannot always convey the right tone. These signs cannot be considered true writing either, because true writing is symbolic and indirect.

A true writing system uses a written symbol to represent a unit of language and not an object, event, or emotion directly. All true writing systems were great advances in human technology. We are not used to thinking of writing as a technology, but in fact, it is. Technology is defined as the following:

> a general term for the processes by which human beings fashion tools and machines to increase their control and understanding of the material environment.... Innovations [in technology] tend to transform traditional cultural systems, frequently with unexpected social consequences. Thus, technology can be conceived of as both a creative and a destructive process. (Merritt, 1999)

Writing is a tool that increases human control of communication and knowledge. It is creative in so many ways, but it also tends to be destructive of oral traditions relying on memory.

WRITING SYSTEMS

Over time, three types of writing technology have developed: logographic, syllabic, and alphabetic. Each technology is based on segmenting individual words from the flow of speech and representing them somehow in a more permanent manner on stone, clay, or paper. Segmentation is not necessarily easy or intuitive, and that's why people can make funny confusions when they write down spoken phrases, like "pullet surprises" for "Pulitzer prizes." The written symbols in each of the three writing systems represent different linguistic units, although it is probably safe to say that most writing systems use more than one type of symbol. The different writing systems are summarized in Figure 2.1.

Logographic Systems

In logographic writing systems, one symbol represents the concept or meaning of an individual word or part of a word. Although the symbol can be read out loud with the sounds of the word represented by its meaning, a

Technological Basis	Script Name	Region of Use
Meaning-based		
Logographic	Sinograms	China, Taiwan
	Kanji	Japan
	Hanzza	Korea
	Arabic Numbers	World
	Math operations	World
Syllable-based		
Syllabary	Kana	Japan
Alphabetic-syllabary	Hangul	Korea
Phoneme-based		
Consonantal Alphabet	Arabic, Hebrew	Middle East/Africa
Roman Alphabet		Europe, Americas
Transparent	Spanish, Finnish	
Opaque	English	
Cyrillic	Russian, Serbian	Eastern Europe
Greek	Greek	Greece

Figure 2.1   Summary of some writing systems.

logographic writing system is largely independent of any spoken language. We can understand the characteristics of logograms by looking at those we are most familiar with. English writing uses certain logograms: 1, 2, 3 (and all numerical writing), !, #, $, and so on. These symbols do not really have a pronunciation (as the artist Prince found out when he tried to change his name to a logogram).

Instead of a pronunciation, most logograms have a name. The term "dollar sign" is the name of $, not the pronunciation of $. The term "question mark" is the name of ?, not the pronunciation of ?. When reading these logograms, we can understand the meaning of them without accessing the name. (Unfortunately, the logogram selected by Prince did not have such a name, so people didn't know what to call him and his symbol never became commonplace enough for people to understand by a direct link to meaning. Recently, he has reclaimed the use of his real name, with its pronunciation and written form.)

Chinese. A standardized largely logographic system of approximately 60,000 **sinograms** (and still growing) is used to represent Cantonese, Mandarin, and the other languages and dialects we group as Chinese. The reason the system is still growing is that each time a new word is invented or borrowed, a completely new symbol must be invented as well to represent the word in writing. However, according to Mair (1996), only 6,600 sinograms are sufficient to convey most meanings in most texts. The script reflects the properties of classical Chinese well, but it corresponds poorly to the contemporary vernacular languages and regional varieties of Chinese. Because of the poor correspondence, "each character is a distinct entity and must be stored as a separate unit in memories or fonts" (p. 200) (Figure 2.2).

Chinese characters are more accurately called sinograms (and not logograms) because they are not completely logographic. Eighty-one percent of the Chinese sinograms consist of a combination of a *radical*, one of 200 or so symbols representing an element of meaning, and a *phonetic complement*, which indicates the sound by means of an analogy. Henderson (1982) gives a useful explanation: "It is as if we represented corn by means of a complex sign combining a semantic pointer to cereal crops and a phonological cue: rhymes with 'horn'" (p. 17). Chinese people are said to use the shape of the sinograms as gestures in the air as they speak, in order to disambiguate speech, so in some ways the gestural use of sinograms may resemble a sign language. Aebersold and Field (1997) note that Chinese characters are used not only for communication, but also for artistic expression.

According to Mair (1996), Chinese writing has been standardized and therefore largely unchanging since approximately 200 B.C.E., but the spoken language has changed quite a bit since that time. Therefore, there is considerable difference between the way the words are actually pronounced

Sample of Modern Mandarin Chinese

1. Chinese:	我	時常	記	起
2. Transliteration:	wǒ	shícháng	jì	qǐ
3. Transcription:	uo	ʂr ʂaŋ	ji	ʂü
4. Gloss:	I	frequently	remember	rise

1.	你	對	我	的	鼓勵,
2.	nǐ	duì	wǒ	de	gǔlì
3.	ni	duei	uo	də	guli
4.	you	toward	I/me	(Possessive)	encourage

1.	我	想	無論	生活	給予
2.	wǒ	xiǎng	wúlùn	shēnghuó	jǐyǔ
3.	uo	ɕiaŋ	u lun	ʂəŋ xuə	ji ü
4.	I	think/feel	no matter what	life	render/bestow

1.	我	們	多少	磨難,
2.	wǒ	men	duōshǎo	mónàn
3.	uo	mən	duə ʂau	mo nan
4.	I	(Plural)	how much	hardship/tribulation

1.	我	們	都	應該	勇敢	的
2.	wǒ	men	dōu	yīnggāi	yǒnggǎn	de
3.	uo	mən	dəu	iŋ gai	ioŋ gan	də
4.	I	(Plural)	all	must	brave/courage	(Possesive)

1.	去	面對。
2.	qù	miànduì
3.	ʂü	mian duei
4.	go	face/confront

'I often remember the encouragement you gave me, and I feel that no matter what hardships life bestows upon us, we all must have the courage to confront them.'

Figure 2.2   Sample of Chinese writing. Personal letter (translated by Charles Ettner).

and the written phonetic complements that are supposed to help the reader. He said the following:

Neither the semantic nor the phonetic components of the sinograms provide an exact indication of meaning or sound, but only give a vague approximation....Readers must guess or memorize the appropriate sound of the phonetic complement for each character in which it occurs; they must also associate the graph with a word that they already know. Only then can they arrive at the meaning of the sinogram in question. (pp. 201–202)

Some phonetic complements have more than one pronunciation, and, even more confusing for the reader, hundreds of sinograms may represent different meanings but the same sound, because Chinese has many homophonous words. Also, Chinese writing does not represent grammatical markings that change in different contexts, such as tense markers on verbs. According to Tseng and Hung (1981), Chinese children, in learning to read, learn to associate each spoken syllable or word with a particular syntactically unchanging character of a designated meaning. (However, in the People's Republic of China, there is a "romanized" alphabetic system called *pinyin* that also has many uses, so some Chinese readers have become familiar with alphabetic writing.)

Japanese. The Chinese logographic system is also part of Japanese culture, both historically and in contemporary writing. The Japanese borrowed Chinese writing by way of Korea in a form of writing that is still in use: *kanji.* (I have seen Japanese students and Chinese students communicate ideas in logographic writing when they could not communicate those ideas in their beginning English.) The kanji system is complex in Japanese; it is not a simple one-to-one correspondence between symbol and meaning. According to Smith (1996, p. 209), there are two ways to read each kanji symbol. One represents the pronunciation in Chinese at the time it was borrowed and the other is with a Japanese word or morpheme that corresponds to the meaning. Around 25% of the 2,000 kanji in use have phonological clues to their pronunciation in Chinese. Kanji symbols encode content words: nouns, verb stems, adjective stems, and some adverbs.

Syllabic Writing Systems

In syllabic writing systems, one symbol represents a consonant–vowel sequence or a consonant–vowel–consonant sequence of sounds. Each symbol is a unified whole; it cannot be broken down into smaller parts to represent the individual consonants and vowels. Once individual spoken words are segmented from the flow of speech, they can be broken up into syllables in a way that seems quite intuitive because they have beats or rhythms. Then the sound of each syllable can be represented with a written symbol and the conglomerate represents the word in written form. Syllabic writing is very sensible for a language like Japanese, in which there are relatively few different consonant–vowel syllables that make up the words. Think about the Japanese words and names that you know and you can see that they are made up of the same syllables used over and over in different combinations.

Japanese. Japanese writing has two syllabaries, one called *katakana,* which is used for foreign loan words and one called *hiragana,* for grammatical formatives, although both are complete systems that can represent everything in the spoken language. There are 47 symbols in the kana that stand for CV syllables, a nasal syllable, a symbol to represent a long vowel (i.e., CVV where the second V has the same value as the first V), and a symbol to represent double consonants. The kana systems seem easy for children to learn, because Sasanuma (1984) reports that most children have learned it by age 6 when they enter elementary school. There also appear to be few reading problems caused by dyslexia with Japanese writing. Syllable structure is stable over time, so syllabic writing maintains its connection to the sound system well. In Japanese writing the kanji and the kana are blended together, and to top it all off, words can be written in *romanji*, an alphabetic system used for names, signs, and acronyms. Smith calls Japanese writing "a complexly organized, multi-scriptal (or multi-orthographic) system." (p. 213) (Figure 2.3).

Korean.   Korean is a language with more diverse syllable structures. Koreans developed an alphabetic writing system called *Hangul* in the year 1446. Korean culture is one among very few in the world to commemorate the origin of its writing system. Hangul is very systematic; its basis is 40 alphabetic symbols that in different combinations (called syllabographs) represent the syllables of the language. The Korean writing system is also hieroglyphic; the consonant letter shapes of Hangul represent both place and manner of articulation. The vowels are made through the use of three symbols that are added to

1. Japanese	: 現在	大学の	独自性や	ユニークさが
2. Transliteration	: genzai	daigaku-no	dokujisei-ya	yunikusa-ga
3. Gloss	: today	university-Gen	originality-and	unique-Nom

1. Japanese	: 就職	環境と	共に	大学	選択の	大きな
2. Transliteration	: syushoku	kankyo-to	tomo-ni	daigaku	sentaku-no	ookina
3. Gloss	: job	environment-and	with	university	choice-Gen	big

1. Japanese	: ウェートを	占める	中で	次	から	次
2. Transliteration	: ueito-wo	shimeru	naka-de	tsugi	kara	tsugi
3. Gloss	: weight-Acc	hold	within	next	from	next

1. Japanese	: へと	新	企画を	打ち出し	大きな
2. Transliteration	: eto	shin	kikaku-wo	uchidashi	ookina
3. Gloss	: to	new	plan-Acc	create	big

1. Japanese	: 注目を	集めている	大学が	ある
2. Transliteration	: chuumoku-wo	atsumeteiru	university-ga	aru
3. Gloss	: attention-Acc	getting	university-Nom	exist

"Today there are universities that are gaining much attention because they are hammering out new [recruitment] plans one after another in response to applicants giving greater weight in university selection to the university's originality and uniqueness, as well as to the employment situation."

Figure 2.3   Sample of Japanese writing. Kanda (2000), translation by Dr. Raymond Weitzman with Eiji Koyama.

the consonant symbol. King (1996) suggested that "the simplicity of its graphic elements promotes learnability, while its syllabic organization enhances efficiency in processing and reading" (p. 220). Korean writing also makes use of Chinese characters in writing; they are called *Hanza* (or *Hanja*) (Figure 2.4).

Alphabetic Writing Systems

In alphabetic writing generally one symbol represents one sound, either a consonant or a vowel. The same alphabet itself may be used to write a number of languages with only minor adaptations, so the representation of writing in each case is related to spoken words of the language. That is, unlike logographic systems, which are largely independent of any spoken language, alphabetic writing is uniquely related to a spoken language even if

Hangul (Korean)

1.	나는	여자들이		직장을 다니는	게	싫다.
2.	nanun	yercatuli		cikcangul taninun	ke	silhta.
3.	I-nom	woman-plural-nom	work-obj	go-nom	thing-nom	dislike.
4.	'I dislike that women go to work'					

1.	물론	좋은 면도 있지만,		나는	젠틀맨도	아닌데
2.	mulon	cohun myunto issciman		nanun	centlmanto	aninte
3.	surely	good aspect is-even-though		I –nom	gentleman	not
4.	'surely	there is a good aspect, but even though I am not a gentleman'				

1.	여자들이	고생을	하면서	직장을 다니는	모습을
2.	yercatuli	kosangul	hamyunse	cikcangul taninun	mosupul
3.	woman-plural-Nom	suffer-obj	do-while	work-obj go to	feature(picture)-obj
4.	'the picture that women go to work with suffering'				

1.	그리	편안한	마음으로 보는	편은	아니다.
2.	kuri	pyunanhan	maumuro bonun	pyunun	anita.
3.	so	easy	mind-with look at	rather	not-predicate verb
4.	'I feel rather uneasy looking at'				

Translation:

'I dislike that women go to work. Surely there is a good aspect, but even though I am not a gentleman, I feel rather uneasy looking at the picture that women go to work with suffering.'

Figure 2.4   Sample of Korean writing. Park (1998), translation by Su Min Hong.

the symbols themselves are shared. English writing is unique to English, French writing to French, and so on. An advantage of alphabetic writing is that a small number of symbols (around 26) can be used to represent all of the words of the language, but a disadvantage is that the reader must know the language in order to read the writing system. There are a number of different alphabets in use today: the Roman, as in English, the Greek, and the Cyrillic, used in many of the Slavic languages.

The Alphabetic Principle.   In many ways, alphabetic writing was a very complex technological development in human culture. First of all, as in all writing systems, someone had to get the idea that the flow of speech could be segmented into words, but then someone had to realize that spoken words can be segmented into individual consonant and vowel sounds. There is no inherent rhythmic separation between the various sounds in the words within the rapid flow of speech, in the way that there is with the syllable. Studies with illiterate people show that neither adults nor children find it easy to segment words into the individual sounds (Morais, Cary, Alegria, & Bertelson, 1979). It doesn't seem to be an ability that people are born with, but rather an ability that must be acquired, either as a precursor to, or even as a result of, reading with an alphabetic script. In fact, Castro-Caldas (2004) found that the brains of illiterate and literate people had different activation patterns. Literate people had a more complex pattern of activation while dealing with phonology than did illiterate people. We come back to this issue of segmentation later, when we discuss phonemic awareness.

The originators of alphabetic writing had discovered the alphabetic principle: that one abstract symbol can be made to stand for one sound of a language, and that the symbols can be written together to stand for a word (Byrne, 1998). The relationship between the symbol and the sound is arbitrary and conventional. In other words, there is no inherent reason why the mark *s* stands for the /s/ sound or the mark *o* often stands for the sound /o/. As English speakers and writers, we agree to represent the sounds in one way and not another. By convention, we all write (mostly) the same way. Spelling errors naturally break this convention.

One important point about the alphabetic principle is that, just as its original invention was crucial, so is its acquisition by each child or adult who learns to read an alphabetic language. In fact, this is the first step in reading: that the prereader understand that the squiggles and marks on the page are not random but that they are a consistent system of representation in which each letter stands for a sound, and writing the letters in one particular order together in a line means writing a spoken word composed of a sequence of sounds.

Consonantal Alphabets.   Some modern alphabets consist mainly of consonantal representation, with the writing of vowels fragmentary and incomplete; Hebrew and Arabic are examples of mainly consonantal representation. Modern Hebrew has 22 consonant letters that have remained largely the same since antiquity (Goerwitz, 1996). At present, modern Hebrew can represent vowels only partially through diacritics, marks that occur along with the consonants, but even this use is inconsistent (Levin, Ravid, & Rapaport, 1999) (Figure 2.5).

Standard Arabic has 28 consonant letters that are in a one-to-one relationship with the Arabic consonants and some of the vowels (Bauer, 1996). As with Hebrew, there is a set of diacritics to indicate vowels, but they are of specialized usage, not normal usage. In reading standard Arabic, the lack of vowel letters produces ambiguity. It is not always possible to determine what the word is or what part of speech it is from the writing without using syntactic context. Standard Arabic writing is a kind of lingua franca, a common language that unites the Muslim world, but it is not like any of the re-

SAMPLE OF MODERN HEBREW

1. *Hebrew*	המדף	מן	החפץ	את	הרים	יואל ←
2. *Transliteration*	PDMH	NM	CPXH	TʔЅ	MYRH	LʔWY ←
3. *Transcription*	fadam-ah	nim	cefex-ah	te	mireh	leoy ←
4. *Gloss*	the-shelf	from	the-object	ACC	raised.he	Joel

1.	המתווך	כאבו	עיניו	מקרוב	בו	התבונן
2.	KWWTMH	WBʔK	WYNYЅ	BWRQM	WB	NNWBTHW
3.	xevatem-ah	u-vaak	vane	vorak-im	o-b	nenobtih-ev
4.	the-agent	hurt.they	eyes.his	from-near	in-it	and-examined.he

1.	כן	ועל	שאלתו	את	שמע	לא	שיואל	חשב
2.	NK	LЅW	WTLʔŠ	TʔЅ	ЅMŠ	ʔL	LʔWYŠ	BŠX
3.	nek	la-ev	o-taleeš	te	amaš	ol	leoy-eš	vašax
4.	so	and-on	question-his	ACC	heard.he	not	that-Joel	thought.he

1.	הבית	מאחורי	להציץ	נלך	עליה	חזר
2.	TYBH	YRWXʔM	CYCHL	KLN	HYLЅ	RZX
3.	tiyab-ah	eroxa-em	cicah-el	xelen	ah-ela	razax
4.	the-house	from-behind	to-peak	let's.go	on-her	returned.he

1.	לענות	יואל	מהר	לא	החלי ט	שכבר	למרות
2.	TWNЅL	LʔWY	RHM	ʔL	TYLXH	RBKŠ	TWRML
3.	tona-al	leoy	reham	ol	tilxeh	ravk-eš	tomral
4.	to-answer	Joel	fast	not	decided.he	that-already	despite

1.		תשובותיו	את	להשהות	היה	רגיל
2.		WYTWBWŠT	TʔЅ	TWHŠHL	HYH	LYGR
3.		va-tovušt	te	toʔšah-el	ayah	ligar
4.		answers-his	ACC	to-dally	was.he	accustomed

'Joel raised the object from the shelf and examined it up close. His eyes hurt. The agent thought that Joel had not heard his question and, therefore, repeated it: "Why don't we take a look behind the house?" Although he had already decided, Joel did not answer quickly. He was accustomed to deliberating before answering...'

—*Oz 1989:5*

Figure 2.5   Sample of Hebrew writing. Oz (1989), translation by Dr. Jack Zeldis.

gional modern varieties of spoken Arabic. Thus, in order to read standard Arabic, one must learn it in school.

Transparent Alphabetic Writing.   For many languages, the alphabetic writing system represents both the consonant and vowel sounds of the language with fair regularity; for these languages, the connection between the writing system and the sound system is *transparent*. Although it is probably safe to say that no alphabetic writing system is completely regular, Spanish, German, Serbo-Croatian, and Greek tend toward transparency. German inconsistencies appear to occur mainly in consonant representations.

Opaque Writing Systems.   In contrast to transparent systems, in which the letter corresponds one-to-one to the sounds of the language, in opaque writing systems the correspondence between the sounds and the letters is not one-to-one. Two writing systems that tend towards opacity are Russian and French. However, English is usually considered the opaque writing system par excellence.

You have probably heard that English spelling violates the alphabetic principle in that there are fewer letters than needed to represent the sounds of English. Some letters are not needed: **c**, **q**, or **x** could be substituted by other letters: **s**, **k**, or **ks**. In addition, some letters stand for more than one sound (letter **c** can be pronounced /k/ or /s/ depending on the word: **cat** or **city**); some sounds are represented by more than one letter (the sound /k/ can be written as **c** or **k**: **cat** or **kin**); or some letters represent no apparent sound at all (**g** in the word **sign**). There is, in addition, little pattern in the way that the vowel letters correspond to vowel sounds. English spelling is often considered chaotic or inconsistent; it is most certainly highly complex. How did the English writing system get so opaque?

A BRIEF HISTORY OF ENGLISH WRITING

The earliest writing system used in English was the runic alphabet, but with the Christianization of the English the Anglo-Saxon alphabet was adapted from Roman letters in the late sixth century by missionaries from Ireland (Millward, 1996, pp. 90–91). The correspondence between letter and sound was very transparent at that time, but English orthography (rules or conventions for using letters to spell words) became complicated over time. By the time of Middle English, 1100–1600, there was a great diversity in the way that words were spelled, reflecting the diversity of regional dialects of English. There were few conventions in the way that words were spelled from place to place within England. Writers wrote words however they were pronounced in that area (Millward, 1996).

Development of Opacity   English writing became complicated because of three issues in the history of our writing system: There were outside influences on our writing (and some well-intentioned meddling); English speakers have a propensity for borrowing words from other languages; and sound changes that occurred in English speech were not reflected in the writing system once it became standardized.

Influences and Meddling. When England was conquered by the Norman French, French writers introduced some French writing conventions. They wrote words like **right** with a **gh**, where in Old English it had been **riht**. Furthermore, the /h/ ceased to be pronounced at all by the late 15th century, leaving us with two "silent" letters in words like **right, night** and so on. English scholars who admired classical languages tried to "improve" English spelling by tracing words back to their origins and revealing the origins in the spelling: **comptroller**, **debt**, or **sovereign**. The English word **island** never had an **s**; the letter was added to make the word more Latin-like. Samuel Johnson's 1775 dictionary standardized and conventionalized many of the illogical spellings of his day (Taylor & Taylor, 1983).

Borrowing. Throughout the history of English, there has been a tendency to borrow foreign words. As a result, English has an abundance of loan words from other languages. Sometimes the spelling has been changed to reflect an English pronunciation (**vamoose** and **savvy** from Spanish **vamos** and **sabe**), but sometimes borrowed words are spelled the same as they are in the original language (Sp. **tortilla** [tortiya] or **marijuana** [mɛrɪhwana]), causing more exceptions to English spelling conventions (**ll**⇒[y] and **j**⇒[h]).

Sound Change. Alphabetic systems, because they are linked to sound systems, have one big disadvantage. Phonological systems in a language usually undergo changes over time as people change the way they pronounce words. The problem is that systematic pronunciation changes cannot easily be reflected in an alphabetic writing system that has become standardized in a culture. Once a writing system becomes standardized, it is extremely difficult to change because people resist any change to the system that is familiar to them. Phonological changes that have occurred over the centuries in the spoken language are not reflected in our writing system.

Spelling Reform

It may seem like these problems are overwhelming and that we should advocate a spelling reform that would bring English writing more in line with English speech sounds. However, there are some advantages to the system as it stands right now. For one thing, we said earlier that spelling was agreed on by convention a couple of centuries ago. Thus, we already have an abundance of literature and printed books that use this system and might be inaccessible if the writing system were to change. We said earlier that writing systems were instances of technology, and when technology changes, it makes earlier forms obsolete and unusable. For instance, few people nowadays have record players and there is quite an industry in reissuing "classic" rock-and-roll hits in CD form so that people can still enjoy them. If our writing system were to change, current books, computer files, and the like might become obsolete or at least as inaccessible as Chaucer's writing is to most of us today.

Furthermore, although there are some small differences in spelling across the globe, the English writing system, for all of its complexities, is a convention among English speakers throughout the world. It doesn't represent any standard variety of English better than any other. If English spelling were to be made more transparent, it is unclear which spoken variety would be chosen to represent accurately: standard British English (whatever that is), standard American English (whatever that is), standard Australian English (whatever that is), or any other.

Spelling reform could have other consequences. There is some indication that having different spellings for homophonous words (words that sound the same) may aid in reading the words without ambiguity: pair and pare, night and knight. Furthermore, preserving the spelling between a root word and word derived from it may be helpful in showing the meaning relationship between the two even though the pronunciation is different: **sane, sanity; innate, nation, nationality; telegraph, telegraphy**. More on this topic later.

In fact, English writing is complex but efficient enough for a reader who already knows how to read in English. In other words, once you know how to read, once you get into the system, the fact that English writing doesn't match the sound exactly ceases to be a problem for reading, although it continues to be a problem in spelling and writing. Readers, as they gain expertise in reading, develop processing strategies that allow them to make the best of their writing system. The main challenge to break into that system then is for two learner populations: beginning English-speaking readers and beginning ESL or EFL students. Much has been written about the former; our concern in this book is the latter.

ENGLISH L2 READING

Up until recently, differences in L2 writing systems have not been given much attention in ESL and EFL reading. Wallace (1992) reflected a commonly held idea:

> The languages themselves may be so different in the way they represent meaning in their written form that there is, arguably, no generalization from the first to the target language.... [But]...if we turn to consider the ways in

which different writing systems convey meaning, it has been argued, for example by Goodman (1984) that, while the contexts and functions of written language vary, reading as a process is unitary. Reading is a unitary process both because it cannot be adequately broken down into separate skills and because we draw on similar processing strategies in the reading of all languages, even where the writing systems are very different. Buck (1979), for example, argues that the process of deriving meaning from written or printed symbols is similar across languages and across contexts. And Cummins and Swain (1986) talk of a Common Underlying Proficiency in language development whereby literacy is generalizable from the first to a second language. (pp. 22–23)

Similar points of view about transfer from L1 reading to L2 reading can be found in Coady (1979), Alderson and Urquhart, (1984) and Day and Bamford (1998).

More recent research supports the idea that reading can be broken down into separate skills or strategies that, in the ideal situation, all work together so smoothly that they become one. The operant words in the preceding quote are "similar" and "generalizable." The process of deriving meaning from writing is probably similar in some ways, but it doesn't follow that the knowledge base and low-level processing strategies are identical, nor that transfer of processing strategies from L1 to L2 is impossible. Although a reader's L1 literacy is generalizable to L2, it is possible that the transfer may be either positive or negative. L1 literacy can facilitate or interfere with L2 literacy.

We have seen that languages represent different linguistic units in writing: meaning, syllables, or phonetic segments, consonants or vowels, features of phonetic segments, or more likely, a combination of these. In addition, languages are spaced differently in a variety of directions on a page: vertically or horizontally, and with or without spacing in between "words." The number of symbols needed to represent a language in writing can vary greatly. The methods that schools and teachers use to teach children those symbols vary from country to country. Languages differ in whether syntactic changes to words are represented in the writing. Alphabetic writing systems differ in how "transparent" they are—that is, how accurately they represent the sounds of the language. It is reasonable to think that the knowledge stored in the knowledge base as a source for reading is different for each L1 writing system and that the low-level processing strategies that mediate between the text and the higher level processes are different. We turn to this topic in the next chapter.

DISCUSSION QUESTIONS

1. This is a common visual discrimination task. Identify which of these letter sequences is different from the other two and then verbalize

the mental and visual process that you used to identify the different one:

i.   a.   βατ   b.   βατ   c.   γατ

ii.   a.   κατ   b.   κιτ   c.   κιτ

iii   a.   μαπ   b.   ναπ   c.   μαπ

iv.   a.   ενεραλιζατιο   b.   ενεραλιζατιο   c.   εμεραλιζατιο

Which one was the easiest to discriminate? Which one was the hardest? Why do you think that you got these results? Do you get the same results for the next set? Answer the same questions as before.

i.   a.   ♌♋♦   b.   ♌♋♦   c.   ♑♋♦

ii.   a.   ②♋⓪   b.   ②⓪⓪   c.   ②⓪⓪

iii   a.   ❗✔🚌   b.   ⬤✔🚌   c.   ❗✔🚌

iv.   a.   ♑♏■♏☐♋●   b.   ♑♏■♏☐♋●✠   c.   ♏⚪☐♋●✠
             ✠⌘♋♦✠☐   ⌘♋♦✠☐   ⌘♋♦✠☐

2. This quote comes from Tseng and Hung (1981):

Miller…has pointed out the importance of notational design in the history of mathematics. In Miller's words (1957) "In order to study the interaction of thought and symbol it is not necessary to travel with Whorf to the Zuni Indians; the language of mathematics is rich with excellent examples. Why are Arabic numbers so superior to Roman?" (p. 238)

In that spirit, compare these different representations of the same meaning concept (the number seven): 7, *seven*, *vii*. Which type of writing does each correspond to? (If 7 and *vii* are both logographic, what is the difference between them?) What are the advantages and disadvantages of each type of number? Do you agree that the history of mathematics has been affected by the type of notations developed? Could mathematics have advanced without the symbols like 7?

Could language and culture be similarly affected by the writing systems that evolved in different civilizations? For instance, Logan (1986) argues that alphabetic writing was related to the growth of theoretical science in Western civilization and not in Eastern:

The effects of the alphabet and the abstract, logical, systematic thought that it encouraged explain why science began in the West and not in the East, despite the much greater technological sophistication of the Chinese…the inventors of metallurgy, irrigation systems, animal harnesses, paper, ink. (p. 23)

What do you think?

Chapter 3

Low-Level Transfer
of Reading Strategies

Prereading Questions. Before you read, think about and discuss the following.

1. If you are a nonnative speaker of English, tell the class about the writing system in your native language. Tell the class about your experiences learning English, especially learning to read. How well do you feel you read now? What would improve your reading?
2. If you are a native speaker of English, find an English learner to interview. Ask them the questions just given. Present your information to the class.
3. If you are a native English speaker and have studied another language, what problems did you have with reading it silently? What problems did you have if you tried to read it out loud?
4. If you have studied a language with a different writing system, what problems did you have learning to read it?

Study Guide Questions. Answer these questions while or after reading the chapter.

1. What evidence is there that different writing systems require different knowledge and processing strategies?
2. What are the four different ways that logograms could be read?
3. What low-level strategy might develop in readers of consonantal scripts?
4. What low-level strategy might readers of transparent scripts be using?
5. Do processing strategies transfer if the L1 and the L2 are very different? If they are similar?
6. What is the evidence from brain activation?
7. Will preference for different processing strategies transfer?
8. What is the significance of the evidence about Japanese readers' preference for a meaning-based strategy for unpronounceable (to them) words with regard to their acquisition of English?
9. Does brain activation evidence indicate any problems for Chinese readers? What does it say?
10. What are some implications for English L2 readers?

Given the differences in writing systems in the world discussed in the last chapter, it is not surprising that learning to read a new script can be problematic for the language learner. When thinking about our ESL and EFL students, we find there are really two preliminary issues and some further questions that follow from these issues:

- Do the demands of reading different writing systems cause readers to develop different knowledge and different low-level reading strategies when they are learning to read in their native language?
- If so, do these strategies transfer from L1 to L2 or not?

If readers acquire different knowledge and develop different processing strategies in L1, then we must consider first whether they transfer to L2 or whether they remain isolated. If they don't transfer, there will be no facilitation but also no interference in L2 reading. If they do transfer, there could be either facilitation or interference with L2 reading. We might expect facilitation if the writing systems are similar in L1 and L2, but how similar do they need to be for facilitation to take place? Is interference in fact more likely even if a learner is moving from a transparent alphabetic L1 to an opaque alphabetic L2 such as English? These concerns lead us to a conclusion that many beginning English-learning readers who are already literate in their native language may need direct instruction in the strategies that expert English readers form in order to read English most efficiently.

DIFFERENT KNOWLEDGE AND STRATEGIES

To answer the first question, we look at evidence from two sources: psycholinguistic experiments and studies of brain activation.

Psycholinguistic Evidence for Differences

In the last chapter we saw that languages differ in their writing systems and we concluded that it is reasonable to think that these differences can result in the development of different knowledge and different low-level processing strategies. There is some evidence that this is so. Taylor and Olson (1995) report the following humorous anecdote:

> Proctor and Gamble have a well-known advertisement for laundry detergent, which shows a pile of dirty clothes on the left, a box of Tide in the middle, and clean folded clothes on the right. The ad worked very well in North America and Europe. But in Arabia, sales of P & G products dropped. Why? Arabic readers viewed the ad from right to left, associating the Tide not with the clean folded clothes but with the dirty ones on the left! (p. 13)

There have been a number of research studies of the question, and many show that subjects use different word recognition strategies depending on their L1 orthography (Chikamatsu, 1996). Each writing system provides the mind with different tasks to perform, so the mind responds by developing different strategies to work with the different input.

Logograms.   One question that researchers have tried to answer is whether logograms (Chinese sinograms, Japanese kanji, or Korean Hanza) can be read by visually associating the symbol directly with the meaning stored in memory without any reference to the sound of the word. That is, the written symbol would be decoded and recognized without any recoding into sound. It is a complicated question because there are actually four possible orthographic/lexical processing strategies. In the first, the logographic symbol is decoded, recognized, and associated with a word meaning directly, which is then used to access the sound of the word in recoding. In the second, the symbol is decoded and recoded with sound first, and the visual/auditory image is used to access the meaning of the word. In the third, the symbol is decoded and associated simultaneously with both the meaning and the sound. In the fourth, the logogram is associated only with meaning and not with sound at all.

Some researchers have found some evidence that reading logograms is more like processing pictures than reading (Henderson, 1982, p. 196). Morton and Sasanuma (1984) also generally conclude that for Japanese writing, although the kana are read phonetically, the kanji are read visually, that is, like a picture. To them, there seems to be "a strong *dissociation* between the processes involved in reading the two scripts" (p. 40). But Leong and Tamaoka (1995) argued that both visual and phonetic processing can occur in accessing difficult kanji with phonetic elements. Sakuma, Sasanuma, Tatsumi, and Masaki (1998) concluded that kanji characters were processed both orthographically and phonologically.

Koda (1995) explains how logograms are read in a way that unifies these apparently conflicting results. In Koda's opinion, all writing systems are recoded into phonological information in reading because studies show that short-term memory is better for phonological material than for visual material. However, alphabetic writing is recoded to a phonological representation *prior to* or *at the time* that the word is accessed in memory. Logographic writing is converted to phonology only *after* the word is accessed because that is the time when phonological information becomes available to the reader. It is, in fact, impossible to pronounce an unknown sinogram because the phonetic cues are not enough.

In simpler terms, logograms are accessed through the meaning of the word first, and only afterward does the sound of the word become available to the reader, which means that logograms are read as in 1 in Figure 3.1. (In contrast, only the most frequent of words written in alphabetic scripts may be accessed with a direct connection between the decoded visual image of the word and the meaning of the word, as in 1. Less frequent words written in alphabets are decoded and recoded into a visual/auditory image, then

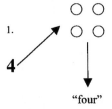

1.

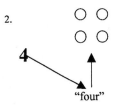

2.

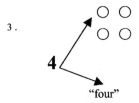

3.

4.

Reader associates logogram with meaning first, then with the sound of the word. Sinograms are probably read this way. This is a <u>meaning-based visual strategy</u>.

Reader associates logogram with meaning and sound simultaneously. Sinograms are probably NOT read this way.

Reader associates logogram with sound first, then meaning. Sinograms are probably NOT read this way.

Reader associates logogram only with meaning. Sinograms (like numbers) may be able to be read this way. This is also a <u>meaning-based visual strategy</u>.

Figure 3.1   Summary of four ways logograms could be read.

the meaning becomes available to the reader, as in 2 or possibly 3.) Logograms can also be read without access to sound, as in mental math calculations, where thinking of the name of the number symbol only slows down and complicates the process. This is shown in number 4 in Figure 3.1.

This evidence supports the claim that readers use different processing strategies to handle logograms (a meaning-based strategy) and alphabetic words (a sound-based strategy).

Syllabic Writing.   There is some evidence that syllabic writing is processed differently also. Kang and Simpson (1996) found, in comparing Korean grade school readers with English-speaking grade school readers, that word recognition processes for Korean sixth-grade readers were different from those found for English-speaking sixth-graders.

Consonantal Alphabetic Writing.   There may be some variation in the way the differing alphabetic systems are processed also. The demands of those scripts that represent consonants primarily may produce different reader strategies from those writing systems that encode both consonants and vowels. Shimron and Sivan (1994) studied English and Hebrew bilingual graduate students and faculty reading texts translated into Hebrew and English. The English native speakers read the English texts significantly faster than the native Hebrew speakers read the same texts in their Hebrew version.

Ben-Dror, Frost, and Bentin (1995) found that Hebrew speakers, when given a task to segment complete words into their component sounds (e.g., *kite* into /k/ /ay/ /t/), segmented words into sounds differently from English speakers for both Hebrew and English words. The variation was attributed to differences in the way that writing systems represent phonological information. Ryan and Meara (1991) found that Arabic readers reading English confuse words that have similar consonant structures. Their hypothesis was that because of the orthography of Arabic, readers tend to rely heavily on the consonants when attempting to recognize English words, a partial alphabetic strategy that is not very effective for English because of our numerous words that are differentiated merely by vowel, our extensive use of vowel spellings, and overall complicated writing system (Figure 3.2).

Transparent Versus Opaque Alphabetic Writing.   Alphabetic languages tend to be read with phonological recoding, meaning that the words are read by associating sounds with the letters. This makes sense because it is the best way to take advantage of the information the writing system provides. It is possible, however, that the demands of dealing with an opaque script such as English might cause English readers to develop strategies different from those of readers of transparent scripts. Oney et al. (1997) suggested, from their research with readers of Turkish (transparent) and English (opaque), that readers become less dependent on phonological processing with experience and that this reduction is more rapid for readers of opaque orthographies.

Naeslund and Schneider (1996) found differences in the emergence in phonological processing skills among beginning readers of German when

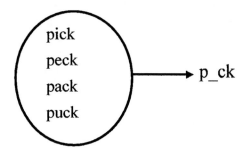

Arabic or Hebrew readers might use a partial alphabetic strategy.

Figure 3.2   Hypothetical strategy used by readers of consonantal L1s.

compared to beginning readers of English. One reason for this, they offer, is the differences between German writing (generally transparent) and English writing (opaque). Chitiri and Willows (1994) reported on a study of Greek and English monolingual readers in which they concluded that the reading process is not uniform across languages and that readers are influenced by orthography. There is reason to think that readers with an L1 transparent script may develop a transparent fully alphabetic strategy, one in which each letter or syllable is read and recoded directly into its predictable sound. This strategy also is not effective for English, because English writing is opaque. Readers of transparent alphabets like German or Greek also rely heavily on the syllable as a unit (Nunes, 1999). This is probably less useful as a strategy for English (Figure 3.3). In a later chapter, we discuss the best strategies for decoding English writing.

Thus, the psycholinguistic research suggests that yes, readers do develop different strategies in order to cope with differing orthographies: a visual meaning-based strategy, a syllabic strategy, a partial alphabetic strategy, and a fully alphabetic strategy. There is also evidence from brain activation studies.

Brain Activation Studies

Several recent studies of brain activation support the idea that readers have some similar brain activation during reading different writing systems, but also that they have differing activation as well. It seems that the brains of readers get programmed with certain knowledge and processing strategies in response to the L1 writing system. There is considerable interest in these studies because they show the effect of culture learning (i.e., writing system) on the structure and functioning of the brain. However, we are just beginning to know how to interpret the results from brain activation studies.

Logographic Writing.   Tan et al. (2001) studied brain activation in Chinese readers reading Chinese and found that there was more activation in the right-hemisphere cortical regions, the right visual systems, than is found in English readers reading English. Tan et al. attributed this to the square shape of the logogram, made up of various strokes that must be ana-

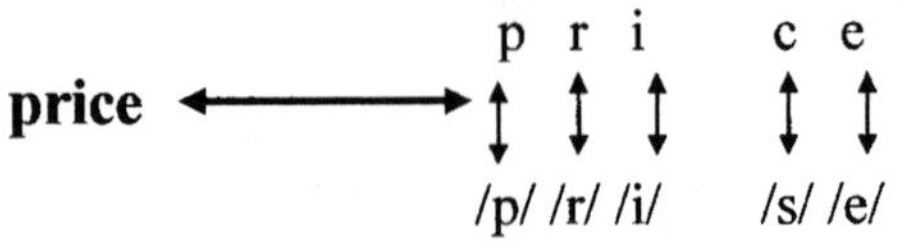

Readers of Greek, Spanish, and other languages with transparent writing systems might develop a fully alphabetic strategy with reliance on syllable structure.

Figure 3.3   Hypothetical strategy used by readers of transparent L1s.

lyzed and processed. There was also left middle frontal activation that they hypothesized showed intense visual and spatial analysis of the logogram's configuration as well as the semantic and phonological analysis demanded by the task in their study. They cited other studies that have found different cortical areas associated with the processing of different languages.

But several studies also show that there are common neural networks used to recognize written language. The study done by Tan et al. implicated brain regions that were the same for both logographic and alphabetic languages, and also regions that were specific to reading logographs. Other studies they cited also had this finding.

However, the finding of similar locations of activation for reading does not mean that the brain is doing identical processing tasks. For instance, the studies imply that for Chinese there is visual processing unlike English, and there is phonological and semantic processing that is similar to English. Nevertheless, it is quite possible that the processing direction for English is mainly phonological first and then semantic. This means that English readers start with phonology to access the word, unless it is a very common word, and then access the meaning.

But in Chinese the direction may be more heavily weighted toward semantics first and then phonology, because it seems that the meaning of the word is more readily apparent in the character and must be accessed in order to recognize the word. In other words, some people report that the character must be recognized first as a meaning before it can be assigned a pronunciation. Brain activation studies don't necessarily distinguish between these processes, because they might show similar activation patterns. However, another study did try to get at differences in processing activations.

Syllable Processing.   Both syllable processing and phoneme processing go on in reading some writing systems, but the information is of varying importance in the different systems. For instance, Japanese kana systems are based on the relatively small number of common syllables in Japanese. Spanish writing also seems to involve both phonemic and syllabic processing: **sa/be**, **pe/ro**. However, English words don't have a common consonant vowel syllabic pattern; instead, they generally have common onset/rime patterns based on common spelling and pronunciation patterns across words. For instance, a common "rime" such as **–an** appears with many different onsets: **p-**, **f-**, **sp-**, as in **pan**, **fan**, **span**.

The problem is that brain activation studies of the processing of alphabetic languages fail to distinguish between phonemic, syllabic, and onset/rime processing because the activation patterns overlap. Syllables and onset/rimes are both made up of phonemes.

However, it seems that one group of researchers, Siok, Zhen, Fletcher, and Tan (2003), using Chinese readers again, was able to design a task that allowed them to distinguish syllabic processing from phonemic processing.

When these researchers were able to pull the systems apart, they found different patterns of neural activation for the two types of processing. The left middle frontal cortex contributes to syllabic processing, but the left inferior prefrontal gyrus contributes to phonemic processing. Therefore, we might hypothesize that an L1 reader of Japanese, which relies heavily on the syllable for processing, would need reprogramming to read English, which relies on phonemic processing and onset/rime patterns.

Alphabetic Processing.   For alphabetic languages, evidence reported by Paulesu et al. (2000) showed

> the first cross-cultural anatomical information about a common reading system for different alphabetic orthographies. Reading in both complex and transparent orthographies depends on a distributed network of primarily left-sided language areas. Within the common network, however, some brain areas were more highly activated by one orthography than the other. (pp. 92–93)

Paulesu and his colleagues studied English readers and Italian readers. Italian writing is transparent, but as we have seen, English writing is opaque and involves a strategy of separating onsets and rimes. In two brain activation studies, the Italians had greater activation in left superior temporal regions associated with phoneme processing. In contrast, English readers showed greater activation in the left posterior inferior temporal gyrus and anterior inferior frontal gyrus, areas associated with word retrieval.

In other words, it seems that the Italians can read by matching letters to sounds in a straightforward way (along with a syllabic strategy similar to Spanish). English readers, on the other hand, are doing something besides simple letter-to-sound processing. The additional activation involving word retrieval could indicate that English readers must rely on comparisons of the words being read with known spelling patterns stored in the brain. This processing for English is discussed in greater detail in later chapters.

L1 TO L2 TRANSFER

These psycholinguistic and brain activation studies show that there are very good reasons to think that readers of different languages use different knowledge and processing strategies to read their first language. Now we come to the question of transfer and the related issues of interference and facilitation. There is evidence that in some cases, no transfer occurs if L1 and L2 are very different. Abu-Rabia (1997) reports that although syntactic and working memory skills show a significant correlation between Hebrew and English skills for Hebrew–English bilingual children, phonological and orthographic tasks show no such positive correlation. Instead,

Abu-Rabia concluded that some language-dependent features do not transfer from one language to another.

There is evidence of transfer and facilitation if the L1 and L2 writing systems are similar. Muljani, Koda, and Moates (1998) studied English word recognition in Indonesian and Chinese students of English in order to find out whether the alphabetic writing system of Indonesian would facilitate reading in English when compared to Chinese writing. Their results suggested that there was some positive transfer from the L1 reading processor to the L2 when both the L1 and the L2 were alphabetic systems. There was no positive transfer from Chinese to English reading because those systems are so different. Thus, they found that L1 knowledge of the alphabet aided the Indonesian students, but L1 knowledge of sinograms did not aid reading alphabetic writing.

Visual Processing

Preference for different processing strategies also transfers sometimes. Chikamatsu (1996) studied American and Chinese learners of Japanese, using Japanese kana because it would be a different writing system for both learners. Kana is syllabic; the American learners would have learned an alphabetic system and the Chinese learners a logographic script of sinograms. Chikamatsu found that Chinese subjects relied more on the visual information in L2 kana words than did the American subjects and that American subjects utilized the phonological information in kana more than did Chinese subjects. The conclusion was that there are different strategies involved in reading different orthographies and that these strategies transfer to L2 word recognition. The Chinese readers transferred their preference for a meaning-based visual processing strategy. The English L1 students transferred their sound-based strategy.

Unpronounceable Words

Similarly, Koda (1995) studied Japanese, Arabic, Spanish, and English readers of English and found that symbols that had no phonological cues and unpronounceable words interfered less with the Japanese readers than with the alphabetic readers. It is well established that unpronounceable words interfere with English reading because of the difficulty they pose for phonological recoding. If you are a native speaker of English, you may have stumbled over unpronounceable foreign names in the novel *War and Peace*, for example. You may have tried to process them without recoding into phonology, by remembering the appearance of the name and associating it with a certain character, which would mean a more direct visual and meaning connection. Or you may have tried a laborious alphabetic strategy of sounding out the names and remembering them by sound. Which did you choose, a visual meaning-based strategy or a sound-based strategy?

However, unpronounceable words did not cause difficulty for the Japanese readers, Koda concluded, because they treated the problem words as they did kanji. They did not try to pronounce them; they tried to remember them visually. In a footnote, Koda reported that Japanese ninth graders extended the same strategies they had developed to deal with unfamiliar kanji to guess the meaning of unfamiliar words in English. Also, ESL reading comprehension among Japanese college students was unaffected by the unpronounceability of English words, suggesting a strategy of relying little on phonological information in the letter representation. The strategy these Japanese students were applying to unknown English words was visual and meaning-based, discarding the very strengths of the alphabetic writing system with its cues to sound.

The short-term strategy of treating unfamiliar words as logograms may assist these ESL and EFL readers at first, but over time, it is more efficient to be able to decode unknown words and assign a pronunciation to them. In short, there is evidence for transfer of processing strategies from L1 to L2 if the writing systems have some similarity, but facilitation only occurs sometimes, and it may only offer a short-term benefit.

Brain Activation

Tan et al. (2003) studied moderately fluent-speaking Chinese/English bilinguals who began learning English after the age of 12. They were graduate students at a North American university and they were compared with a set of English monolinguals. First, Tan et al. found that processing of Chinese characters involves regions of the brain that contribute to the representation and working memory of spatial information. They concluded that this activation is because a Chinese character has a square pattern that is related to a Chinese word.

Next, they found that when the bilingual students performed a phonological task on English words, the same neural system was activated. In contrast, when English monolinguals were tested with the same task, there was only weak activation in that area. Tan and his colleagues suggested that the bilingual students applied their Chinese strategies to reading in English. Furthermore, they felt that the Chinese readers were less capable of processing English because they did not have the same processing strategies that the English monolinguals did.

Tan et al. reported that the English L2 graduate students applied a processing strategy developed in response to Chinese to their reading of English words. They did not automatically use the letter-to-sound conversion rules like the English monolinguals did. In other words, it seems that the Chinese graduate students were using their habitual visual and semantic processing to read English—not taking advantage of the alphabetic writing system and not using those processing strategies that are most effective for English, presumably because they never acquired them. It remains unclear, however, what the relationship is between brain activation patterns and fluent reading. It is possible that for these moderately fluent and successful graduate students, English L2 reading was problematic.

Nakada, Fujii and Kwee (2001) studied 10 Japanese volunteers and 10 American English speakers. First they found that the brain activation patterns in the Japanese reading Japanese (their L1) and the patterns in the Americans reading English (their L1) differed substantially from each other. Then they found that the activation patterns of the highly literate Japanese and the Americans reading their L2 (English and Japanese, respectively) were virtually identical to the patterns seen when reading their L1. These researchers concluded that second-language reading is an extension of the same system employed in reading L1.

The accumulation of evidence from brain activation and psycholinguistic studies supports the hypothesis that L1 readers develop their knowledge and processing strategies in response to their L1 writing systems and that these processing strategies can transfer from L1 to L2. Positive transfer can occur if writing systems are similar, for example, Chinese characters to Japanese kanji and vice versa, or Spanish to Italian and vice versa. However, the more different the L1 and L2 writing systems are, the more likely it is that the transfer from L1 will interfere with L2 reading. Thus, the answer to both questions from the beginning of the chapter is that people do develop different low-level decoding strategies in response to different L1 scripts, and the strategies do transfer from L1 to L2. The open question is: To be a fluent reader of English, is it necessary to have English brain activation? Clearly, more research on this topic is essential. In the absence of clear answers, we can only assume that reading instruction should help readers acquire the knowledge and processing strategies that best fit the L2 system, whether it shows up in brain activation or not. We return to the topic of instruction and its effect on brain activation again later.

ENGLISH L2 READERS

How can we understand what this means to students who need to learn to read the more or less opaque English script? We have seen that in general, ESL and EFL students bring with them different types and amounts of prior knowledge and strategies from their L1 literacy. We can discuss these differences by referring to hypothetical case studies of four typical ESL or EFL reading students: MariCarmen, Despina, Mohammed, and Ho. What these students have in common is that they have all learned to read their own L1 script accurately and quickly. They are all now in the process of becoming good readers of English as a second language.

Many students enter English classes having already learned an alphabetic script to read and write their native language or for another language that they have learned. These students can transfer quite a bit of this knowledge directly from that experience into their English learning experience.

There are two types of students within this category: those who have learned a script a lot like English (Spanish speakers, Italian speakers, German speakers, etc.) and those who have learned an alphabetic script unlike English (Russian speakers, Greek speakers, etc.).

L1: Roman Alphabet

For those students coming from languages with a Roman script, it is reasonable that there will be some positive transfer or facilitation; in other words, much transferred information from L1 to L2 would aid these ESL learners in beginning to read English. For example, readers would know that reading goes from left to right across the page. They would know the alphabetic principle and they would recognize letter shapes and fonts. However, many languages have a more transparent writing system than English does; the letter-to-sound correspondences are more regular. So students who have learned such a transparent system may experience some negative transfer of their reading strategies when they begin to experience the more opaque English writing. It is possible that they need to develop additional strategies to cope with the opacity of English writing.

> *MariCarmen.*   MariCarmen is a 12-year-old student from Mexico who has been studying English for a year. Because Spanish uses the same alphabet as English, she is catching on fairly quickly to English reading and writing. Much of what she already knows about reading would help her in the new task of reading English. In order for MariCarmen to begin reading in English, she needs to learn the few English letters or letter combinations that are not used in Spanish (k, x) or that are used in English associated with a very different sound (g, h, j, ll, rr, th). She needs to recognize English sounds. (We see later why she doesn't need to pronounce them perfectly.) She needs to begin learning English vocabulary and phrases orally, and for a while, she needs to read and write very simple selections that replicate the words she knows orally. MariCarmen also needs to learn how to deal with the "opacity" of English writing: that English letters represent sounds with less regularity than Spanish. This is a topic of later chapters.

L1: Other Alphabets

Students who speak languages that use alphabets other than the Roman alphabet may find the early stages of reading development more problematic because they need to learn to recognize new letter shapes quickly and efficiently. These students must also learn to recognize the new sounds of English. The associations between the new letters and new sounds take a while to become automatic, as in Chall's reading stages 1 and 2 (described in chap. 1), so that bottom-up reading can occur with fluency. Until this happens, these students must spend most of their attention on the bottom levels of the reading processor and have less attention to spare for the higher levels. It is unfair for the reading teacher to require a great deal of reading comprehension from students in these stages. Reading passages should be simple and easy to understand.

Despina.   Despina is 14 and recently traveled with her family from Greece to the United States. She is in eighth grade at a middle school. Her language arts teacher is Ms. Gordon and her ESL teacher is Ms. Linder. Despina knows only a few words of spoken English although she studied English for several years in school before coming. Despina's native language is Greek, which she knows how to read and write well. Greek is written with an alphabet, but it is very different from the English alphabet. Like MariCarmen's, much of Despina's reading abilities would transfer directly and positively to the task of reading English. Despina's knowledge of the world is similar to MariCarmen's and similar to any American 14-year-old's. She knows how to hold a book and how to read left to right across the page. Despina's knowledge of sounds derives from her experience with her native language, and the knowledge would transfer with some modification to English. Where Despina differs greatly from MariCarmen, though, is in her lack of knowledge of English letters. There is little overlap between the Greek alphabet and the English one.

In order for Despina to become a good reader of English, she must learn to recognize English sounds quickly and accurately. She must read and write English selections that do not contain words that are unfamiliar to her. The crucial thing for Despina to learn, however, is the English alphabet: the letter shapes in various fonts and the correspondence between the letters and the sounds of English. In addition, Greek, like Spanish, has a more transparent connection between writing and sound, so Despina may need to acquire some new procedures and mechanisms for coping with English writing system opacity.

Mohammed.   In many ways, Mohammed, from Egypt, is like Despina. His writing system is alphabetic, but it uses different symbols. It is also consonantal. So Mohammed must learn the same things that Despina must learn, but he must also learn to look at vowels and process them efficiently. However, Mohammed also presents some additional challenges because his eyes are trained to process writing in the opposite direction from English. Furthermore, standard Arabic writing is very different from spoken Arabic dialects. In fact, some consider written Arabic and spoken Arabic to be different dialects entirely and as a result, it is very difficult to learn to read and write. There is a lot of illiteracy in the Arab world, and this is considered one reason why. So Arabic writing is opaque (in consonants), but in a different way from the way that English writing is opaque (in vowels). The strategies that Mohammed may have developed to deal with the opacity of Arabic may not be useful for reading English, but I know of no research on this topic.

L1: Logographic Writing

Most Chinese L1 ESL and EFL students are not very familiar with alphabetic writing at all until they try to learn English or another alphabetic language. There is compelling evidence that the processing of sinograms and kanji is different from the processing of an alphabet. The implication is that those ESL and EFL readers whose L1 is Chinese, Japanese, or Korean may try a strategy of memorizing English written words as unitary wholes (like sinograms or kanji) that may or may not also involve some kind of memory for the pronunciation of the word. In fact, some beginning English-speaking children try this also as a strategy, but they usually don't become proficient readers using it. They must develop an alphabetic strategy.

Chinese L1 students may use their prodigious memories to learn English words as if they were whole entities and unreduceable to letters and sounds. In other words, there is reason to believe that they try to read English words without any modification to the reading processor they have already acquired through reading Chinese. The situation for the Japanese and Korean readers is somewhat different because of the multiorthographic nature of Japanese and Korean writing, but research cited earlier suggests that they use a visual and meaning-based strategy for unknown words. The transparency of the Japanese and Korean syllabic systems may also affect the development of reading strategies for English.

Ho.   Ho is a Taiwanese graduate student who has come to study at an American university. He can speak and listen well, but reading and writing are a problem for him. Ho takes so long to decide what the word is in English that by the time he has come to a decision, he has lost track of what the sentence means. If he can't recognize a word as a whole and summon up a meaning, he can't sound it out. When Ho has an assignment to read, he looks up each word he is not sure of in his English–Chinese dictionary and writes the Chinese symbol for the word in the line above the word. This takes him forever, but at the end, he can read the English passage as if it were Chinese because in effect, it is Chinese. When he rereads the passage to review, he looks only at the Chinese writing. His slow and laborious reading is having a serious impact on his success in college because of the time it takes for him to read and comprehend his assignments.

For teachers to help students like MariCarmen, Despina, Mohammed, and Ho acquire efficient bottom-up processing, they must first understand that L1 and L2 low-level reading processes are never quite the same. Aebersold and Field (1997) said the following:

> The differences between the writing systems and rhetorical structures of the native language and the target language may be another factor in L2/FL reading. Orthographic systems vary widely, and some systems include strong aesthetic elements—for example, Chinese calligraphy is not only a commu-

nication tool but is also one of the most highly respected arts in that culture. *Readers who use basically the same alphabet or writing systems in their L1 as they are learning to use in the L2/Fl will have less to learn and be able to begin reading faster.* Conversely readers switching from a system with a limited number of symbols to a system with abundant characters will need more time to become proficient.... It is prudent to keep in mind Haynes's (1989: iii) argument that mastery of the L2 writing system "is both harder and more important to L2 reading success than existing theory and research would suggest." (p. 28, emphasis added)

A similar but more complexly worded point is made in Geva (1999):

At the same time, the acquisition of literacy skills may be also propelled by language specific processing requirements at the phonological, orthographic or morphosyntactic levels. In the latter analysis, underlying cognitive resources are tapped differentially, to the degree demanded by the orthographic or linguistic characteristics of L1 and L2.... Considerations of orthographic complexity refine our understanding of L2 literacy skills development. For example, Hebrew and Persian word recognition and decoding are associated with less steep developmental trajectories than those associated with parallel development in English. (pp. 360–361)

The fact for teachers to recognize is that no other writing system is like English; therefore, positive transfer or facilitation from L1 will be either limited or nonexistent, but negative transfer may be great. Teachers who overlook this fact may not have a realistic view of the reading task for their students, even at an advanced stage. Their expectations may be unrealistic, and worse, they may not know how to assist their students beyond supplying background knowledge and activating schemas. They may not know how to begin helping their students improve their reading speed and automaticity. One surprising place for teachers to begin is with their students' listening comprehension. We turn to that topic next.

DISCUSSION QUESTION

1. The Chinese linguist Wang (1973) has observed: "To a Chinese the character for "horse" means **horse** with no mediation through the sound /ma/. The image is so vivid that one can almost sense an abstract figure galloping across the page." Which representation from Figure 3.1 does this quote agree with? Which representation, if any, seems to indicate the way that you recognize and understand the word 'horse' in English?

Chapter 4

Listening Skills in Reading

Prereading Questions. Before you read, think about and discuss the following:

1. Say the words **pat** and **bat**. What is the difference in the pronunciation of these two words?
2. Say the words **peat** and **pat**. What is the difference in the pronunciation of these two words?
3. Can you sing the sequence *ttttttttt*? Can you sing the sequence *mmmmmmm*? Can you sing the sequence *aaaaaaaa*? Why can you sing (or hum) the latter two sequences and not the first?
4. Why do we have accents when we try to speak another language?
5. Do you hear sounds in your head when you are reading words? Or do you have a sense of pronouncing words even though you are reading silently? If so, do you think that it slows down your reading?

Study Guide Questions. Answer these during or after reading the chapter.

1. What property do all voiceless sounds have in common? What property do voiced sounds have in common?
2. What is the difference between oral sounds and nasal sounds?
3. Using the diagram of the mouth and your own mouth, go over the place and manner in which these consonant sounds are produced: /p/, /tʃ/, /f/, /ð/, /ŋ/, /l/.
4. Make the vowels [iy] and [uw]. What is the difference in how they are made? Are these true diphthongs or phonologically created diphthongs?
5. Define these terms: *phone, phoneme, allophone, minimal pair.*
6. Do you pronounce the names Don and Dawn the same? What vowel sounds do you have in these two words?
7. What is phonemic awareness? How can it be developed?
8. What are the suprasegmental features of English? How are they important to the nonnative speaker?
9. Why does pronunciation not matter in silent reading?

In some ways it makes sense to believe that phonological processing in reading is linked to the reader's ability to pronounce words accurately (Freeman & Freeman, 1999; Hatch, 1979), but Wallace (1992) quite rightly argued:

> "Phonics," as the method is popularly called, involves the ability to match up letters (or "graphemes") to some kind of sound representation. It tends to be assumed that phonic skill is displayed by the ability to read aloud with a "good" —that is native-like, standard English—pronunciation. (p. 54)

Wallace is more properly referring to phonemic-to-graphemic awareness, the ability to match letters and sounds. (Phonics is a teaching methodology.) However, she is correct in disconnecting reading and pronunciation, and here's why. The fact is that phonological processing in reading is more heavily dependent on accurate perception and recognition of sounds in listening than it is on the production of sounds in speech (Bradley & Bryant, 1983).

For native readers of English, listening ability is a good predictor of reading performance; better listeners tend to be better readers (Bond, Tinker, Wasson, & Wasson, 1989). This may be because language knowledge and listening strategies form a framework to which knowledge of written language and reading strategies are added as they are acquired. Knowledge of sounds, morphemes, words, syntax, and the world stored for listening can be used to bootstrap reading, because the written form "attaches" to the sound form. The strategies for identifying sounds, words, and sentences and tying them to meaning by ear may be similar to those needed by the eye. This indicates the importance of beginning reading instruction with written materials that are similar to spoken language. Therefore, for most readers and reading tasks, accurate pronunciation of the sounds of English is largely irrelevant, but accurate listening is not. This chapter explores the issue further by looking at the development of phonemic processing, the types of reading people generally do, the phonemic inventory of English, and the relationship between listening and reading.

THE DEVELOPMENT OF PHONEMIC PROCESSING

Studies show that infants can discriminate (perceive the difference) between different sounds from birth and that the innate ability to discriminate is applied to the sounds of the language that surrounds them. As infants begin to comprehend and later to produce their own language, they lose their ability to discriminate between sounds that are irrelevant to their own language. For example, infants discriminate between many sounds that are not used in English, but they lose this ability as their knowledge of English sounds develops and as they gain the ability to understand the speech that is directed at them and the speech that goes on around them. They usually master the comprehension of spoken language before they can produce all of the sounds of English accurately. Slowly they begin to be able to produce the sounds with accuracy, although many children's production of difficult sounds like /r/, /y/, and /l/ can be delayed until the age of 6 or 7.

Speakers of other languages also lose the ability to discriminate between sounds that do not occur in their native language, but if the ESL and EFL instruction that they receive has a strong oral/aural focus, they too will master the discrimination of English sounds, although completely accurate production of English sounds can be challenging and may, in fact, never occur. Accurate pronunciation seems to be highly correlated with the age of acquisition; the earlier in life English is acquired, the more accurate the pronunciation of the speaker is. Luckily for our students, accurate silent reading is more dependent on accurate discrimination of sounds rather than accurate production of sounds. I know of no evidence that the ability to develop accurate aural discrimination in an L2 diminishes with age unless hearing becomes impaired.

However, discrimination of English sounds, especially vowels, can be problematic for ESL and EFL learners because most languages have fewer vowels than English does. A common vowel system in the languages of the world has five spoken vowels, roughly those in Bach, bait, beat, boat, and boot. Another common vowel system has three vowels, those in Bach, beat, and boot. Although there is quite a bit of dialect variation even in so-called standard English, English is thought to have 12 vowels. There are also some consonant sounds in English that can cause discrimination difficulties because they are uncommon: the initial sounds in **th**is, **th**in, **sh**ip, **ch**ip, **g**enre, **j**et, and the final sound in si**ng**.

For accurate listening comprehension and reading, the learner's knowledge base must contain an inventory of English sounds, each sound in the form of a generalized mental image learned from a number of different memories of experiences with the sound in different contexts (Baddeley, Gathercote, & Papagno, 1998). Learners need not be able to verbalize or describe the difference between two sounds, but they need to be able to discriminate two sounds. In addition, learners don't need to be able to pronounce sounds perfectly. In silent reading of familiar words, only the abstract mental image of a sound may be used in recoding. It is in oral reading that pronunciation and fluency become relevant. Articulation of sounds is also important in reading and learning new words, as we show in later chapters, but for now, let's explore the question of silent versus oral reading in more detail.

THE TYPES OF ENGLISH READING

We have hypothesized that for most words, the squiggles on the page (Figure 4.1A) are identified as letters (decoding), and matched with the abstract mental images of English sounds stored in memory (recoding), as in Figure

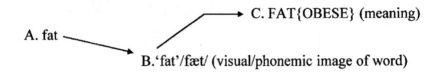

Figure 4.1 Silent efficient reading of the word "fat."

4.1B. This creates a visual and aural image of the word, which then undergoes lexical processing to identify and retrieve the word and its correct meaning, as in C. This means that no real physical sounds need to be involved in silent reading; only the abstract sounds stored in the head are processed. If only abstract sounds are processed, reading is quicker.

However, there are three other possibilities for reading, and each possibility involves slightly more processing work.

"Hearing" the Words

In the first type of reading (Figure 4.2D), readers proceed to summon up a memory of the physical sounds in the word they are reading. They have the sensation of hearing the words in their heads. Naturally this slows the rate of reading down because reading only takes place at the speed of speech. Recalling how the words sound also requires more cognitive work, so there may be less attention available for comprehension.

Subvocalizing

In the second type of nonsilent reading (as in Figure 4.2E), readers proceed even further to activate the motor commands to the mouth that are associated with the sound, so that the reader has the sensation of saying the words, but nothing is audible. This is called *subvocalizing*. As with "hearing" the words, fast readers sometimes use subvocalizing as a method to slow down their reading so as to comprehend better, but in general, subvocalizing is less efficient than pure and simple activation of the abstract mental image because it requires more processing effort and attention. However, subvocalizing unknown words may be a important strategy to learn new words (Baddeley et al., 1998).

Oral Reading

The third way of reading is oral reading, in which the motor commands to the mouth are actually realized and the read words are pronounced audibly, as in Figure 4.2F. Sometimes oral reading is intentional, to accomplish a task like reading a story to someone. However, sometimes the words are unintentionally whispered under the reader's breath almost as an extreme form of subvocalizing, which is not a good way to read. (Subvocalizing and whispering during reading can be inhibited if readers put something in their mouths while they are reading so that they become more aware of their mouths.)

Intentional oral reading requires quite a bit of processing work, effort, and attention to achieve careful clear pronunciation and intonation. Many ESL and EFL students find oral reading difficult and stressful because they must process the squiggles into letters, match the letters with abstract mental images of sounds, activate the right motor commands to the mouth, and put those motor commands into effect with the most accurate pronunciation. Is it any wonder that comprehension of orally read material suffers? Another problem is that the way the word looks is more likely to affect the pronunciation of the word, which, for English, is sometimes counterproductive because the pronunciation is distorted. There are some occasions in which oral reading is useful as a pedagogical tool, for instance, in learning new vocabulary, but it is not useful either for testing pronunciation or for testing reading comprehension. The topic of oral and silent reading fluency is taken up again in chapter 10.

THE PHONEMIC INVENTORY

Phonetics is the study of the sounds of the flow of speech. Even though it seems like we perceive individual sounds as we hear them, the flow of speech is actually continuous. The sounds are not really discrete segments, but we learn to discriminate discrete sounds in the flow of speech as we acquire a language. If we hear speech in a foreign language that we do not understand, at first we cannot segment the speech into words, and we often

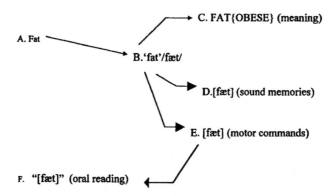

Figure 4.2   Other types of less efficient reading follow: hearing the words mentally (D), subvocalizing (E/F), and reading out loud (F).

cannot even segment the speech into discrete sounds because we have lost the ability to discriminate between sounds that are not in our native language. As we acquire knowledge of the L2, we acquire the ability to segment the flow into separate words and sounds because our phonological and lexical processing strategies can draw on knowledge about sounds and words stored in the knowledge base.

Segmenting the Flow of Speech

One of the strategies that we use to distinguish sounds in the flow of speech is to notice certain invariant properties that each sound has. Thus, every time we hear a [d], even though it might be different from speaker to speaker or from environment to environment, we can recognize it as /d/. (Linguists use square brackets to "write" sounds as they are actually produced in speech and slanted lines around symbols for abstract mental images of sounds, so that we keep them separate in our thinking and we know that we are not talking about ordinary written letters.)

When we hear someone with an accent, we can understand their speech as long as they more or less pronounce the main invariant properties of the sounds (or at least substitute a sound with some similar acoustic properties). The speech of each individual is unique. It's called a "voiceprint." The pitch of a person's voice depends on the length of his or her vocal tract. That is why small children have very high-pitched voices. The resonance in the vocal tract depends on the shape of it, so that will also vary from individual to individual. Yet these individual variations in speech and accent do not stop us from understanding, because the invariant properties of the sound are maintained no matter who the speaker is.

It is possible that the invariant properties that linguists use to classify English sounds are similar to the unconscious and informal knowledge that is stored abstractly in the reader's knowledge database to be accessible in processing both spoken and written language. We also need knowledge of the sounds of English for our discussion of letter-to-sound correspondences in the following chapters.

English Consonants

We describe consonants based on the way the sound is produced and the place that the sound is made in the mouth, as shown in Figure 4.3. To make most of the sounds in human language, the airstream has to pass through the trachea and the glottis, the opening between the vocal folds.

Voicing. *Voiceless* sounds are those that pass through the glottis unobstructed by the vocal folds, so they do not vibrate. Voiceless sounds are /p/, /t/, /k/, and others. *Voiced* sounds are produced when the airstream

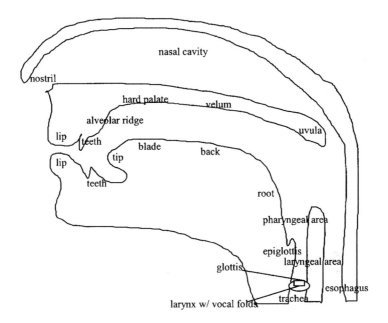

Figure 4.3   The vocal tract.

causes the vocal folds to vibrate because they are pulled together and ob-
struct the airstream. Voiced sounds are /b/, /d/ and /g/ and others. The
voiced/voiceless distinction accounts for the difference in the first sound of
following word pairs: **fat** and **vat, sit** and **zit**. If you say these words carefully
and focus on the sounds and how you are producing them you will note that
each pair is identical except for the vibration or lack of vibration in the first
sound. All sounds are either voiced or voiceless.

Orality Versus Nasality.   If the uvula is closed, the airstream passes
through the mouth. Those sounds are called *oral*. If the uvula is open and if
the airstream is stopped somewhere in the mouth, the airstream passes
through the nasal cavity and out the nose; those sounds are called *nasal*. All
sounds are either oral or nasal. Nasal sounds are /m/, /n/, and /ŋ/. They are
voiced and nasal. Oral sounds are /b/, /p/, /t/, /k/, /l/, /r/, and others. So all
sounds can be divided according to their manner of articulation (how they
are made) into voiced or voiceless, oral or nasal. Consonants have other dis-
tinguishing manners of articulation also.

In Figure 4.4 we see a chart of the English consonants. The place of articulation is across the top, the manner is down the left side. We talk about
manner first.

Manner of Articulation	Place of Articulation						
	Bilabial	Labiodental	Interdental	Alveolar	Palatal	Velar	Glottal
Stops	p b			t d		k g	ʔ
Affricates					tʃ dʒ		
Fricatives		f v	θ ð	s z	ʃ ʒ		h
Nasals	m			n			ŋ
Liquids				l	r		
Glides	w				y		

Figure 4.4   The Consonant Inventory.

Manner of Articulation.   Going from the top to the bottom of the chart, the manner goes from maximal obstruction of the air flow to minimal obstruction, or a mere shaping of the vocal tract. In other words, in making a *stop*, the air flow is stopped completely at some point in the mouth. Air pressure is built up and then released. In an *affricate*, the air flow is stopped briefly to build up a little pressure, but then quickly released with a small force of air that passes through the mouth, which is shaped to produce friction. *Fricatives* are produced by bringing two parts of the mouth very close together, making a small channel for the air to go through. When the air goes through the small channel, a lot of friction is produced in the airstream. Stops have maximal obstruction or stoppage; affricates have maximal obstruction and then constriction; fricatives have a continuous airflow that is highly constricted.

Recall that *nasals* are produced by allowing most of the air to flow through the nasal cavity, but a little air goes through the mouth, where it is stopped by the two lips for /m/, by the tongue tip and the alveolar ridge for /n/, and by the back of the tongue and the velum for /ŋ/. *Liquids* are produced by bringing two parts of the mouth very close together so that they may even be touching, but the channel that the air goes through is large and no friction is produced. Instead, a kind of resonance or musicality is produced by the shape of the tongue and mouth. *Glides* are like liquids, but the opening through which the air flows is even greater. The continuum of "aperture" or opening, as I call it, explains why liquids and glides are similar to vowels. As we will see, vowels also are produced more by mouth shape than by stopping or constricting the air flow.

Place of Articulation.   Across the top of Figure 4.4 are some terms that refer to the parts of the mouth that are involved in producing the sound. *Bilabial* refers to sounds produced by the two lips; *labiodental* means that the lower lip and the upper teeth are involved. *Interdental* sounds are produced with the tongue tip between the two sets of teeth. *Alveolar* sounds are produced with the tip of the tongue on the alveolar ridge, the bony part just behind the upper teeth. *Palatal* sounds are produced at or near the hard palate with blade of the tongue and *velar* sounds are produced at or near the velum with the back of the tongue. *Glottal* sounds are produced in the pharyngeal or laryngeal areas. Besides the glottal fricative, there is also a glottal stop, written with the symbol ? (a question mark without the dot at the bottom). It is a sound that has no correspondence with any letter in the alphabet; it is the sound at the beginning of each syllable in the word **uh-uh**. If you say this word, you will sense a closing, a build up of air pressure, and an opening in the glottis before the vowel sound. Although the glottal stop is not a contrasting meaningful sound in most dialects of English, I include it on the chart for completeness.

As you read through the descriptions of the individual consonants in Figure 4.5, make each sound and focus on what you are doing to verify the place and manner of articulation. (The best way to learn this information is in two steps. First learn to associate the symbol with its sound, and second, learn the descriptors and their definitions. With this information, when you see the symbol, you can pronounce the sound, and come up with the descriptions based on the sound you have made. This is more efficient than trying to memorize the descriptions for each symbol or sound.)

English Vowels

English vowels form the nucleus or musical center to the syllable. The principal vowels of English are distinguished from each other by the shape of the vocal tract when they are produced. The main articulator is the tongue, which is capable of very precise, rapid, and small movements. These movements take only a tiny fraction of a second, but they are enough for us to tell the difference between vowel sounds based on tongue height and tongue position. Pronounce the word in parentheses to understand the value of each symbol in the chart (Figure 4.6).

Tongue Position.   The high front vowels are produced with the tongue relatively high and forward in the mouth, as opposed to the low back vowels, in which the tongue is relatively low and back. So the vowels are not distinguished in absolute terms but in relative terms. They are defined with respect to their relative position when compared with each other.

Phonetic or Phonemic Symbol	Description	Example words
p	voiceless bilabial stop	pig, dipper, lip
b	voiced bilabial stop	big, fiber, rib
t	voiceless alveolar stop	tick, fatty, fat
d	voiced alveolar stop	dig, laddie, lid
k	voiceless velar stop	kid, sicker, snack
g	voiced velar stop	get, digger, dig
tʃ	voiceless palatal affricate	chick, kitchen, birch
dʒ	voiced palatal affricate	John, wedges, sage
f	voiceless labiodental fricative	fat, sniffle, sniff
v	voiced labiodental fricative	vat, swivel, believe
θ	voiceless interdental fricative	thick, ether, teeth
ð	voiced interdental fricative	then, either, bathe
s	voiceless alveolar fricative	sing, kissing, hiss
z	voiced alveolar fricative	zip, buzzer, buzz
ʃ	voiceless palatal fricative	ship, bushes, bush
ʒ	voiced palatal fricative	genre, treasure, rouge
h	voiceless glottal fricative	hat, ahoy, ___
m	voiced bilabial nasal	milk, simmer, dim
n	voiced alveolar nasal	nun, sinner, fin
ŋ	voiced velar nasal	___, singer, sing
l	voiced alveolar liquid	lap, spilling, spill
r	voiced palatal liquid	right, terror, car
w	voiced bilabial glide	wide, slower, slow
y	voiced palatal glide	yes, layer, stay

Figure 4.5   Consonants and their properties.

			Front	Central	Back	
High	Tense	(beat)	i		u	(boot)
	Lax	(bit)	ɪ	ə (telephone)	ʊ	(soot)
Mid	Tense	(bait)	e		o	(boat)
	Lax	(bet)	ɛ	ʌ (putt)		
Low	Tense				ɔ	(bought)
	Lax	(bat)	æ	ɑ (sod)		

Figure 4.6   The Vowel Inventory of Standard American English.

Tension.   We use the terms *tense* and *lax* to get at a very subtle difference in vowels, but it is not useful to spend much time trying to understand these two terms or their definitions. One difference between the tense and lax vowels is a very slight repositioning of the jaw as you make the tense sound and then the lax.

True Diphthongs and Diphthongization.   Some vowels are composed of a simple vowel followed by a glide; they are called diphthongs. In English there are three true diphthongs and four phonologically created diphthongs. The three true diphthongs that occur in English are /oy/ as in **boy** or **poison**, /aw/ as in **house** or **now**, and /ay/ as in **night** or **sky**. True diphthongs are phonemes.

Phonologically created diphthongs are also composed of a simple vowel followed by a glide but they come about as a result of the way that tense vowels are pronounced. A process of diphthongization causes tense vowels to be longer in duration because a glide is added to the simple vowel. The front tense vowels in English /i,e/ are made longer in duration through the addition of a palatal glide /y/. So, /i/ is really pronounced [iy] and /e/ is really [ey]. The back tense vowels /u,o/ are made longer in duration with the addition of the bilabial glide /w/. /u/ is actually pronounced [uw] and /o/ is pronounced [ow]. (Remember the slashes are placed around mental images of sounds and square brackets are placed around actual pronunciations.) If you have ever tried to learn to pronounce Spanish vowels, you know the difficulty English speakers have in removing the glides to pronounce the shorter and purer Spanish vowels. In fact, a major part of the English "accent" in speaking Spanish and other languages comes from transferring these diphthongized vowels to the other language. Diphthongized tense vowels are not phonemes because they occur in pronunciation.

Rounding.   The term *rounding* refers to the position of the lips when the vowel sound is produced. If the lips are somewhat pursed, the vowel is round. Make the sound of /o/; notice the position of the lips. /o/ is a round vowel, as opposed to /a/, which is not. All the back vowels in English are round. When English speakers try to pronounce French, we may have difficulty with front round vowels in French, because we associate roundness with backness. The tense back round vowels in English /u/ and /o/ are pronounced with a "round" bilabial glide [uw] and [ow]. The round glide, like the palatal glide, causes trouble for the English speaker who is trying to learn any language, like Spanish, that has pure tense simple vowels. In my classes, I usually contrast the way an English speaker pronounces the word *taco* and the way that a native Spanish speaker says it.

Nasality. When a vowel is produced right before a nasal consonant, say in the word **band**, the vowel is actually nasalized in pronunciation, although we don't notice it very much in English. Nasalization is marked with a wavy line or tilde ~ over it.

Schwa. In addition, there is very little difference between /ʌ/ and /ə/. The former occurs in positions where there is stress on the vowel, as in words of one syllable like **putt**; the latter occurs in positions where there is little or no stress on the vowel, as the second vowel sound in the word **telephone**. In fact, as we discuss in a later chapter, many vowels that are nonstressed in English are "reduced" to /ə/, so it is a common sound in English.

Variation. There is a lot of dialect variation in the vowel system in English as it is spoken across the globe and even within one country. For instance, many American English speakers don't make a distinction between the vowels in **pin** and **pen**. Many don't have the sound /ɔ/ as in the words **bought** or **coffee**. Instead, speakers of this dialect have /ɑ/. (Another factor in dialect variation is the pronunciation of the /r/.) It is helpful for ESL teachers to train students to hear the distinctions in the primary local dialect, but they also need to be able to understand other speakers of English. Students can be instructed that the word **bought** can be pronounced /bɔt/ or /bɑt/, and similarly for other variation. One problem I've had as an ESL and EFL teacher is that my students learn to understand me, but they don't understand the English on the radio or in the streets. Tapes, videos, guest speakers, and team teachers can alleviate that problem. EFL programs should employ native and nonnative teachers, as well as supplemental resources from a variety of origins, so that students have the chance to acquire the flexible recognition strategies based on the invariant properties of sounds.

PHONES, PHONEMES, AND ALLOPHONES

We have been using the word "sound" somewhat loosely in order to keep our discussion simple, but the word is inadequate for a more accurate and detailed understanding of the unconscious knowledge stored in our memory database. First, we need to be more precise than we have been about the relationship between *language*, the abstract mental system of linguistic knowledge, and the concrete representations that are expressions of it in its different modalities: reading, writing, speaking, and listening.

Language is a complex, abstract, rule-governed knowledge system that humans have in their minds. It consists of unconscious and informal knowledge of the words, syntax, and meanings, among other things. Language is mental, but it has several "real-world" representations: a phonetic system for oral production and listening comprehension, and a writing system for writing and reading. Our concern right now is to describe the relationship between these two systems of representation in a way that is helpful for reading teachers. As we have seen in chapter 2, logographic writing represents the meanings of language and syllabic writing represents the syllables of a language. Alphabetic writing represents units of language, too, but what exactly are these units of sound?

Phones

Any discussion of the phonetic system of a language requires an understanding of three important concepts, which are among the most complex within the field of linguistics: *phone, phoneme*, and *allophone*. A phone is a sound as is it pronounced in speech. In pronouncing the word **fat**, for example, we pronounce three phones. Phones are the real articulations, or vocal noises, that we represent with phonetic symbols inside square brackets, [fæt]. We write phones in square brackets to show that we are talking about sounds as they are actually pronounced, to distinguish them from both mental images of sounds (phonemes) and written letters.

Phonemes

In contrast, a phoneme is an abstract symbol, something that is not actually pronounced, but that has a mental reality only. A phoneme is a meaningful symbol in a language, but it is meaningful in a special sense. It is not that the phoneme itself has a meaning like a word does, but rather that the phoneme makes a meaningful difference in comparing two words. Phonemes are the symbols written inside of slanted lines or slashes, /fæt/.

Thus, each phone as it comes out of a mouth is an instance of a mental abstraction, the phoneme. Each [t] that I say is unique, different from any other [t] that I might say on other occasions. But each [t] is an instance of the same mental abstraction, /t/. It is clear that the number of phones is infinite, but the number of phonemes in a language must be finite. The number of phonemes in English is actually quite small.

Allophones

Phonemes are mental abstractions; they are never pronounced because when we try to produce them, we are forced to produce phones! For instance, the tense vowel phonemes /i/, /e/, /u/, and /o/ are always pronounced as their allophones /iy/, /ey/, /uw/, and /ow/.

Sometimes when we pronounce the phones in the context of a word, the surrounding sounds form a context that can produce a change in a phone. Sometimes phones vary freely from instance to instance (they are in *free variation*), but they are still associated with one phoneme. Sometimes phones are not in free variation; instead a certain phone must occur in one context and another phone must occur in another context. They are in *complementary distribution*. Phones that are related to each other by being different context dependent or free varieties of the same phoneme are called *allophones* of a phoneme. One such phone is called an allophone of a phoneme. An example will make these concepts more concrete.

One English phoneme is /t/. We know that it is a phoneme of English because we can find a lot of *minimal pairs* that show it to be a meaningful contrasting sound. A minimal pair is a set of two different words that are identical except for two phones. If such minimal pairs exist then it is good evidence that the contrasting phones belong to different phonemes. The contrasting phonemes /t/, /d/, and /k/ are illustrated in Figure 4.7 with the minimal pairs **lit** and **lid, ten** and **den**, and **lit** and **lick.**

When we look closely at the phoneme /t/, as in Figure 4.8, we find that the situation is more complicated. For one thing, compare the [t] as pronounced in the word **tick** and the [t] as pronounced in the word **stick**. In the first case, [t] is *aspirated*, or pronounced with a puff of air, so a more accurate phonetic symbol would be [tʰ], where the ʰ represents the aspiration of the puff of air. In the second case, the puff of air is missing. This is an example of *complementary distribution*.

We also see that in the word **write**, the [t] may or may not be aspirated, but it doesn't seem to make any difference in meaning to the listener because these sounds are in *free variation*. The word still means the same thing; the words are not minimal pairs, so the sounds do not contrast with each other. In the word **writer**, the [t] seems to sound more like a flap [D] for most Americans, but not for most British English speakers. In fact, we can find no minimal pairs in English that contrast the aspirated version with the unaspirated version or the flapped version of /t/. Therefore, we know that we are dealing with allophonic variation and not different phonemes. The different ways that /t/ is pronounced in different contexts (of the words **stick**, **tick**, and **writer**) are allophones of the phoneme /t/, which can be written phonetically as in Fig. 4.8.

You may have already seen the connection between allophones and "accent." American English has these allophones for /t/, but other dialects of English and other languages have different allophones. Few other languages have the aspirated stop or the flap [D] for /t/, for instance. Because

Figure 4.7   Minimal pairs as proof of the status of phonemes.

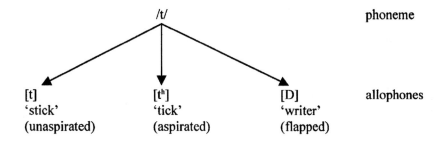

Figure 4.8   Some allophones of the phoneme /t/.

we transfer our knowledge of our native allophones to other languages when we are speaking them, we have an accent.

Phonemic (Not Phonetic) Writing.   It is crucial for the reading teacher to understand that individual phones or allophones are not represented by the English writing system; instead, the unit of language that is represented by our spelling is the phoneme. That is why English spelling is called *phonemic* and not phonetic. Some linguistically unsophisticated educators argue that a phonetic system would be better, but that is untrue. First, a phonetic system would require at least three different symbols to represent the allophones of /t/, so the number of symbols needed to write English would increase substantially.

Second, English speakers know the allophonic variation in their dialect and it is mostly predictable, so it is redundant to represent it in writing. For example, earlier we discussed how vowels can be pronounced with nasalization if they occur in proximity to a nasal consonant. We don't need to represent that nasalization in writing because that allophonic variation doesn't carry any meaning to us. It is an accident, as it were, of the way that our vocal tract works. We sometimes open the uvula early or close it late in making a nasal consonant sound, so the nasalization leaks onto nearby vowels. This accidental "leaking" is called *co-articulation*.

Third, we don't want to represent allophonic variation in writing because it differs greatly from English dialect to English dialect. English consonant phonemes are quite constant, but allophones may be different in different dialects. All dialects have the phoneme /t/, but not all dialects have all of the same allophones. Around Hartford, Conn., for example (and elsewhere), some speakers have the phone [ʔ] as an additional allophone of /t/. When some speakers say the word Britain, they say [brɪʔən]. A writing system that tried to represent phones would be hopelessly confusing and complex; it is more efficient to represent our mental system of abstract phonemes, which is more consistent.

It is true, however, that allophonic variation may cause children and nonnative speakers some difficulty in learning to read and write, because they might have incorrect expectations. For instance, there is an aspirated [tʰ] in the word **truck**, which sounds a great deal like another phoneme, /tʃ/. It sounds to many children that the word **truck** is really something like **chruck**, so they would expect it to be written with a **ch** and not a **t**. Someone who advocated a strict phonetic spelling would agree with the child. For teachers, however, it is helpful to understand that spelling errors (or "creative spelling") often follow the phonetic and allophonic values of the sounds, so when students write **chruck** they are using sound-to-letter correspondences, but they are not following our conventionalized spelling system. Similarly, the ESL and EFL student may use creative spelling that reflects the allophones they hear instead of the phonemes of English.

SUPRASEGMENTAL FEATURES OF ENGLISH

Besides the inventories of consonants and vowels, each language has different ways to encode other information in the flow of speech. Some languages use systems of tone to differentiate words that otherwise have the same consonants and vowels. A sequence of [ma] is a different word if it is pronounced with a "falling tone" or if it is pronounced with a rising tone:

$$\overset{\backsim}{\text{ma}} \quad \overset{\diagup}{\text{ma}}$$

For tonal languages, the tones are suprasegmental phonemes of the language. Suprasegmental means that they "float" above the phonetic segments, the consonants and the vowels. English does not have phonemic tones, but it does have two suprasegmentals: *stress* (word-level and phrasal) and *intonation*.

Word-Level Stress

English words are composed of one syllable or more than one syllable. One syllable of a multisyllable word is pronounced with more stress or emphasis. Stress is a combination of loudness, duration, and effort in pronunciation. The more highly stressed a syllable or word is, the louder and longer it is and the more effort it takes to pronounce it. Stress differences are relative; they are defined with respect to each other and not in some absolute way. Usually there is one syllable that has primary stress and another may have a secondary amount of stress. In **photograph**, **pho-** has primary stress, **-to-** is unstressed, and **graph** has secondary stress.

Phrasal Stress

English sentences are made up of different phrases: noun phrases, verb phrases, and the like. Each main word in a phrase receives more stress than the less important words in the phrase. That means that the stressed word is longer in duration, louder in intensity, and pronounced with more effort than the other words in the phrase. In the following sentence, the phrasal stress is marked with bold print.

In the **morning**, I have a **cup** of **coff**ee and **read** the **paper**.

Phrasal stress is involved in the timing of phrases. Each phrase takes more or less the same amount of time to pronounce, but the stressed word takes up more of the time than the unstressed words. This means that the unstressed words are shorter and mushed together. This contrasts sharply with a language like Spanish, which is syllable timed. In Spanish, each syllable receives approximately the same amount of time. It is for this reason that Spanish sounds more staccato than English does. It is possible that English speakers cue into the phrasal stress to help them determine the phrasal structure of the sentences that they hear because word order and structure are important for understanding English.

Intonation

Sentences in English also have intonation, which is a cue to meaning. Typically, declarative sentences and Wh- questions have a falling intonation and yes/no questions have a rising intonation. Phrasal stress, timing, and intonation can also be used for emphasis and contrast in English. Prosody (phrasal stress and intonation) is available to listeners but not to readers. In reading, intonation patterns are represented imperfectly by punctuation: Periods reflect falling intonation, commas reflect pauses, and question marks may mark rising intonation in the absence of other syntactic cues. Other languages, of course, have other characteristic intonation patterns.

PHONEMES AND PROCESSING STRATEGIES IN READING

Processing strategies in listening comprehension draw upon the knowledge of English phonemes and processing strategies that match incoming phones to the phonemes and understand speech (Figure 4.9). This occurs automatically, effortlessly, and unconsciously most of the time for native speakers, but we can grasp how it works because sometimes we need to process difficult speech more consciously. If you are listening to someone with a heavy unfamiliar accent, you may need to decide what word you have heard if you are not sure. I have a friend from Atlanta and at first her words "blind" and "blond" sounded the same. On several occasions, I had to decide if she was talking about someone who couldn't see or someone who had blond hair. I used the sound cue, but I also had to use other areas of my knowledge base, like context and world knowledge. It made for some interesting misunderstandings.

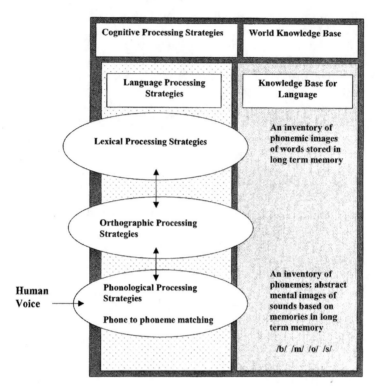

Figure 4.9   Phonological knowledge and processing strategies.

Phonemic Awareness

The knowledge that words are made up of discrete sounds, along with the strategies that allow discrimination and segmentation of the sounds, is called *phonemic awareness*, which has become a "buzz word" in English reading research and classroom practice for native readers. Phonemic awareness is an important precursor for alphabetic reading, but paradoxically people often acquire it as a result of learning to read an alphabet. ESL and EFL learners need to acquire the knowledge base of English phonemes so that their aural discrimination of sounds can proceed effortlessly, quickly, and unconsciously. Note that they need to distinguish the phones in hearing based on the mental image of the sound (phoneme), but they don't need to produce phones with complete accuracy. That is, learners need to be aware of phonemes, but they don't need perfect pronunciation of phonemes in English.

The idea that pronunciation is important in reading stems from a common misunderstanding of the concept of the phoneme, that it is a real sound and not the mental representation of a sound. Still, more research is needed in this area. Bernhardt (1991) is correct in pointing out that "the extent to which readers' own accents interfere with, facilitate, or have no impact on their reading process remains uninvestigated" (p. 77). The suggestion made here is that readers' own accents will not affect their silent reading, but their aural discrimination of sounds will. Only their oral reading will be affected by their ability to pronounce what they read. Findings by Baddeley et al. (1998) support the idea that phonological accuracy in pronunciation is not crucial for learning new words either.

Phonemic Awareness Activities

For quick and efficient silent reading, the ESL and EFL learner should acquire an accurate mental image of the phonemes of English. As noted earlier, the image should be based on experiences with different speakers and different situations, but other activities can also help. These activities are very similar to each other.

Segmentation. One part of phonemic awareness is the segmentation of a spoken word into component sounds. In chapter 1, it was noted that the ability to segment words into component sounds is not very intuitive and that its initial discovery was crucial to the invention of the alphabet. English L1 children often learn segmentation through preschool word play, rhyming games, nursery rhymes, and books like those of Dr. Seuss. These prereading activities prepare them to learn the alphabetic principle. For ESL and EFL learners, there is evidence that Hebrew speakers have difficulty segmenting the beginning consonant of an English word from the rest of the word because of their consonantal writing system (Ben-Dror et al., 1995). Arabic readers may have similar difficulties, as well as Chinese readers, who also may not have good segmentation skills because of their sinographic script. (But see Wallace [1992, pp. 54–57] for an opposing point of view on the value of segmentation activities for Arabic readers.) ESL and EFL learners can also learn to segment words into component sounds by identifying (with a number of fingers or a number of claps) how many sounds they hear in a word, by trying to pronounce the sounds in a word separately, by playing oral rhyming games, and by learning rhymes and songs.

Identification. Teachers help learners identify whether a particular phoneme has occurred or not in a context. She might say, "Hold up your YES sign if you hear the sound of /p/ in this word/sentence. Hold up your NO sign if you don't hear the sound. *Sit down please.*"

Manipulation. In addition, English L2 learners can practice manipulating the sounds of words by taking off sounds at the beginnings, in the middle, or at the ends of words. This is an oral task, even a kind of a game, not a reading task. For instance, students can learn to answer "ick" to the question: "What happens if I take the /t/ off of the beginning of the word 'tick?'" They can answer "his" to the question, "What happens if I take the /l/ out of the middle of the word 'hills'? And they can answer "sing" to the question "What is left if I take the /s/ off of the end of 'sings?'"

Discrimination. Many of these activities are based on minimal pairs like **ship** and **chip**, or **chip** and **cheap**. Recall that minimal pairs are different words in which there is only one different phoneme or sound difference. (Don't be distracted by spelling; minimal pairs are not letter differences.) Minimal pairs are used to teach learners to discriminate similar sounds or to test whether the sounds are accurately discriminated. For instance, learners practice identifying whether the teacher has said ***ship*** or ***chip***, ***sheep*** or ***cheap*** in a given context. They don't need to pronounce the phonemes correctly at this point. For preliterate learners, pictures can be used; for literate learners, the words can be written on the blackboard next to numbers. The learners use the number to identify the correct answer.

Is this sandwich cheap? Is this sandwich sheep? (Note that this sentence is absurd or "funny." Encourage learners to laugh at absurd sentences. This makes the exercise more fun.)

Do you want a ship? Do you want a chip?

Do you eat dip with a ship? Do you eat dip with a chip?

English L2 Learners

Which of our students benefit from instruction in phonemic awareness activities? MariCarmen and Despina are already sophisticated readers of an alphabetic writing system, so we can presume that they have acquired phonemic awareness. If they have accurate mental images of English phonemes, their phonemic awareness will probably transfer to their new language. They may need some instruction and practice to acquire accurate mental images of English vowels. Mohammed, the Arabic reader, may need phonemic awareness activities like segmentation to expand his knowledge of English vowel and consonant segments. Ho, coming as he does from a writing system based on sinograms, may benefit from phonemic awareness/segmentation activities in English to improve his bottom-up reading skills. In addition, Chinese is a tonal language, so Ho may benefit from instruction in phrasal stress, timing, and intonation.

The discussion in this chapter leads to the conclusion that strategies for accurate listening comprehension are more relevant to reading than accurate pronunciation. Pronunciation, in fact, only comes into play in oral reading. Here are more specific ideas for teaching auditory perception and discrimination.

SPOTLIGHT ON TEACHING

Teachers often use phonemic awareness exercises in listening comprehension: segmentation, identification, manipulation, and discrimination.

Segmentation

1. The teacher asks learners to clap their hands for each sound they hear in a word: hill (3), taps (4), an (2), very (4), and so on.
2. The teacher asks learners to say the words with a short pause between each sound. If learners can read and write, they should be cautioned not to spell the word. Hill should be something like [h ɪ l]. Taps should be [t æ p s]

Identification

1. The teacher asks students to put up one finger if the first word has **tʃ**. Then she (or he) gives a list of words like: *at, chat, apple, chapel, chin, in*. (This can be short.) The teacher can also draw students' attention to the fact that these word pairs rhyme.
2. The teacher asks students to raise their hands whenever they hear the sound **tʃ**. The teacher then reads the following sentence and similar ones slowly: Chucky likes to share his chocolate candy bars with Charlotte and Charles. (If some students are waiting to see what other people do before putting their hands up, the teacher should give the students two cards, one with an *x* and one that is blank. They must put up the card with an *x* on it whenever they hear the sound.) This can be fun because even if the sentence is read slowly, students will need to listen carefully and respond quickly. It can also be a competitive activity with two or more teams. The team that responds most quickly or accurately wins. Then the teacher does a similar activity for ʃ. (Note that in some ways it is hard to differentiate an identification activity like this from a discrimination activity like those given later in this section.

Manipulation

1. Teachers ask learners to find words within words. This is sound manipulation, not spelling manipulation. What word is left if I take the [br] off of the beginning of these words or names? *break (ache)*; *bride (I'd)*; *Brill (ill)*; *broke (oak)*.
2. Teachers ask learners to manipulate sounds and see if what is left is a word or not a word. What sounds are left if I take the [br] off of the beginning of these words or names? Is what is left a word or not a word in English? *Brenda (-enda)*; *brim (-im)*; *brew (-ew)*.

Auditory Discrimination

1. Teachers make up a list of minimal pairs, such as these pairs with /i/ and /ɪ/. They have learners indicate in some way which they hear: *chip/cheap, bean/bin, will/wheel*. Students who cannot read or write might do this by pointing at the appropriate picture. When the contrasting sound is at the beginning of the minimal pair the words rhyme, which can also be pointed out to students.

2. In an *odd-man-out* task, students hear four words in a series and they are asked to determine which one of the four words doesn't rhyme with the others (*cheap, deep, leap, dip*) or which one begins with a different sound (*pill, pan, bill, pot*) or ends with a different sound (*hug, pick, dig, pig*). (The last task is the hardest.)

Now *you* select an English consonant or vowel contrast that causes difficulty for a certain population of English language learners: (tʃ and ʃ, θ and ð, or s and ʃ; i and ɪ, ɪ and ɛ). Make up creative and interesting identification and discrimination exercises like these examples to teach the sound. Practice your exercise with another student in your group. Remember that this practice is auditory; successful pronunciation of the sounds is not necessary. As always, try to make your practice as creative and fun as possible.

Alternatively, make up a rhyming game or song or a story like Dr. Seuss (for your age level) that can be used to teach phonemic awareness. Follow it up with phonemic awareness activities such as those described in the chapter.

DISCUSSION QUESTIONS

1. Listen to someone with a foreign accent with great attention. How easy or hard is it to understand them? What kind of mental processing do you do when you are trying to understand them? Do you "get used to" someone's accent so that you are aware of it less and less? Describe what must be happening in your mind if you get used to someone's accent.

2. Some people find it easy to pick up regional or foreign accents. It's also a skill that some actors have perfected. Discuss about what it means to be able to do that in terms of the acquisition of phonological knowledge and motor commands.

3. Say these sentences with different phrasal stress and timing and different intonation. How does the structure and/or meaning of each change?

   a. Time flies like arrows.

   b. The man turned on his friend. (Two meanings: One is bawdy.)

   c. This is your handbag, isn't it?

Chapter 5

Processing Letters

Prereading Questions. Before you read, think about and discuss the following:

1. Do you remember learning your letters? How did you learn them? What difficulties did you have? Did any particular letters cause you problems?
2. Look at several letters (a, b, c, f) in a variety of fonts on your computer. What properties do the letters consistently have? What differences are there?
3. How do you read illegible handwriting, if it is important information?

Study Guide Questions. Answer these questions while or after reading the chapter.

1. Explain the idea that readers just sample the text as they are reading. Where did this idea come from? Why is it unhelpful for ESL and EFL students?
2. What are graphemes? What are graphs?
3. Consult Appendix A to answer these questions:

   a. What are the major phoneme correspondences for ch, c, k, g, j, and s?
   b. Why are vowel grapheme-to-phoneme correspondences less predictable?
   c. Which tense and lax vowel phonemes correspond to the graphemes i, e, and a?
   d. What are markers? Give two examples of markers.
   e. What is the main rule describing the alternation between i and y? u and w?

4. What are saccades? What are eye fixations? What are regressions?
5. What knowledge does the orthographic processor draw on to recognize graphs?
6. What strategies does it use?
7. What is the most salient information we use to recognize graphs?
8. What accounts for the differences in reading speed between beginning and expert readers?
9. What is pattern recognition?
10. What is the word superiority effect? What causes it?
11. Why is it easier to read a pseudo-word like *blash* than a nonword like *hsalb*?
12. What implications are there for ESL reading instruction?

We need to understand how expert English readers cope with reading an alphabetic system to know how to help beginning EFL/ESL readers master the same system. What knowledge do English readers acquire or learn in order to decode the text? What processing strategies do they use? One idea that has been important in recent years is that good readers just pass their eyes quickly across the text, focusing on a few letters or words here and there and forming predictions based on background knowledge. Reading is thought to be a process of "sampling the text" in order to confirm or disconfirm these top-down predictions. In this chapter I attempt to show that the sampling metaphor is largely untrue for many typical ESL and EFL readers.

SAMPLING THE TEXT

Carrell's 1993 characterization of the history of reading theory in the field of English as a second language traces the roots of the sampling metaphor to Goodman's early discussions of the "psycholinguistic guessing game." According to Carrell, citing Goodman (1973):

> In this model, the reader need not (and the efficient reader does not) use all of the textual cues. The better the reader is able to make correct predictions, the less confirming via the text is necessary. According to this point of view, the reader reconstructs meaning from written language by using graphophonic, syntactic, and semantic systems of the language, but he or she merely uses cues from these three levels of language to predict meaning, and most important, confirms those predictions by relating them to his or her past experiences and knowledge of the language. (p. 2)

Goodman and other early researchers were characterizing good native English-speaking readers, and they did not minimize bottom-up processing, but by the late 1970s and early 1980s, according to Carrell, second-language reading specialists

> began to view second language reading as an active process in which the second language reader is an active information processor who predicts while sampling only parts of the actual text.... The introduction of [this] top-down processing perspective into second language reading has had a profound impact on the field. In fact, it has had such a profound impact that there has been a tendency to view the introduction of a strong top-down processing perspective as a *substitute* for the bottom-up, decoding view of reading, rather than its complement. (pp. 3–4)

The expression "sampling the text" caught on quickly, and it, like the term "psycholinguistic guessing game," created an impression that still prevails among many ESL and EFL reading practitioners today. Some teachers seem to believe that if students have enough cultural background knowledge and prereading strategies, they will be able to make predictions, confirm them, and therefore read, almost without looking at the text at all. For example, in a widely reprinted and excellent article, Clarke and Silberstein (1979) said the following:

> The reader, therefore, does not use all the information on the page but rather must select the most productive language cues in determining the message of the writer. From this it follows that reading is necessarily a rapid process that could not proceed word by word…. [R]esearch has shown that reading is only *incidentally visual* (Kolers 1969). More information is contributed by the reader than by the print on the page…. The reader forms a preliminary expectation about the material, then selects the fewest, most productive cues necessary to confirm or reject that expectation. This is a sampling process in which the reader takes advantage of his knowledge of vocabulary, syntax, discourse, and the "real world." (pp. 48–49)

In fact, the word *sampling* is as misunderstood as the word *guessing*. Both are extremely complex and cognitively demanding processes that are minimized by the metaphors chosen to talk about them. The idea that readers just sample the text is not very helpful, in a number of ways. First, as Carrell points out, it places too much emphasis at the top of the reading process, skimping the bottom. Although it may be true that expert native English-speaking readers can make top-down predictions and confirm them while reading, they do not just sample the text, as we might sample a variety of the offerings at a banquet table, picking and choosing at random what catches our eye. Reading is not a bit of this and a bit of that thrown onto a plate. As we show later, expert readers are diligent about looking at the text even though they may not fixate their eyes on each and every word. Much of this diligence is unconscious. Good readers' bottom-up processing has gone underground, beneath their awareness, but that does not mean that it isn't happening.

Second, the term *sampling* does not describe the reading process for beginning or intermediate readers, or ESL and EFL readers, who must process more of the cues in the text in order to grasp the meaning. Readers must acquire automaticity through ample experience with reading diverse texts before they can make the predictions to be confirmed in the reading process.

Third, if teachers believe that readers just sample the text, their instructional methodologies will lack a solid foundation in linguistic knowledge and low-level processing strategies. If they believe that readers are just "guessing" and just "sampling," attention to the nitty-gritty details of English letters and sounds may seem to be a topic to be dispensed with as quickly as possible.

Fourth, students are sometimes told explicitly to "sample" the text and to rely on strategies like predicting or skimming. These may work for easy reading for pleasure, but when students must comprehend difficult textbooks or journal articles, these strategies by themselves will not do. In this chapter, we look at the knowledge that beginning English language readers must learn and the low-level processing strategies that they must acquire in order to read English. At the end of the chapter we return to the evaluation of this idea again.

GRAPHS AND GRAPHEMES

For this discussion, we need to discard the word *letter* in favor of the more technical words *grapheme* and *graph*, which parallel our usage of phoneme and phone in the last chapter. In Figures 5.1 and 5.2, we can see that neither graphemes nor graphs are the same as alphabet letters: There are 26 alphabet letters but more than 65 graphemes and a potentially infinite number of graphs.

English Consonant Graphemes

simple						compound
b	g	kh	q	t	wh	ck
c	gh	l	r	th	y	dg
ch	h	m	s	u	z	tch
d	j	n	sh	v		x
f	k	p	sch	w		all geminated consonants (pp, tt)

Notes: **u** is a consonant unit when it corresponds to /w/, as in **qu**ack or lang**u**age.

wh is mainly used as a simple consonant corresponding to the voiced /w/ or the voiceless /ʍ/. In some dialects, **wh** seems to have a compound usage /hw/ as in the "voiceless" pronunciations of the beginning consonants of **wh**at, **wh**ich and **wh**en.

sch is a simple consonant grapheme when it is used as in **sch**ist or **sch**wa.

gn is a simple consonant grapheme when it is used as in **gn**ome, co**gn**ac or poi**gn**ant

Geminated consonants are compound consonants which are simple consonants doubled: **bb, dd, ff, gg, ll, mm, nn, pp, rr, tt, zz**, as in e**bb**, e**dd**y, ga**ff**er, e**gg**, fe**ll**, di**mm**er, di**nn**er, a**pp**le, pu**rr**, be**tt**er, bu**zz**.

In fact, **ck, dg,** and **tch** actually stand for geminate consonants as well: **ck** = **cc** and **kk, dg = jj**, and **tch = chch**. For some reason, our writing system has resisted writing true geminates for these and has preferred to use **ck, dg,** and **tch**, as in ba**ck**, e**dg**e, and wa**tch**.

Figure 5.1   Main English consonant graphemes from Venezky, 1970. Used by permission of Mouton de Gruyter.

English Vowel Graphemes

primary	secondary		
a	ai/ay	ie	ue
e	au/aw	oa	ui
i	ea	oe	ae
o	ee	oi/oy	eau
u	ei/ey	oo	eo
y	eu/ew	ou/ow	uy

Figure 5.2   Main English vowel graphemes from Venesky, 1970. Used by permission of Mouton de Gruyter.

The number of graphs is infinite because a graph is a real-life written mark on a piece of paper, a page, a billboard, or any other surface that can be written on. A graph is a concrete instance of a grapheme in the same way that a phone is a concrete instance of a phoneme. Nevertheless, in general, we use the term *grapheme* more often, reserving the term *graph* to refer specifically to written marks.

A grapheme is an abstract mental symbol of writing that corresponds to a phoneme in our spoken language, and thus, it represents all of the allophones of that phoneme. It is not accurate to say that a grapheme represents a sound, because it really represents more than one sound, usually. A grapheme is an abstraction that we use to recognize graphs. There are four types of graphemes.

First, there are two types of *simple graphemes*, that is, graphemes that represent a single phoneme at a time: single graphemes and double graphemes.

Single graphemes use one grapheme to represent the phoneme. Examples are **t, d, f, s, a, o,** and so on.

Double graphemes (also called *digraphs*) take two graphemes together to represent a phoneme. Examples are **ch, sh, ph, th,** and a few others.

Second, there are two other types of graphemes: compound and complex.

Compound graphemes are simple graphemes doubled (or geminated), as in **gg, tt,** or **ck.** Although compound graphemes are also pronounced as one phoneme, as graphemes, they serve an important purpose in spelling to mark pronunciations (**diner** vs. **dinner**) or to maintain pronunciation and meaning, as in the difference between *striping* (with stripes) or **stripping** (from the verb **strip**).

A *complex grapheme* is **x,** which uses one grapheme to represent a sequence of two phonemes, namely /ks/.

(There is more extensive information about the correspondence between graphemes and phonemes in Appendix A, which is an updated and abridged version of Venezky's 1970 monograph titled *The Structure of English Orthography*, long out of print.)

DEVELOPING GRAPHEMIC KNOWLEDGE AND PROCESSING STRATEGIES

Accurate reading requires both knowledge of graphemes and a number of different strategies to recognize and identify graphs.

Knowledge Base

As a first step, prereaders must learn to identify and write the letters of the alphabet. It is often helpful for students to make the shapes in a number of different visual, tactile, or physical ways and also to identify them in different fonts. We use the alphabet letters to write English, but students also need to acquire the system of graphemes listed earlier. That is why early reading and writing books must contain information about the simple, compound, and complex graphemes that make up the English system of writing. This is true for the native English and ESL and EFL prereaders alike.

Graphemes, like phonemes, have invariant properties, and the knowledge base for language must include an inventory of graphemes and their invariant properties. The grapheme **b**, for example, is a lower case grapheme, a visual symbol made up of a vertical line on the left and a shorter curved line on the right. Our mental image of a **b** must be abstract enough to allow us to read many different real-life **b**s, no matter who writes them, just as our mental image of a phoneme /b/ must be abstract enough to allow us to understand many different voiced bilabial stops, no matter who pronounces them and what position they hold in a word. We must be able to read a **b** in different fonts because of the invariant properties of its shape that remain constant throughout its different appearances. ESL instruction in graphic shapes must extend to at least the variety of fonts available on most computers.

We have seen that the knowledge base needs stored information about English graphemes and their properties in order to identify graphs in what is called orthographic processing.

Processing Strategies

In addition to knowledge of graphemes, readers use quite a few low-level processing strategies to recognize and identify graphs.

Eye Movements. One source of information comes from the study of the eye movements that take place during reading. The eyes do not move smoothly across a line of words; instead they move across print in very quick jerks, which he called *saccades*. During saccades no real sight is possible because the eyes are moving, but between the saccades there are also times, called *eye fixations*, when the eyes are stopped on the print. During eye fixations light energy bouncing off of the page is received in the eye and transmitted to the brain, where the visual stimuli are processed.

The adult expert reader has about four eye fixations per second and identifies around one word per fixation, even though it is theoretically possible for the eye to read four or five words in a single fixation. This means that the average reader takes in around 240–300 words per minute even though, theoretically again, it would be possible to read at a rate of 900 to 1,200 words per minute (Crowder & Wagner, 1992). Presumably, readers prefer a slower speed because it allows for better comprehension of the material that is being read. There is always a trade-off between speed and comprehension, and good readers can adjust fixation speed to accommodate to comprehension needs.

In perceiving the graphs on a page, our eyes do not just move from left to right. Our eyes also perform *regressions*, or backward movements, possibly to check information or to reanalyze something we have perceived (Crowder & Wagner, 1992). In addition, we do not use all of the information from the text equally (Weaver, 1994). For instance, it seems like consonant graphs provide a better cue to the identity of a word than vowel graphs do, at least for English. In English, consonants are more frequent than vowels in most words and the consonant spellings are more consistent and predictable than vowel spellings, so it may not be accidental that expert readers use consonant cues better than vowel cues. Consonant graphs carry more "meaning" for readers; the vowel graphs only have meaning when they occur within a framework of consonants. For example, note that sentence (a) is much easier to decipher than sentence (b).

a. Th- qu-ck br-wn f-x j-ump-d -v-r th- l-z- d-gs.
b. —e —i— —o- -o- -u—e- o-e- —e -a-y -o—.

Selective Fixating and Projecting. At first, early readers probably look carefully at both vowels and consonants, but soon they develop a strategy of fixating more on the more informative consonants than on the vowels, tolerating incomplete information and *projecting* vowel information from the peripheral cues they get and from their ample experience with English spelling patterns. Projecting roughly means that the processor makes a best guess about what the graph is based on partial information. Another example of the use of partial information is that readers get more information from the tops of graphs than the bottoms (Weaver, 1994). Again, note the difference between reading sentence (c) and sentence (d).

c. The quick brown fox jumped over the lazy dogs

d. The quick brown fox jumped over the lazy dogs.

Furthermore, readers fixate more carefully on some words than on others. Stanovich (1991) reports research that indicates that content words receive a direct fixation and that even though short function words and highly predictable words are often passed over, there is quite a bit of fixation on them as well.

During an eye fixation, there is a "window" of 10 graph positions on the right of the fixation point where perception takes place (Crowder & Wagner, 1992). (The window is to the left for scripts that go in that direction, like Hebrew, which may require some retraining for the eye for English learners from those languages.) The reader can see word length information a word or two beyond where his or her eyes will be next. The fixation provides a "snapshot" of the text before the eyes move on.

The fixated and projected information from the sequence of snapshots must be merged together by the mind at some higher level of processing, maybe at the lexical and syntactic levels. The 10 or so graphs are perceived and recognized, and then held in short-term memory until the next snapshot of 10 or so graphs is processed and recognized. The lexical and syntactic levels of the reading processor supplement any other incomplete information from the snapshots by projecting possible additional data from the previous linguistic knowledge and experience the reader has acquired. The more the reader has, the better he or she can do this. This accounts for many of the differences between the beginning and the expert reader.

A few years ago, I had an experience while reading that shows some of this in action. While reading a description of bat navigation, I picked up peripheral cues from a later word while fixating on an earlier word. The later word was actually something different, but the peripheral cues from the graphs activated the word **chocolate** in my head. I felt an instantaneous sense of surprise that the substance (chocolate) would occur in a discussion of bat navigation, but in the same instant I fixated on the word **echolocate**. I remained fixated on the word for a long time while I processed the graph **ch** correctly, and processed the graphs in the correct order, and then identified the unusual verb. After about a millisecond, I succeeded in analyzing the word two ways. First I saw that it was a compound of **echo** and **locate**, and second I saw that it was a back formation from echolocation, the noun form I am more familiar with. I noticed myself regressing to that point frequently until I moved onto the next page.

Reading Speed. This view of the complexity of "sampling," as summarized in Figure 5.3, is confirmed when we look at differences in reading speed between beginning and advanced English readers. Crowder and Wagner (1992) told us that there are many differences between the fixations of beginning readers and expert readers. In a study that compared eye

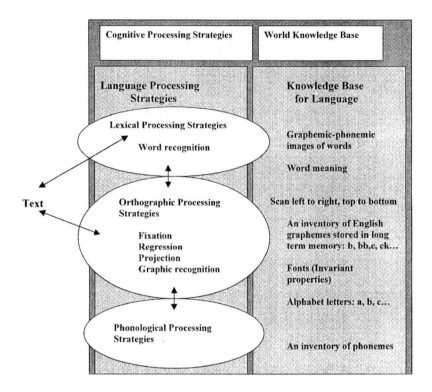

Figure 5.3   The knowledge base and processing strategies for "sampling" the text.

movements from native language readers of all grades from Grade 1 to college, beginning readers had about three fixations per second, while college students had four. Fixations took about 0.33 seconds for the beginning readers but they took 0.25 seconds for the college students. So beginning readers had fewer snapshots per second, and each one took longer. It is reasonable to think that these beginning readers are looking at the visual cues on the page more carefully and or that they aren't as fast at information gathering, processing, and projecting.

In a text, beginning readers had more fixations and also more regressions, showing that they process information slowly but carefully, correcting mistakes that they might have made. Readers in Grade 1 had 183 total fixations with 42 regressions for a 100-word passage, but college students had only 75 fixations with 15 regressions for 100 words. The number of words seen in one fixation also changes as readers gain expertise.

Beginning readers seem to be reading 0.55 words in each fixation, whereas the college students were reading 1.3 words in each fixation, with the adults reading 300 words per minute. So beginning readers have more and longer eye fixations than do advanced readers, but they are actually reading a smaller amount in each fixation. The efficient and expert readers have fewer, shorter eye fixations in which they can read more than one word; they have truly mastered the process! The so-called sampling of the text, instead of being haphazard and cursory, is actually "dense," with rather complete processing of graphs during each fixation. Efficient readers, it seems, depend on the information from each graph and word that is visible in the fixation. Along with low-level processing strategies like fixation, projection, and regression, readers also acquire other processing strategies that operate below conscious awareness. One such strategy is called *pattern recognition* (Crowder & Wagner, 1992; Underwood & Batt 1996).

Pattern Recognition.   The human brain seems well suited to recognizing patterns and similarities in the environment. Pattern recognition in reading means matching the shape of a graph with the mental concept of a grapheme stored as linguistic knowledge. There seem to be two possibilities. One is that the graphs are perceived holistically and identified by matching the perception with a "template" or visual image of the whole grapheme stored in memory. The other type of theory suggests that the features of the graph, the shapes of the lines and so on, are detected separately and compared with a visual image of a grapheme stored in memory. The comparison is not done serially, or one by one, but in parallel, a number of features at a time.

In either case, pattern recognition, like the phonemic recognition we discussed in the last chapter, seems to rest on associating the token (graph or phone) with the invariant properties of the type (grapheme or phoneme). Each instance of a graph is recognized because its properties are similar to the abstract properties of the grapheme, whether it is done holistically or not. Graphic recognition is really a decision-making process in which a lot of different information and strategies come into play.

In fact, there are further connections between graphemes and phonemes. The orthographic processing, which takes the printed text as direct input, is connected to the phonological processing, which was discussed in the last chapter. In orthographic processing, the graphs in the printed text are perceived and recognized, a grapheme is activated, and because graphemes are associated with phonemes, the activation of the grapheme spreads to the associated phoneme. The phonemic activation is how we know the sound or pronunciation of the grapheme even if we do not actually pronounce it out loud. The visual and sound cues are both used to decide the identity of the word that is being read. Once we have recognized some of the graphs in a written word or a partial word, a phonological representation is also associated with the part of the word. Soon there is enough graphemic and phonemic information for the reading processor to begin forming a hypothesis about what the full word is. This is the essence of how alphabetic writing works.

Word Recognition.   There are a number of theories about how words are recognized. For example, it is possible that recognition of graphs causes activation of a graphemic image in our linguistic knowledge, and then the activation spreads to those words that have those graphemes in them, causing them to be recognized (Underwood & Batt, 1996). It seems that at this level of word recognition in the reading process, bottom-up and top-down processing show their greatest overlap. This is because word recognition, like graphic recognition, is a complicated interactive and integrated decision-making process to which the reading processor tries to contribute as much information as possible. The graphemic and phonemic cues are necessary for reading, but the interactive reading processor can also draw on world, semantic, and syntactic knowledge for cues to what the words are that are printed on the page. Many processing strategies also come into play. For instance, the reader can use information from the context of the paragraph to decide what a word is or which of several meanings is the most suitable. The fact that all of this knowledge and these strategies overlap doesn't minimize the bottom-up recognition that must take place. Readers must start with the print and stay close to the print in reading. Anything else is not reading, it is imagination.

When we recognize graphs and words, we don't work on each in isolation. It has been found that we cannot process individual graphs as well in isolation as we can when they appear in the context of the word. We process in chunks because information that is organized into a unit is easier to process than the individual bits of information that compose the unit. That graphs are perceived more easily in the context of a word is called the *word superiority effect* (Crowder & Wagner, 1992).

The Word Superiority Effect.   If we assume that readers remember how words typically look, there would be storage in long-term memory of a visual image for each word that is frequently read. There is a lot of support for the idea of a visual or graphemic image of words stored in memory. For example, people can read letter sequences that have meaning better than those that don't: **YMCA** is read more easily than **YSSU**. However, that reading advantage disappears if the sequences are presented with mixed typography: **ymCA** is read the same way as **ysSU**. The explanation is that **ymCA** doesn't quite match the pattern of our graphemic image of **YMCA**, so the graphs must be read individually, as in **YSSU** or **ysSU** (Henderson, 1984, cited in Crowder & Wagner, 1992). It seems that the development of a graphemic image based on prior experiences with a word gives an advantage to the reader. (And the writer too, because one spelling strategy for words we are uncertain of is to write out alternatives and pick the one that "looks right.")

It is interesting that word superiority effects can also be found for nonwords that could be possible English words, or, as they are called, *pseudo-*

words. It is easier to read **blash** than it is to read **hsalb**. To explain this, we need to suppose, as Crowder and Wagner (1992) do, that the activation that spreads from the graphemic images to the word level activates words that are visually and phonologically similar—**lash, slash,** and **splash**. When these other images are activated, they facilitate the reading of the pseudoword. Facilitation also comes from the fact that pseudowords are pronounceable—a hypothetical phonemic image can be assigned to them. Later on, we pick up on this detail again; this process turns out to be quite important for the English as a second/foreign language learner.

Word Beginnings. Research also suggests that readers find the beginnings of words more useful than the middles or the ends in identifying words (Weaver, 1994). There may be a number of reasons for this. First, we read from left to right, so the beginning of the word is what we encounter first. The ends of words often contain grammatical morphemes that are largely predictable from context, for the native reader at least. It may not be necessary, for example, for the expert English L1 reader to process each verb ending once the context has established that the reading is in the past tense. The morphological information can be projected. Another possible reason has to do with the way that word identification may take place. It may be that the visual images of words are accessed from the beginning to the end and once a word is accessed and identified and the meaning confirmed to fit the context, the rest of the information from the word is not as necessary for identification purposes.

If we think of the reading processor as an expert decision-making system, this use of multisource and extensive, but also incomplete and projected, information makes sense. We have world and linguistic knowledge and different processing strategies that allow us to make a best guess about the graphs and words we are reading. Our best guesses are confirmed by adding in further information from a later fixation. If there is some problem, we can always fall back on the regression strategy to check for a misread graph or a misidentified word.

What can we conclude, then, about the idea of "sampling" the text? It is true that readers do not read every graph or every word, and that their projections and expectations supplement incomplete information. It doesn't take a complete perception to activate stored knowledge, but fairly complete perception may be necessary to store new knowledge. But it is also true that being able to comprehend the message in the text is a complex decision-making process involving many types of knowledge and processing strategies that interact at different linguistic levels. If we understand the word "sampling" in this more complex and respectful sense, we might say that only the best English readers read by "sampling" the text, especially if they are reading something unchallenging, with little new information to be processed.

THE ENGLISH L2 READER

There is little research on eye movements in the reading of ESL and EFL learners. One study (Tullius, 1971, cited in Hatch, 1979) with university level ESL students found that they did not have more eye fixations per line and they did not have more regressions than monolingual students, but their eye fixations lasted three times longer. This indicates that more processing was involved for them to identify the word or that their processing was not as automatic and effortless. It is probably the case that beginning and intermediate ESL students will require more fixations and regressions in their beginning reading, but that the number and frequency will decrease if they succeed in passing into the later developmental stages. World knowledge and activated schemata will only do so much to help their processing if they cannot learn to read quickly with efficient and short eye fixations, accurate projections, and few regressions. These lowest level processing strategies are as crucial to reading success as the higher level cognitive strategies.

Can ESL and EFL readers read by sampling the text? Yes, they can if they have the knowledge, experience, and low-level reading strategies of the best native English-speaking readers. If ESL and EFL readers are lacking knowledge, experience, or strategies, and/or if these do not interface automatically and effortlessly, their reading cannot be described this way. In the research discussed in previous chapters, we found that there is evidence to conclude that readers develop strategies for reading their L1, but that these strategies might not be the same for English. We saw that readers often transfer their L1 strategies to English, which probably interferes with their reading. Furthermore, English learners might not have developed the most efficient strategies for reading English. It is hard to imagine that anyone but the most proficient English L2 reader can "sample" the text and get much from it.

To read English, readers must match a graph on the page to a grapheme stored in their heads, which is matched to a phoneme to form a graphemic–phonemic image of the word, which is then matched to an image stored in our word memory to access the word. For ESL and EFL readers, things can go wrong at any point in this process. The strategies of fixation and regression may transfer if the learner's L1 writing system is similar to English, or they may require some retooling if, for example, the symbols are written right-to-left or top-to-bottom in columns.

Some students may need to learn to fixate on both consonants and vowels, but mainly on consonants. They need to fixate more on the tops of graphemes than on the bottoms. They need to fixate more on content words than on function words. Efficient fixation and regression (e.g., to detect an error that requires regression) requires extensive L2 knowledge, and the ability to project, say, vowel information from incomplete, uncertain, or missing information does, too.

ESL and EFL students may have trouble with graphic pattern recognition. Teachers often assume that students have already learned how to identify graphs when they come into our beginning reading classes, but they should not take this skill for granted. Learners may not know the alphabet letters or how alphabetic writing works and may be using other cognitive or linguistic strategies that compensate for not being able to recognize the graphs on the page.

Illiterate people are not stupid. They become specialists at hiding their illiteracy by memorizing information that is given to them verbally or by memorizing words as holistic units. This is true for English-speaking nonreaders, and it may also be true for some English learners. People who "read" in these ways do not advance into the later stages of reading proficiency. Students may have learned the alphabet letters, but don't understand how they are used to form graphemes in English. For example, they may not know that **ph** is often /f/, or that **dd** indicates the quality of the previous vowel. They don't have the knowledge of English graphemes stored as units and cannot process them in reading.

Another problem is that some ESL learners have *learned* the graphemes of English, but they have not *acquired* them. By that I mean that they know what the graphemes are consciously and formally and can identify them, but they cannot use them to identify graphs quickly and effortlessly as they are reading. The associations between their perception of the graph on the page and the grapheme stored in their memory do not work fast enough, and the associations between grapheme and phoneme may also be missing, faulty, or too inefficient for automatic reading. An ample store of graphemic/phonemic images for frequent words may be nonexistent, which is be the topic of a later chapter.

Thus, for many ESL and EFL learners, being able to read by sampling the text must be the ultimate goal to which they aspire, in order to read quickly and effortlessly. They need low-level L2 knowledge and processing strategies and ample practice to achieve this goal.

SPOTLIGHT ON TEACHING

Texts for English-speaking children use different orders when presenting the consonant grapheme-to-phoneme correspondences. Some of the factors that guide the order of presentation are, according to Gunning (1988), single before digraphs before complex, frequency of occurrence in general, ease of auditory discrimination (stops are least discriminable), frequency of occurrence in the children's reading materials, and not teaching graphemes easily confused together (b, p, and d). Are these factors equally important for ESL and EFL learners? In which order would you teach the consonant graphemes?

According to Gunning (1988), there have been at least three distinct methods of teaching the grapheme-to-phoneme correspondences to English-speaking children over the years. For each one, discuss what might be the advantages and disadvantages for the ESL and EFL learner in terms of what you have learned so far in this text about phonemic awareness, segmentation, and so on. Take notes on your discussion. After discussing each one, put your notes aside until you have read the next two chapters. Then come back and check them to see if you would change your ideas or add more advantages or disadvantages for the ESL and EFL learner.

Three Methods of Presenting Grapheme-to-Phoneme Correspondences

a. The *analytical* method, in which the graphemes and phonemes are never isolated from the context of a word. The teacher says things like "The letter M stands for the sound at the beginning of 'man' and 'monkey.'" The teacher never isolates the sound /m/ for the students.

b. The *synthetic* method, in which the consonant and vowel sounds are isolated and taught separately. The teacher might say, "The letter M stands for /m/." Once the sounds are mastered, then they are blended (synthesized) together (em-aaa-t) to pronounce the whole word: *mat*.

c. The *linguistic* method, in which a series of words are placed on the board in a vertical column: *cat, fat, mat*. Each word is read out loud and contrasted with the one above it. Children learn each spelling pattern (-at) and "induce" (learn on their own from the examples) the grapheme-to-phoneme correspondences in the patterns.

A lesson plan for presenting a consonant grapheme-to-phoneme correspondence might include the following steps: phonemic awareness activities (/b/ vs. /p/), visual discrimination of the grapheme (b vs. p), grapheme-to-phoneme linkage within a word (bat = /bæt/), controlled writing practice, and guided application.

a. Phonemic awareness means that the ESL learner can perceive, identify, and discriminate the sound, as in chapter 4.

b. Practice visual discrimination of the grapheme, picking it out from other similar graphemes, picking it out in various fonts, underlining examples of it in sentences, and so on.

c. Grapheme-to-phoneme linkage within words means that the grapheme is presented visually as the first letter in a word written on the blackboard and pronounced only as part of the whole word. The grapheme-to-phoneme pattern is reinforced several times with different words, including words in which the grapheme is not word-initial. (This is an analytical presentation.)

d. Practice printing or writing upper case and lower case graphemes, make the grapheme shapes in sand, from beans or other objects, label objects with names that begin with the grapheme, and so on.

e. Read stories with words that have the grapheme in them, draw pictures of things that start with that grapheme and write the word, other writing practice, and so on.

Now *you*, individually or in groups, discuss a lesson plan for a common consonant grapheme-to-phoneme correspondence that you pick from Appendix A. Create the materials you would use, with any of the three types of presentation methods. Make sure you make them as interesting, meaningful, and "real" as possible. Use cooperative learning in your activities.

DISCUSSION QUESTIONS

1. In this chapter I described an unusual experience while reading the word **echolocate.** Do you recall any similar experiences while reading? Pay attention to the reading that you do in the next few days. What do you become aware of? What problems do you resolve?

2. Are you a fast reader or a slow reader? If the latter, what do you think slows you down—subvocalizing, "hearing" the words, or something to do with the knowledge or processing strategies discussed in this chapter?

Chapter 6

The English Spelling System

Prereading Questions. Before you read, think about and discuss the following:

1. What complaints have you heard people make about our writing system? Make a list.
2. Some people advocate spelling reform. What are the pros and cons of that? Do you think it will ever happen?
3. How would you pronounce these pseudowords: **habb, spack, hobe, loce**. How did you know how to pronounce these nonwords?
4. Compare your pronunciations to those of a classmate. Are there any differences?
5. What is phonics instruction? What is your impression of it?

Study Guide Questions. Answer these questions while or after reading the chapter.

1. What is the myth that English spelling is chaotic? Where does it come from?
2. What does it mean to say English writing is phonemic? Why is it not phonetic?
3. How do readers use probabilistic reasoning in reading? What are *raw* probabilities? What are *adjusted* probabilities?
4. What knowledge do readers need to have in order to reason probabilistically?
5. Which English consonants have the most unpredictable pronunciations? What increases their predictability?
6. How is reading different from spelling? How is it similar?
7. Give the probabilistic reasoning that might be involved in reading the **c** or **ch** in the words **clad, city, pack, chorus, chlorine, channel**.

In an earlier chapter, we saw that the English writing system is called *opaque* because the correspondence between graphemes and phonemes is not one-to-one. Because of borrowings, historical changes in English, scribal preferences, and so on, our writing system has complexity. If you examine the information from Appendix A carefully, you will see that the consonant graphemes correspond more regularly with phonemes than do the vowel graphemes. Although the consonant system in spoken English has remained fairly stable for the past centuries, spoken English has had a very unstable vowel system. One change was the Great Vowel Shift, which influenced the pronunciation of many vowels, like /i/, /e/, and /a/. Although the change took place in speech, our writing system had been standardized by that time and the changes in pronunciation were not reflected in our writing system. This is why, in other European languages, the letter sound corresponds to the letter name: **i** = /i/, **e** = /e/, and **a** = /a/, but in English, the names and sounds are different: **i** tends to be /ay/, e = /iy/ and **a** = /ey/.

For the reasons just given and others, it is a common idea that the English writing system is hopelessly chaotic and random. People point to the old remark attributed to George Bernard Shaw that in English the word **fish** could be written **ghoti**: the **gh** from **lau<u>gh</u>**, the **o** from **w<u>o</u>men**, and the **ti** from **ac<u>ti</u>on**. In the second-language field, many reading practitioners believe that there is no system that can be taught to English learners to make English reading and writing easier. In fact, English writing is largely systematic; but there are a few anomalies that attract attention and give people the impression of chaos. Many of these anomalies cause more problems for spelling and writing than they do for reading. However, if people expect to perceive chaos in the English writing system, they will. If they want to perceive the order, they must learn to see it.

The English writing system is phonemic, but the relationship between graphemes and phonemes is not one-to-one. The consonant grapheme-to-phoneme relationship is quite consistent, however. In fact, for most of the consonants in the English writing system, the probability that a consonant grapheme will be read in a certain way is quite high. The English reader takes advantage of that consistency and uses knowledge of those probabilities in a certain processing strategy to read them. The processing strategy is called *probabilistic reasoning* and is a common strategy in judgment and decision tasks (Rachlin, 1989; Edwards & von Winterfeld, 1986).

PROBABILISTIC REASONING

To use the strategy of probabilistic reasoning in reading, readers need to learn the probabilities that certain graphemes will represent certain phonemes. Many English L1 readers learn this information directly from their teachers in their earliest reading instruction in preschool or kindergarten (called *phonics*), or they acquire it unconsciously, mainly through exposure to many graphs and words in print. Phonics instruction is instruction in the most common graph–grapheme–phoneme connections in English writing, but not the actual probabilities in the chart in this chapter. Teachers vary as to how much phonic information they present and practice with pre-readers. At first, in Chall's first reading stage, reading takes place out loud (the learning stage), and it probably continues as such until there has been enough exposure to words for rapid mental processing of graphemes to take place (the acquisition stage). Once readers have internalized the main associations between graphemes and phonemes, they begin to read silently (Figure 6.1).

Raw Probabilities. To begin our discussion of probabilistic reasoning in expert reading, and later in reading instruction, we need to get an

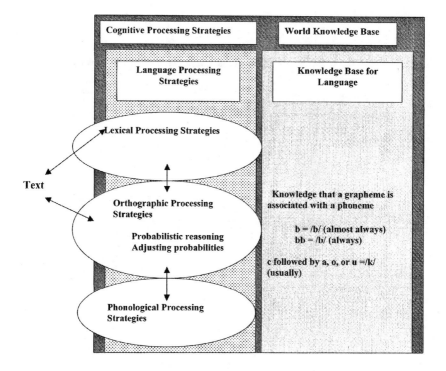

Figure 6.1   The knowledge base and processing strategies for English consonants.

idea of what some of the probabilities are that graphemes will represent certain phonemes. In Table 6.1, you see a chart of English consonant grapheme-to-phoneme correspondences based on, but considerably different from, information in Dewey (1970). Dewey studied a set or *corpus* of 100,000 running words, in which he found 10,119 different words. Function words or frequent content words were presumably repeated more than once, which accounts for the difference between the total corpus and the number of different words he studied for the purposes of the information that I adapt in Table 6.1. Column 1 has the main simple and compound graphemes of English. Column 2 shows the phoneme that the grapheme corresponds to. The last column gives the percentages of times that the grapheme corresponded to that phoneme in the corpus that was studied by Dewey.

These are called *raw probabilities* because the information about them comes from the statistical analysis of a written text and its pronunciation. In computing raw probabilities, there is no accounting for the abilities of the human mind to bring special knowledge and processing strategies to the task of assigning pronunciations.

TABLE 6.1

English Consonant Grapheme to Phoneme Correspondences

Grapheme	Phoneme	Approximate Percentage of Times that the Grapheme Spells that Phoneme:	
bat	**b**	100	
e**bb**	**b**	100	
de**bt**	**0**	100	
cat	**k**	72	
city	**s**	28	
ba**ck**	**k**	100	
church	**tʃ**	90	
choir	**k**	8	
dot	**d**	98	
a**dd**	**d**	100	
fat	**f**	60*	*Note: this result is skewed by three
o**f**	**v**	40*	very frequent words in the corpus in which f
cu**ff**	**f**	100	=>/v/. One is **of**. Except for those frequent words, the correspondence between f and /f/ is probably very high.
got	**g**	73	
general	**dʒ**	26	
e**gg**	**g**	99	
e**dge**	**dʒ**	100	
lau**gh**ter	**f**	100*	*Note: in syllable final position. There were no occurrences of words like bough or daughter in the corpus.
ghost	**g**	100*	*Note: at the beginning of a syllable.
gnome	**n**	100	
hat	**h**	100	
jet	**dʒ**	100	

keep	k	100	
know	n	100	
leap	l	100	
hill	l	100	
met	m	100	
lamb	m	100	
hammer	m	100	
never	n	100	
sing	ŋ	100	
dinner	n	100	
pat	p	100	
phone	f	100	
pneumonia	n	100	
happy	p	100	
quick	k	100	
run	r	100	
purr	r	100	
sat	s	54*	*Note: /s/ is frequent when s is syllable
as	z	45	initial; /z/ is much more frequent when s is syllable final. The frequency of the word **as** may have affected the results.
sword	s	100	Note: This result is questionable.
less	s	93	
pressure	ʃ	5	
shirt	ʃ	100	
tap	t	99	
putt	t	100	

Table 6.1 (continued)

action	ʃ	96	
thimble	θ	20*	*Note: 113 items with **th** => **ð** account for
then	ð	80*	80% of the pronunciations of **th**. These will be high frequency function words like **the** and **that** which distort the figures.
vat	v	100	
water	w	100	
who	h	100	
what	w	No figures	
write	r	100	
tax	ks	No figures	
yes	y	100	
zebra	z	96	
buzz	z	100	

The table is to be read the following way: Each time the grapheme **b** occurred in the corpus, 100% of the time its pronunciation was /b/. There were no exceptions. Similarly, each time the compound grapheme **bb** occurred, 100% of the time its pronunciation was also /b/. There were no exceptions. My findings are very similar to those of Berndt, Reggia, and Mitchum (1987; see also Carney, 1994, pp. 280–381).

In Appendix B, my adaptation of some tables from Groff and Seymour (1987) shows that out of another corpus, **b** will occur 97% of the time and **bb** will occur approximately 3% of the time overall. That means that overall in our spelling, we spell /b/ more often with *b* than with *bb*. We probably have expectations of that based on the knowledge of English writing that we acquire from our experiences with texts, but that information is really irrelevant to the orthographic processor because it knows that every time it encounters a **b** it will access the phoneme /b/ and every time it encounters a **bb** it will access the same phoneme /b/. It should be obvious that this will not cause any difficulty for the orthographic processor.

Spelling Versus Reading Rules.   Note that the variation between **b** and **bb** can a problem for someone who is trying to *spell*, but not for someone who is trying to *read*. One way to look at it is that the reading "rule" is quite regular, but the spelling rule may be more difficult to apply. In our discussion of the reading processor, our concern has been with a unidirectional correspondence of grapheme to phoneme, because that is what we do in reading. We match incoming printed graphemes to abstract mental units, phonemes, in order to access words and meanings. These correspondences can be called *reading rules*.

Reading rule: grapheme ⇒ phoneme

b or bb ⇒ /b/

But the relationships between graphemes and phonemes are really bidirectional. In other words, the relationships can be stated the other way as well, and when they are, they are called *spelling rules*.

Spelling rule: phoneme ⇒ grapheme

/b/ ⇒ b or bb

The learner may be able to read **b** and **bb** with ease, without knowing exactly when to write **b** or **bb** unless the learner has acquired the generalization that the compound grapheme occurs after lax vowels, before certain suffixes, and so on. The English writing system is therefore more complex for the writing decision-making system than it is for the reading decision-making system, which may account for the impression of chaos surrounding the system.

Spelling rules have some similarities with reading rules. For one thing, they draw on the same linguistic knowledge of raw probabilities that readers have in their heads about graphemes and phonemes. Reading rules and spelling rules are often taught at the same time. But reading rules and spelling rules are fundamentally different in their functions and application. The correspondence that goes from grapheme to phoneme in reading is far more predictable, because, for the most part, there are fewer phonemes than potential graphemes associated with them.

Patterns in English Writing. People also think that the English writing system is chaotic because of their somewhat unrealistic expectations of what an alphabetic writing system should be. Many people have the idea that a perfect writing system would have a certain number of symbols, 26 say, with one symbol for each sound and one sound for each symbol. Very few writing systems are that simple and certainly, English writing is not like that for various reasons. First, we have more phonemes in our spoken language than we have alphabet letters for writing. Second, we have more graphemes than alphabet letters too. As we have already seen, graphemes far outnumber the alphabet letters that make them up.

A radical solution would be to double or triple the number of alphabet letters by inventing some new ones, assign each symbol ambiguously to each phoneme, and begin writing in this new way. Indeed, some naive reformers have advocated this and other similar solutions. However, reforming our spelling has proven to be as resistant to change as the U.S. conversion to the metric system, so such a radical spelling reform is highly unlikely. While the spelling of some words could benefit from some "pruning," the system itself works well enough.

To see the pattern in English spelling, we must rid ourselves of the expectation that alphabet symbols must have a one-to-one correspondence to phonemes in order for that alphabetic writing to be regular and consistent. Instead, let's think about a complex system in which, first of all, there are more graphemes than alphabet letters. For instance, both **b** and **bb** are graphemes made up of the alphabet letter b—that is, two graphemes per one letter. Second, most consonant graphemes (except **c**, **g**, and **gh**) are read unambiguously because they do correspond to one phoneme of English. Sometimes the phonemes correspond to more than one grapheme (as in the case of **b/bb** corresponding to /b/), but that is not the problem for reading as it is for writing, as we have seen. In general, the raw probabilities that a consonant grapheme will be pronounced a certain way are high.

When the charts just shown are examined in this new light, the high raw probabilities mean that regular and consistent patterns of correspondences between graphemes and phonemes (despite their complexity) make it fairly easy for the reading processor to make decisions about assigning a phoneme to a grapheme in reading. The human mind can handle such complexity because once the orthographic processor is trained (through experience, practice, and direct instruction) to the point of automaticity to recognize graphemes, the correspondence is predictable. That mind exploits the fact that the raw probability that a consonant grapheme will correspond with a certain phoneme is high.

PROBABILITIES ADJUSTED BY CONTEXT

The human brain does not just rely on knowledge of raw probabilities, however, because it also takes advantage of *contextual information* to interpret consonant graphemes, especially when the raw probabilities are lower. Contextual information can add to or subtract from the raw probabilities that aid the reader in assigning a pronunciation to a particular word encountered in print. Knowledge of these *adjusted probabilities* also needs to be added by readers to their knowledge base, either directly through instruction, or indirectly based on extensive exposure to reading practice. For accurate reading, the reading processor needs to acquire the strategy of using context to adjust the raw probabilities that a grapheme will be pronounced a certain way higher or lower. Here are some examples of how the processor uses stored knowledge and processing strategies to do just that.

The Grapheme c in Context. The grapheme **c** can stand for either /k/ (72% of the time) or /s/ (28% of the time). However, the pronunciation of the grapheme is correlated with the following vowel; the following vowel gives us a context for interpreting the phonemic value of the preceding consonant. If **c** is followed by **a**, **o**, or **u**, it is likely to be pronounced as /k/. If the c is followed by **i**, **e**, or **y**, it is more likely to be pronounced as /s/. Although we don't know from the information we can find in Dewey (1970) what the adjusted probabilities are, because he doesn't provide information about the contexts for these pronunciations, it is safe to say that they would be much higher than the raw probabilities. The adjusted probabilities are encoded as if/then statements in the knowledge base:

> If **c** is followed by **a**, **o**, or **u**, then increase the probability that it is pronounced /k/.

> If **c** is followed by **i**, **e**, or **y**, then increase the probability that it is pronounced /s/.

The Grapheme g in Context. An almost identical example can be seen in the reading rule involving the grapheme **g**. The raw probabilities are 73% that it will be pronounced as /g/ as in got and 26% that it will be pronounced /dʒ/ as in **general**. But the context for this grapheme is the same as for **c** as already described. If **g** is followed by **a**, **o**, or **u**, it is likely to be pronounced as /g/ and if it is followed by **i**, **e**, or **y**, it is likely to be pronounced /dʒ/. The exceptions to this rule are very common words like **girl** and **get**, which can be learned as sight words. It is safe to assume that the reading processor, when it encounters an unknown word, can rely on this contextual information to choose whether are certain **g** will be pronounced either as /g/ or /dʒ/.

The Grapheme s in Context. There are also problems in the raw probabilities for the correspondence between spelling and pronunciation for **s**, which can be either /s/ or /z/. Again, if we know where in the word the grapheme occurs, we can adjust the probabilities higher or lower. The pronunciation of /s/ is much more frequent when **s** is syllable initial; /z/ is much more frequent when **s** is syllable final.

In this case, the "structure" of the word also plays a part. Plural or possessive nouns and third person singular verbs in the present tense end in **s** (as in book**s**, *John's*, and go**es**). The case is complicated, as shown in a later chapter, but sometimes the suffix is pronounced /s/ (books) and sometimes /z/ (John's, go**es**). The native English reader usually knows which pronunciation to assign to the suffix -s depending on what context it is in. This stored knowledge about the suffix allows the reading processor to adjust the probabilities that the grapheme s will represent /s/ or /z/ if it is a suffix.

C, g, and **s** are commonly thought of as exceptions or problems, because of their lower raw associations with phonemes. However, adding contextual information to the mix means that there is less irregularity than previously thought. The correspondence between grapheme and phoneme in the English writing system is patterned, but the pattern is complex. It is crucial to note that human brains are willing and able to store this much information and more in their knowledge base to use as a basis for probabilistic reasoning and decision-making. (However, reading problems are more frequent in English readers than in readers of more transparent systems, so this is not true for everyone.) In general, our minds are capable of handling much more complexity; indeed, many of the decisions and judgments we are asked to make instantaneously every day are far more complex than the interpretation of **g** or any other grapheme, which become, for expert readers, nothing more than routine. Just as we can gauge the probability of getting caught if we go through a red light, or the probability that we will be late if we have that extra cup of coffee in the morning, we can gauge the probability that a certain grapheme will correspond to a certain phoneme. The basis for this knowledge is experience and learning, through which we build up expectations that aid us in future situations.

The Grapheme ch in Context. Let's examine another example of probabilistic reasoning. This case involves the storage of more sophisticated linguistic knowledge about words and spelling patterns and also advanced processing strategies involving context. From Appendix A we see this information about the grapheme **ch**:

a. **ch** in fuchsia or yacht = /0/: less than 0.5%
b. **ch** = /k/ before l, n, r, and in words of Latin or Greek origin: 8%
c. **ch** = /ʃ/ in words of French origin: less than 1%
d. **ch** elsewhere = /tʃ/: 90%

When the orthographic processor sees **ch** in a word that it is processing, the main (or default) option it has learned is /tʃ/ [as in (d)], so it will assign **ch** a pronunciation of /tʃ/ until further notice. Recall in this regard the relevant example of **echolocate**, from the last chapter, in which I first assigned the **ch** the pronunciation of /tʃ/ and then had to regress to repair it to /k/ once I realized that it was in the context of the word **echo**. That means that, in general, if further information from other graphs and the lexical processor contradicts that first assignment to /tʃ/, the lexical processor will override the first assignment to correct it.

For example, say the processor perceives an **l** after the **ch**, as in the word **chlorine**, and realizes that this is a contingency that it knows about, as in (b).

In addition, the processor also begins to form the hypothesis that it is reading a Greek or Latin chemical word. At some point, the orthographic processor or the lexical processor assigns **ch** the correct pronunciation of /k/.

Let's say the reader has had some unfortunate experiences with the pronunciation of French words, so he or she is attentive to them in reading. Over time, based on these cases, the reader has developed the expectation contained in (c). When encountering for the first time the word **chamois**, the reader identifies it as a French word because of the unusual **ois** at the end. The first attempt at pronunciation /ʃamoy/ is not too far off (but still not quite right).

Probabilistic Reasoning With Vowels. Although probabilistic reasoning works well for consonants, it is less useful for vowels. An examination of Table 6.2 shows that although the correspondence between vowel graphemes and vowel phonemes is less predictable than the correspondence between consonant phonemes and spellings, the orthographic processor does have some expectations to work with. Let's say the processor comes across a new word: **tun**. How would we pronounce it? By consulting with the table, we can see that there are three alternatives: /tʌn/ with a vowel like **pup** (63%), /tʊn/ with a vowel like **put** (10%), or /tun/ with a vowel like **truth** (2%). The processor will choose /tʌn/ because the grapheme-to-phoneme correspondence has the highest raw probability of occurrence.

However, context also plays a part in adjusting these probabilities. The vowel graph **o** has the raw probability of 40% of having the phonemic value of /ɑ/ according to the first part of Table 6.2. That is its most consistent correspondence. The main phonemic value for **o**, when placed in the context of **o-e**, is 60% for /o/, which is its most consistent pronunciation. This tallies with our expectations that over all, our graph **o** is most commonly pronounced as in **pot**, unless it is followed by a consonant and a "silent" **e**, as in **tone**. This is the major reading rule for vowels as reported by Venezky and reprinted in Appendix A. The orthographic processor can use this raw and adjusted probabilistic information about vowel graphs to assign pronunciations to the flow of incoming graphs while reading, as it does with the more predictable consonants. Nevertheless, another type of reasoning is thought to be more valuable for vowels: reasoning by analogy to known spelling patterns. We take up that topic in the next chapter.

PROBABILISTIC READING FOR ESL AND EFL READERS

Seidenberg (1990) says that orthographies in different languages differ as to how much phonological information they encode. He cites a number of languages with alphabetic writing systems that are more regular than English in their grapheme–phoneme correspondences. We have called these writing systems, like Spanish, German, or Greek, *transparent*. According to

TABLE 6.2

English Vowel Grapheme to Phoneme Correspondences

Grapheme	Phoneme	Approximate Percentage of Times that the Grapheme Spells that Phoneme
a	æ	52
	ə	22
	e	8
	ɔ	5
	ɑ	4
	ɛ	1
e	ɛ	50
	ə	23
	i	15
	ɪ	12
i	ɪ	89
	ɑy	9
	ə	1
o	ɑ	40
	u	15
	o	15
	ə	12
	ɔ	11
	ʌ	3
	ʊ	2
u	ʌ	63
	ʊ	10
	yu	8
	w	6
	ə	6
	u	2
	ɪ	1

y	ɪ	78
	ɑy	22
ai	ey	71
	ɛ	23
	ɪ	6
au	ɔ	49
	ɑ	42
	o	4
	æ	4
aw	ɔ	100
ay	ɑy	95
	ɛ	4
ea	i	63
	ɛ	18
	ey	11
	ə	6
	ɑ	1
ee	i	76
	ɪ	24
ei	e	77
	i	17
	ɪ	5
eo	i	97
	ə	2
ie	ɪ	53
	ɑy	24
	i	17
	ɛ	6

Table 6.2 (continued)

oa	o	94
	ɔ	5
oe	ʌ	56
	o	37
	u	10
oi	oy	99
oo	u	50
	ʊ	45
	o	3
	ʌ	2
ou	aw	38
	u	30
	ʊ	15
	ʌ	14
	o	3
ue	yu	33
	u	27
	ʊ	25
	ɛ	13
ui	ɪ	69
	yu	**17**
	u	**12**

Seidenberg (1990), readers "adjust their processing strategies in response to the properties of writing systems…[and] there are very basic differences in the types of knowledge and processes relevant to reading different orthographies" (pp. 49–50). What potential differences are there in the knowledge and processes of L1 and English as an L2?

We have already seen that L1 logographic reading doesn't transfer at all or negatively to alphabetic writing, so those readers must start from square one.

Readers of consonantal systems must learn to look at vowels and know something of their pronunciations. Readers of different alphabets must learn the Roman alphabet. Everyone must learn to discriminate English phonemes.

But there are more subtle differences based on our discussion in this chapter. Some ESL and EFL readers may be accustomed to the Roman alphabetic writing system, but it is likely that they are not accustomed to all of the strange English graphemes listed in the last chapter and this: **gg, ck, gh, x.** Readers from an L1 transparent writing system will have learned to assign a phoneme to a grapheme, but it is a fairly straightforward process of matching one-to-one. The knowledge base for their L1 will not contain information about the probabilities that a certain grapheme will be pronounced a certain way because that information is moot if all the probabilities are 100%. The knowledge base will not contain information about the contextual information which plays a role in assigning pronunciations in English.

Similarly, ESL and EFL readers may not have needed to use a strategy of probabilistic reasoning to read their L1, if the matching between grapheme and phoneme is completely regular, or they may have relied on probabilistic reasoning only exceptionally. If this is true, they will most certainly not have acquired the ability to apply the strategy continuously, assigning phonemes to graphemes by weighing probabilities and examining the context, adjusting probabilities higher so that a decision can be made, and all of this with little if any conscious effort.

All of the students we have been considering (MariCarmen, Despina, Mohammed, and Ho) may require extensive experience with reading in English in order to achieve the knowledge base of probabilities and contextual information, processing strategies, and the automaticity that depends on them. Braten, Lie, and Andreassen (1998) report a study that showed automatic orthographic word recognition was directly dependent on the amount of leisure reading children did while away from school. This suggests that unless ESL readers are reading an abundance of English inside and outside of the classroom they may not develop efficient grapheme-to-phoneme knowledge and processing strategies. Naturally, students like MariCarmen, Despina, Mohammed, and Ho should be encouraged to read as much as possible, but it may also be helpful to provide direct phonics instruction in the classroom as an entry point to enable them to do extensive reading without frustration. Such phonics instruction should obviously emphasize the visual recoding of the graph into a phoneme, but it should involve accurate listening discrimination activities and only secondarily pronunciation, even though students will probably read out loud.

As a primary background for phonics instruction, teachers should be more optimistic about the learnability of the English writing system. At least for the purposes of reading, it is a patterned and consistent system, although the system is complex. It should be presented to students as such, and not as a confusing mass of contradictions no one can learn. The next chapter explores the system for reading English vowels, another complex but fairly consistent system.

SPOTLIGHT ON TEACHING

A reading rule like "bb→/b/" or an if/then statement like "If c is followed by a, o, or u, then it is pronounced as /k/" are linguistic generalizations. A lesson plan involving such linguistic generalizations may have these components: presentation of the generalization, practice with presented data, application to new data, common exceptions, controlled and free practice, and assessment of learning.

The presentation of a linguistic generalization may be either inductive or deductive. In a *deductive* lesson plan, a generalization is presented first, and then it is applied to examples to show how the rule works. With the generalization (reading rule) bb→/b/, we have: The consonant b is doubled in some contexts, but the pronunciation of the doubled consonant is the same as the single consonant.

Examples include *ebb* (the b is doubled because otherwise the word would have only two letters, which is discouraged in content words; also, the vowel is short) and *rob/robbing* (the b is doubled because of the addition of the suffix -ing.)

In an *inductive* lesson plan, the examples are presented first and then the rule is presented by the teacher or "induced" by the learners on their own.

Examples: *cake, cinnamon, cookies, cellophane, cupcakes, cyclone*.

Generalization: What is the pronunciation of the *c* at the beginning of each word in the data set just given? What clue tells you how to pronounce the word?

In groups or as individuals, invent either deductive or inductive presentations for the following examples. Think of an original activity to present or practice with one of the generalizations that follow and examples in order to increase contextual knowledge that "adjusts" probabilities.

a. gain   gym
   go   giant
   gun   gentleman

b. cap   city
   copper   cement
   cup   cycle
   came   cinder

c. lace   picnic
   peace   Lac
   nice   tarmac
   fleece   comic

d. cage	bag
huge	hug
change	log
village	Ag

After you have finished the deductive or inductive presentation/practice, think of several other examples that follow the same generalization. Add these new examples to model reasoning by probabilities. An example is provided for you: If *cap* is pronounced with a /k/ at the beginning, how do you think *car* is pronounced? Then think of some counterexamples, if you can, to the generalization and find a way to practice with these exceptions.

Your next activity should be designed to have the students practice writing the words that follow the generalization and those that don't. The activity might be a dictation, a structured language experience approach (in which students write a communal composition using specific words and then practice reading), a spelling bee game, or something similar.

You can then assess whether the generalization has been learned through an activity in which students restate the generalization that they have learned in their own way. Assess whether the generalization has been acquired (although consciously) through an activity that requires them to apply the generalization to unknown words. Build in other activities throughout the school term to apply the generalization until it becomes unconscious.

DISCUSSION QUESTIONS

1. This chapter touches on the relationship between spelling and reading. Some researchers believe that learning to spell should take place within the context of reading and writing because spelling and reading are based on the same data: the visual images of words we have stored in the mental lexicon. The following words are particularly difficult to spell. Discuss various reasons why these words may be difficult to spell. Do you have difficulty with any of them?

lieutenant	sergeant	receipt	aisle
unnecessary	accommodate	muscle	yacht
conscientious	noticeable	pneumonia	vacuum

These words are also difficult—why?

beautiful	input	debris	grammar

What words do you find difficult to spell? Articulate what makes them difficult for you.

Chapter 7

Approaches to Phonics

Prereading Questions. Before you read, think about and discuss the following:

1. How old were you when you learned to read?
2. What activities do you remember? Make a list of activities and evaluate their purpose and effectiveness. If you have ESL and EFL learners in class, compare how they learned to read in English.
2. What reading materials did you read in preschool, kindergarten, or first grade?

Study Guide Questions. Answer these questions while or after reading the chapter.

1. What is phonics?
2. What are phonic generalizations? Why did many teachers stop using them? What is blending? Why did teachers stop using it as a strategy to sound out new words?
3. What is reasoning-by-analogy? What knowledge is necessary for the strategy? Why it is better for reading vowels?
4. What are Ehri's stages of development of reading strategies?
5. What is the structure of the syllable for English?
6. How do the strategies ESL and EFL learners develop for their L1 reading relate to Ehri's stages of English L1 acquisition?
7. How can reading instruction for vowels be taught most efficiently?

In previous chapters, I introduced the idea of teaching phonics to expose beginning readers to the predictable consonant grapheme-to-phoneme correspondences and contextual information in English writing. In this chapter we see that context is important for another type of reasoning that is useful for reading vowels in English with maximum efficiency. Before going on to that, let's compare and contrast two phonics methodologies. Finally, we take a look at how phonics information can be taught to ESL or EFL learners in the most efficient way.

I often call phonics the "f-word" in reading instruction because it has such a bad connotation for many reading practitioners. This bad connotation stems, I think, from the way some phonics instruction was done in the past or people's somewhat muddled ideas about the way that phonics instruction takes place at present. The prevailing idea for many seems to be that phonics instruction is useless (because English writing is so chaotic), pointless (because readers are just guessing anyway), time-wasting (because readers will automatically learn grapheme-to-phoneme correspondences), and boring (because it involves memorizing rules that don't work or reading sentences that don't make any sense). Other chapters have shed a different light on some of these ideas; this chapter is about the last idea. Phonics is not about memorizing rules that don't work. It is not about reading sentences that are meaningless.

PHONICS METHODOLOGIES

There have always been a number of phonics methodologies (Adams, 1990; Hatch, 1979; Tierney & Readence, 2000). These methods evolved before there was much information about how people actually process letters and words in reading. One method involved first, an analysis of words into their component separate sounds, which were then associated with letters by means of rules, and second, a synthesis of those sounds back into words, blending them together. Let's call this method and similar ones "synthetic."

Synthetic Method.   In this method, grapheme-to-phoneme correspondences were taught directly and explicitly through the use of rules that were called *phonic generalizations*. Here are a few examples of phonic generalizations (from Clymer, 1963, followed by their percentage of utility or percentage of times that the rule actually works) derived from a certain corpus of words. (The complete list can be found in Adams, 1990, and Weaver, 1994.) "When there are two vowels side by side, the long sound of the first one is heard and the second one is usually silent." (45%) "When there are two vowels, one of which is final e, the first vowel is long and the e is silent." (63%)

Phonic generalizations were taught as part of an explicit deductive phonics program for children learning to read. Often the rule was explained in terms the beginning reader could understand. The first generalization was a common one taught as "When two vowels go walking, the first one does the talking." Then the rules were applied in worksheets and workbooks, which had many examples of words that illustrated the generalization. Once the phonic generalizations had been learned, they were applied as part of a strategy to sound out words. Each individual graph was assigned a pronunciation and then the individual pronunciations were blended together (synthesized) by saying them quickly in sequence. For example, to sound out the word **cat**, the learner was taught to say something like "kuh æ tuh." This method of teaching phonics is often called "blending."

When we consider the phonic generalizations in English, we must recognize that their percentages of utility will inevitably range from high to low. The utility of the 45 phonic generalizations studied by Clymer (1963) ranged from 0 to 100%, but the high range was mainly for consonants, and lower ranges were found for vowels, as we might expect. There is much we can say about phonic generalizations, but the long and the short of it is that the low or unpredictable utility of many of them made teachers feel that they were not useful to teach and practice. Sometimes even though the generalizations were often true (when a word begins with **kn**, the **k** is silent) it seemed a waste of class time to explain it and then do a worksheet on that one pattern. Many teachers were eager to turn away from this type of phonics instruction and embrace whole language methods that often assumed that beginning readers would just learn phonic generalizations on their own through exposure to print (Weaver, 1994). It is true that readers do unconsciously acquire knowledge of these phonic generalizations through exposure to print, but they are not in the form of overt rules. Rather, they form the unconscious probabilistic and context-dependent knowledge and processing strategies we saw in the last chapter.

From our current perspective in ESL and EFL, we can see that phonic generalizations and the deductive synthetic phonics instruction that accompanied them fall into the category of learning about the language rather than acquiring the use of the language. We think it commonplace now that learning a grammar rule doesn't necessary imply that the learner will be able to apply the rule in speaking or writing. Likewise, learning the phonic generalizations such as those previously mentioned doesn't lead to automaticity, so those teachers who found these phonic generalizations tedious and unhelpful were probably right. When the teaching of phonic generalizations was largely discarded, however, an important thread of reading instruction was also lost for some teachers. In their eagerness not to teach phonic generalizations, some teachers stopped explicit phonics instruction altogether.

A similar thing has happened with the blending strategy that used to be quite commonly taught in English L1 reading instruction. Teachers saw that trying to figure out the pronunciation of a graph in isolation led to many errors and problems. Some children would say the letter name instead of the sound; siy ey tiy for **cat** will never "blend" into its proper pronunciation. Some children, although they could assign a sound and not a letter name, chose the wrong sound to assign and they also encountered problems when trying to blend the sounds together to figure out what the word was. For many teachers, blending also went out the window as they began to prefer whole language methods.

Linguistic Method.   Although some phonics instruction in the past was rule-based and synthetic, another phonics instructional method, called the *linguistic method*, was based on learning key spelling patterns like -at, bat, cat, sat, fat, and so on (Tierney & Readence, 2000). Although this has turned out to be a good method of teaching reading in English, at the time the method was first in vogue the materials were based largely around meaningless nonwords or silly stories with sentences like "Dan can fan Nan." Teachers quite rightly criticized this phonics method because it did not provide early readers with much motivation to read. It was dull and unrealistic. The purpose of these stories was to illustrate and practice spelling patterns, but that is not an authentic purpose for literature or any other types of written material. The purpose for this phonics-based reading was to acquire low-level reading skills, but the purpose for real reading is getting the meaning, enjoying a story, learning about a subject matter, and so on. The whole language methodology, with its focus on real children's literature, was much more attractive.

"Smart" Phonics.   The good news is that reading researchers have now given us a justification and a methodology for teaching the grapheme-to-phoneme correspondences and sounding out strategies in a way that leads to acquisition rather than learning. We do not need to choose either phonics or whole language because we can do both. In modern phonics instruction, the consonant grapheme-to-phoneme correspondences are taught because we know that readers apply a probabilistic reasoning strategy acquired through direct instruction and through extensive reading for pleasure. It involves reading graphs in word and sentence contexts and not in isolation.

Modern phonics instruction also involves a different kind of knowledge of basic English spelling patterns and using reasoning by analogy to similar patterns to decode words. Phonics can be taught in an efficient way if we understand how readers read, and it can be embedded as one element within a whole language reading program. The next part of this chapter details the rationale and methodology of "smart" phonics.

REASONING BY ANALOGY

When the correspondence between a grapheme and a phoneme is not very predictable, as is the case with vowel spellings in English, probabilistic reasoning can take place as we saw in the last chapter, but expert readers also use another strategy: reasoning by analogy using contextual information in the form of frames (Goswami, 1998, and others). The frames are the typical rimes, morphemes, or syllables that show consistent spelling patterns over a number of English words. Frames provide a context that allows for easier graphic recognition. Frames are also very useful because they provide a context to disambiguate the pronunciation of vowel graphemes. This information is illustrated in Figure 7.1.

An example will make this clear. Take the grapheme **a**. When we see it in isolation, we cannot assign it a pronunciation with accuracy. It could be pronounced [a], as in **father**, [æ], as in **hat**, [ey], as in **rate**, and in fact, some other pronunciations are also possible. However, as soon as we provide the bare grapheme **a** with a context, _at, we instantly seem to know how to pronounce it. We have stored the chunk _at in our linguistic memory as a graphic image with a strong connection to its pronunciation, /æt/, so that as soon as we see it, we know how to pronounce it.

Stages of Development

Ehri (1998) hypothesizes that there are four stages in the acquisition of expert English L1 reading, shown in Figure 7.2. At first, readers "read" by re-

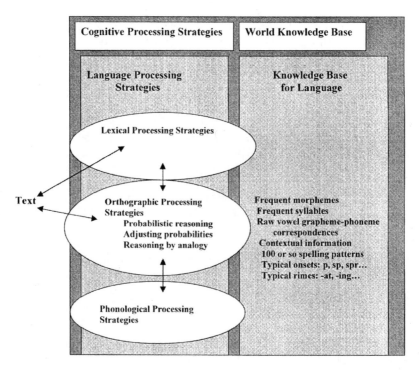

Figure 7.1   The knowledge base and processing strategies for reading English vowels.

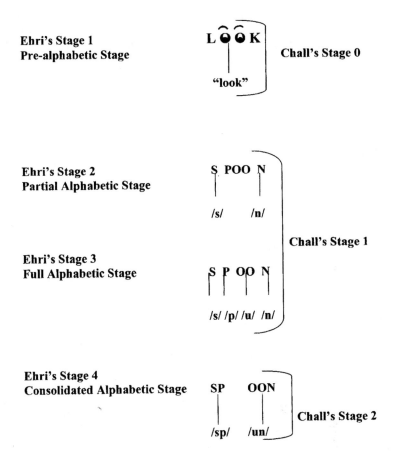

Figure 7.2   Probabilistic reasoning restructured as Reasoning by Analogy. Figure adapted from Ehri, 1998, p. 18.

membering certain features of the way words look; this "reading" is nonalphabetic (as in, say, Chall's Stage 0). As readers learn the alphabet, they begin to use their knowledge to connect the graphs on the page to the phonemes in their heads. Early on (in Chall's Stage 1), the connections between graphs and graphemes and phonemes are partial, but later the connections are complete and sophisticated. At Ehri's third stage (which might still be in Chall's Stage 1), we might hypothesize that readers have a good knowledge of probabilities and contingencies that allow them to read accurately and automatically. In Ehri's fourth stage of reading (which may occur in Chall's Stage 2), as we acquire extensive knowledge of graphemic/phonemic patterns that hold true over a number of words, frames that can be used for reasoning by analogy emerge in our knowledge base.

It is in the full alphabetic phase that rapid growth in our knowledge of printed words becomes possible. As we become more and more knowledgeable about words and spellings through more and more exposure to print, grapheme-to-phoneme patterns that occur again and again begin to merge and "consolidate." Information in our knowledge base is restructured into chunks of information called *frames*. Frames may be morphemes (-tion, -ness, pre-), syllables (at, in, ten), or smaller parts of syllables called **onsets** and **rimes**. The onset is the first consonant or consonant sequence in a one-syllable word if there is one; the rime is the vowel and final consonant or consonants. Words that share the same rime with different onsets are called *word families* or *phonograms*.

Rime: _at. Examples: at, bat, cat, chat, fat, hat.

Rime: _in. Examples: in, bin, din, chin, fin, spin.

Cognitive Restructuring

Probabilistic reasoning can take English readers only so far, but it is not the most efficient way to deal with English vowel graphemes, so English readers develop different knowledge and a different strategy. We might say that *cognitive restructuring* takes place because of the demands of reading an opaque script. That is, up to a certain point, readers get by on their knowledge of how individual graphemes are to be read, along with some contextual information. After a while, readers realize unconsciously that there is an even more efficient way to read vowels if the common spelling patterns of English are stored in memory too. So, along with the probabilities discussed in the last chapter, readers begin amassing a store of chunked information in the form of frames with which to assign vowel pronunciations by analogy. The strategy of storing frames and relying on analogy allows the reader to resolve important decision-making problems quickly and accurately in the incoming textual data.

Ehri believes that the larger grapheme-to-phoneme units reduce memory load and increase our ability to understand words with several morphemes such as happy + ness or pre + own + ed. Because we have seen that graphs are easier to identify in contexts, she argues that remembering larger units like rimes will make identifying the graphs even easier. Ehri thinks that it is in second grade that English-speaking readers begin the consolidated alphabetic phase. So we might say that most beginning readers begin by learning the shapes and pronunciations of graphs formally. They go through a period of fairly painstaking application of their learning to reading texts and as they acquire automaticity with the graph–grapheme–phoneme connection, they begin to build up speed and read for more enjoyment.

As readers acquire more and more stored knowledge about the way that spelling patterns work in English, it becomes more and more efficient to store larger chunks of words too. Common rhyming games and stories probably facilitate passage into this phase. The awareness of rhyme has been correlated with reading success for English early readers. That is, readers who can segment words into onsets and rimes and pick out or produce words that have the same rime are generally better readers than those who cannot. This is the value of Dr. Seuss books and similar rhyming material for prereaders and early readers.

Seymour (1997) cites a model of the internal structure of the syllable from Treiman (1992) and others, which I adapt for our purposes in Figure 7.3. The discussion so far leads us to posit that both the bottom level of phonemes and the higher level of onset and rime (and other frames, too) are important in English reading. The bottom of Figure 7.3 is the basis for probabilistic reasoning based on grapheme-to-phoneme correspondences and develops first, most likely in Stages 1 and 2 of Chall's stages of reading development. At some point, as a result of restructuring, the higher levels of onset and rime are added, because of the demands of dealing with English vowel grapheme-to-phoneme unpredictability. It is a way of building in context, which is so necessary for reading vowels. At this point, analogy to known rime patterns can become a useful strategy for reading. English-speaking children acquire knowledge of frames and analogical reasoning as they gain automaticity with graphs. But what about our ESL readers?

ESL READERS

Ehri's three first stages of reading development are reminiscent of the strategies described in the brain activation and psycholinguistic studies for some ESL and EFL learners of different first language writing systems.

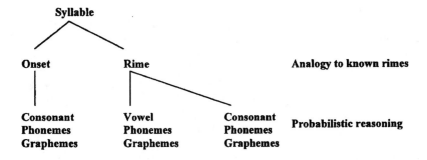

Figure 7.3 The structure of the syllable for English-speaking readers. Adapted from Seymour, 1997, p. 323.

Meaning-Based Strategy

We have already seen that there is evidence that L1 readers of sinograms and kanji are using a meaning-based strategy in which the written symbol is associated with a meaning and only secondarily with a set of phonemes. The meaning-based strategy is quite similar to Ehri's Stage 1 prealphabetic reading stage, in which the early readers use visual cues in the word to associate with a meaning and thus to figure out what the sound of the word is. We saw evidence that some ESL and EFL readers use the meaning-based strategy for reading English words; they may need assistance to develop more appropriate alphabetic strategies.

Partial Alphabetic Strategy

Likewise, some evidence indicates that Arabic or Hebrew readers might use a strategy very similar to Ehri's partial alphabetic Stage 2 reading strategy, in which readers use their knowledge of consonant grapheme-to-phoneme correspondences to guess what English words are. Consonants are more informative to readers than vowels are, and English readers fixate more on them than vowels, but ultimately the information from vowels must come into play as well. Arabic or Hebrew L1 readers may need a nudge to get from a partial alphabetic strategy to a fully alphabetic strategy.

Fully Alphabetic Strategy

Readers from L2 transparent alphabetic scripts like Italian or Spanish may be using a strategy like Ehri's fully alphabetic strategy when they start reading English. Readers using the fully alphabetic strategy process all of the letters, and this strategy would work for transparent scripts. In fact, there would be no need to develop the consolidated alphabetic strategy based on frames if their L1 writing system is transparent.

For example, Goswami (1998) finds that the correlation between rime awareness and reading ability has not been consistently found for early readers of other alphabetic languages. Goswami theorized that the importance of rime units in reading different languages could be studied by looking at whether familiarity with rimes aided reading for early readers. English, French, and Greek were studied. Greek has a nearly one-to-one correspondence between graphemes and phonemes and French has a closer connection between them than English. Goswami found that rime familiarity aided English readers quite a bit, French readers somewhat, and Greek readers not at all. It seemed that the Greek children were not using rimes in reading their orthography. If we look back at Ehri's (1998) phases, it is possible that because Greek writing has great consistency in grapheme-to-phoneme correspondences, Greek readers can read efficiently at the fully alphabetic phase. There is no need for them to develop further strategies, like English readers do. In fact, Goswami (1998) argued that it is dealing with English writing that causes strategies based on using rimes to emerge. Cognitive restructuring only happens if it is necessary.

Therefore, readers like MariCarmen and Despina may have greater problems with orthographic processing than we had previously thought. Not only do they lack knowledge of English grapheme-to-phoneme correspondences and probabilistic reasoning as a strategy, they may also not be able to read most efficiently by using consolidated chunks of words because the orthographies of their languages may not have required development of that strategy. Rather, there is some evidence that students from transparent alphabetic writing systems acquire a syllabic processing strategy, dividing words into predictable syllables based on the vowels, for the purposes of reading (Aidinis & Nunes, 1998).

For example, a colleague (Andrea Voitus, personal communication) whose first language was Hungarian, which has a transparent orthographic script, reported that when she was acquiring English reading skills as a young immigrant child, she mentally "translated" all the letters of English words into Hungarian sounds and syllables and then "translated" this into the English pronunciation in order to identify the word she was reading. Although Andrea eventually became very adept at reading English fluently (and indeed is now a native speaker of English), it is to be wondered how and when she dropped this reading strategy in favor of more efficient ones. She reports that she still uses this strategy to help her spell sight words such as **Wednesday**.)

We may presume that those of our students who become good readers of English will learn the grapheme–phoneme correspondences in their earliest reading classes, that they may, like English-speaking children, go through a painstaking phase of matching the graphs to graphemes and phonemes, and that this laborious process will become more automatic as the connections between the units become fully defined as probabilistic knowledge and reasoning. Unless learned material becomes acquired material, some of our ESL readers may be blocked at any of these stages. But under no stretch of the imagination can we think that our ESL students like Mohammed or Ho, or even MariCarmen and Despina, will come to us fully prepared to use analogy to known frames to read English most efficiently. Can we expect them to acquire the strategy on their own, as Andrea did? Or can we expect at least some of them to keep on reading English orthography in a fully alphabetic way? That is, can we expect cognitive restructuring to occur naturally or should we help them?

ESL READING INSTRUCTION BASED ON ANALOGY TO FRAMES

Goswami (1998) reported that a few studies have been conducted with English-speaking children that show the potential for instruction in analogy to frames. In one study, children who had had long-term training with a strategy of analogy based on rimes and word families were better at reading new words than an equivalent control group, although the ability to make use of rimes also depended on phonological segmentation abilities. Rime analogy benefited phonological segmentation, as we might expect. In another study, children in the analogy classroom were trained for 1 year and in a posttest were shown to be better in decoding and in reading comprehension than their equivalent control group that had not received the training.

Instruction and practice in using an analogy to frame strategy may benefit ESL and EFL students because it increases their ability to sound out words that they are reading accurately. Earlier we saw that English readers can read pseudowords that are possible more easily than impossible nonwords because of their graphemic/phonemic similarity to real words. The same could work for ESL and EFL students if they store common frames and use an analogical strategy. Sounding out new words is an important skill for ESL and EFL students, but it is one they are often very poor at. If they can sound out the words accurately, they can tell if they know the word in their oral/aural language. If they don't know the word, they can still begin to form a lexical entry with the visual/auditory image of the word, which can't help but improve their reading skill over time. In addition, they may be able to read faster and with better comprehension because more efficient bottom-up reading leaves more attention for higher level processing.

The best way to begin is to introduce the idea of phonological segmentation of spoken words into phonemes and into onsets and rimes. Reading instruction begins with the graphs and their letter names and common sounds associated with them. Learners should read simple words that they know orally. Teachers should provide instruction about rimes in the written language and their connection to pronunciation through the use of word families.

Modeling

Goswami (1998) suggested that teachers should model the use of analogy to frames by asking questions: "How can we use our clue to read this word? What is our clue word? Yes, it's **cap**. What are the letters in **cap**? Yes, **c, a, p**. What are the letters in this new word? Yes, **t, a, p**. So which bit of the new word can our clue help us with? Which part of the words are the same? That's right, the **a, p** part. What sound do the letters **a, p** make in **cap**? Yes, *-ap*. So what sound do they make here? Yes, it must be *-ap*. So now we just need to sound for the beginning letter, which is—yes, **t**. What is the sound for t? Yes, **t** as in **teddy**. So our new word is? Yes, **t**-*ap*, *tap*. We can use **cap** to figure out **tap** because they rhyme" (p. 58).

Analogy

There are many places where teachers can find lists of common vowel spelling patterns. One is from the Benchmark School in Pennsylvania, which has used the decoding by analogy strategy to help children who have had difficulties learning to read (Gaskins, 1997; Figure 7.4).

Teachers can model the use of analogy to sound out new words in the course of their whole language reading/writing class. Rather than spending time learning the words on the Benchmark list, for example, the teacher can select five frames that naturally occur in the reading text that the students are using for that day or week. Take a few minutes to look at the pattern and pronounce it. Talk about other words that have the same pattern or words that have a different pattern.

-a		-e		-i		-o		-u		-y	
gr	ab	h	e	h	i	g	o	cl	ub	m	y
pl	ace	sp	eak	m	ice	b	oat	tr	uck	bab	y
bl	ack	scr	eam	k	ick	j	ob	gl	ue	g	ym
h	ad	y	ear	d	id	cl	ock	b	ug		
m	ade	tr	eat	sl	ide	fr	og	dr	um		
fl	ag	r	ed	kn	ife	br	oke	j	ump		
m	ail	s	ee	p	ig		old	f	un		
r	ain	bl	eed	s	ight	fr	om	sk	unk		
m	ake	qu	een	l	ike		on		up		
t	alk	sl	eep	sm	ile	ph	one		us		
	all	sw	eet	w	ill	l	ong		use		
	am	t	ell	sw	im	z	oo	b	ut		
n	ame	th	em	t	ime	g	ood				
ch	amp	t	en		in	f	ood				
c	an		end	f	ind	l	ook				
	and	t	ent	w	ine	sch	ool				
m	ap	h	er	k	ing	st	op				
c	ar	y	es	th	ink	f	or				
sh	ark	n	est	sh	ip	m	ore				
sm	art	l	et	squ	irt	c	orn				
sm	ash	fl	ew	th	is	n	ose				
h	as			w	ish	n	ot				
	ask				it	c	ould				
c	at			wr	ite	r	ound				
sk	ate			f	ive	y	our				
br	ave			g	ives	c	out				
s	aw					c	ow				
d	ay					gl	ow				
						d	own				
						b	oy				

Figure 7.4 The spelling patterns from the Benchmark Program (Downer, 1991, p. 11). Used by permission.

For example, these are five patterns from the Benchmark list:

fl ag   r ed   kn ife   br oke   j ump

Let's say your reading text contains rag, bed, wife, spoke, and lump. Isolate these words from your text and discuss the meaning if necessary. Then look at the spelling and the sound. Have the students repeat the words while looking at them. Play games with them, make up rhymes with them, use them in oral sentences, use them in a spelling test or dictation. The more familiar the students become with these patterns, the more available the patterns will be for the orthographic processor.

The Benchmark Method rests on teaching students the use of overt analogy to sound out the words that they don't know. Although that method is mainly for native-speaking students, it can be applied profitably to the ESL situation. The pattern words are written on cards and displayed on a wall in the classroom. When the students come across an unknown word, they learn to break it up into syllables and break each syllable up into onsets and rimes. Then they find the rime that is like the rime in the unknown word and they pronounce the new syllable by analogy. Then they reassemble the unknown word, pronouncing each syllable. Again, that seems complex when you describe what the mind is doing, but in actual practice it is simple.

Let's say the student sees the word **ornery**. Its three syllables are **or ner y**. The rimes in the spelling patterns are **for**, **her**, and **baby**. The analogical process the student goes through is:

If **for** is /for/, then **or** is /or /.

If **her** is /hər/ , then **ner** is /nər/.

If **by** in **baby** is /biy/, then **y** is /iy/.

The written word **ornery** is pronounced /ornəriy/.

(If you're from a dialect region that prefers /ɑnriy/, then this is probably best taught as a sight word, a word that must be learned as a whole unit because analogy is not practical.)

In summary, pronouncing the word and looking at its graphemic shape help the student form a new entry in the mental lexicon for the new word. Obviously, meaning clues from context will help the student begin to elaborate an associated meaning in semantic memory. The analogical strategy not only helps the student build up his or her mental lexicon and semantic memory, but it also helps the student recognize words that he or she already knows orally but may not know in written form. As the student gains practice with conscious analogy, he or she also gains practice with using his or her knowledge base of frames unconsciously to read faster and more accurately.

Sight Words

The Benchmark Method also provides a method for learning sight words because they happen to be common and frequent function words like **would, too, they**. Teachers write those words on different colored cards and place them on the wall also. This procedure will help ESL students learn to identify the written forms of common function words automatically.

Reading Texts

While the students are learning the grapheme-to-phoneme correspondences with the contexts they occur in, frames, probabilistic reasoning, and the strategy of using analogy to common spelling patterns for vowels, they need to practice these skills in reading texts, but not texts that are too difficult for them. Instead, the texts should be very easy but age-appropriate. They can be encouraged to read aloud to the teacher and to supportive reading groups, because reading aloud forces the student to associate graphemes with phonemes, but it is imperative that reading aloud not be competitive or graded. Anxiety will lead to mispronunciations and other mistakes because students are too concerned with pronouncing accurately. Comprehension questions and testing on content must wait until students have had a chance to read and study the text silently by themselves. Reading aloud often requires so much concentration on the part of the student that he or she doesn't have much attention left for comprehension.

Reading and Listening

Another good activity is to read along silently while a tape of the story is playing because that not only improves the association between grapheme and phoneme, but it also improves pronunciation, as an added by-product. Students can follow along in their books as other students read aloud also, provided the readers are accomplished and interesting. There is nothing less motivating than listening to a poor reader stumble through a text, no matter how short, so poorer readers should read aloud to the teacher, to their parents at home, and to a supportive and small reading group or reading partner. Another activity is called *shadowing*. In this activity, the beginning reader is matched with a more advanced reader. The advanced reader begins reading the text aloud and the beginning reader follows along reading aloud a few seconds behind the advanced reader, so that they are both reading aloud, but one is slightly ahead of the other. More information about instructional methods that lead to reading fluency is provided in chapter 10. In the next chapter, we continue discussing the system that can be found in English writing.

SPOTLIGHT ON TEACHING

Review: A lesson plan for a set of common spelling patterns may have these components: presentation, practice with presented data, application to new data, common exceptions to the spelling pattern, and controlled and free practice of the spelling pattern, and assessment of learning. The presentation of a spelling pattern is best done inductively: The examples are presented first and then the pattern is presented by the teacher or "induced" by the learners on their own.

Using an inductive presentation, how would you treat the following as onsets and rimes so that your students can use analogy to decode similar words or syllables?

bake	back
lake	lack
rake	rack
make	Mack

Now *you* write an inductive presentation and lesson plan for the spelling pattern *bead* = /biyd/. (Its most common alternative pattern is bread.)

DISCUSSION QUESTIONS

1. We have discussed a couple of strategies for spelling words correctly. What strategies do you use for spelling words? How do you use a dictionary to look up a word if you don't know how to spell it? What kind of knowledge does this strategy rely on?

2. Do this quiz again. What have you learned so far? What remains to be learned?

   - Logogram.
   - Transparent orthography.
   - Phoneme.
   - Phone.
   - Grapheme.
   - Morphology.
   - Derivation.
   - Inflection.

- Onset.
- Rime.
- Tense vowel.
- Morphophonemic writing.

Chapter 8

English Morphophonemic Writing

Prereading Questions. Before you read, think about and discuss the following:

1. The words **naked** and **baked** look much the same but their pronunciations are very different. What can explain the difference in pronunciation?
2. Why do we spell the word **sign** with a **g** in it? If you look back to Appendix A you will see that we had to specify that word final gn = /n/. Could there be another generalization that would make this spelling more explicable? What might that be?

Study Guide Questions. Answer these questions while and after reading the chapter:

1. Define these terms and give examples of each: *morpheme, free morpheme, bound morpheme, derivational morpheme, infix, inflectional morpheme, bound root.*
2. What is the morphological structure of the words *Massachusetts, cannibal, congregational, carpet, disapproval, disproved, proven, Polish, liked?*
3. Give an example from the chapter of pronunciation changes due to derivational morphology for a vowel, consonant, or stem change, and a stress change with vowel reduction. Then give an original example of each.
4. What does it mean to say that English writing is morphophonemic?
5. Give another example of each of the three principles involved in spelling morphemes consistently even though pronunciation changes due to derivational morphology: tensest vowel, stops rather than affricates/fricatives, most complete spelling.
6. Would you, at any point in your spelling career, have benefited from an explanation that English writing is morphophonemic? Would it help you spell better to know the principles?
7. What are the four morphological types of languages?
8. Could a language's predominate morphology type affect the structure of the mental lexicon? How?
9. Could morphological processing in English be problematic for the ESL and EFL learner?

We have been looking at the bottom levels of the reading processor, which deal with the connection between graphemes of written language and phonemes of spoken language. But English is made up of other units of organization that are important in understanding the system of English writing: *morphemes*. We have described the English writing system as phonemic, but, in fact, we show in this chapter that it is actually better described as *morphophonemic*. For teachers, knowing how English morphology affects pronunciation and spelling is essential to presenting English spelling as a learnable system to students.

Readers process morphology while reading based on the level of morphological awareness they have achieved. Levin, Ravid, and Rapaport (1999) and Bryant, Nunes, and Bindman (1999) propose that morphological awareness plays a causal role in the learning of morphological spelling patterns. The causal link is not unidirectional, but rather they bootstrap each other. That is, as children become morphologically aware, they develop knowledge of written spelling patterns. As their knowledge of morphological spelling patterns matures, their morphological awareness is also maturing (Nunes, 1999).

Because morphology differs from language to language, it is reasonable to think that readers develop different strategies to process it in their L1 writing system. After an examination of English morphology, pronunciation, and spelling, this chapter looks briefly at morphology in other languages, the possibility that different languages require different morphological processing strategies, and some suggestions for ESL and EFL instruction.

WORDS AND MORPHEMES: BASIC UNITS IN LANGUAGE

The flow of speech can be segmented into words, but the exact meaning of *word* is complex.

Words

The word is in many ways the most basic unit of language, but in spite of that (or maybe because of it) there is no really adequate definition of what a word is. Part of the problem is that words are very different from language to language. Some languages have very short and simple one- or two-syllable words that mean only one concept, but some languages have words that are formed of many syllables all strung together forming a complex concept. Some languages, like English, show a variety of word structures. Some are simple (sun, moon, chair, man, girl) and some are complex (bookkeeper, antediluvian, developing fluid). People used to think that there might be a millisecond pause between words in the flow of speech and that we could define words that way. However, technology has shown that that is not true; there is no pause between words as we speak unless we consciously make a pause. The pauses in speech tend to mark off phrases or clauses, not individual words.

Morphemes

Because the word is difficult to define precisely, linguists talk instead about *morphemes*. Morphemes can be free or bound. The definition of the word *morpheme* has three parts. First, there must be a form, a unit of language that usually consists of a sequence of sounds. Second, this unit of language must be associated with a meaning, either a grammatical meaning or a meaning with real content. Third, the form must be minimal in that it cannot be broken down into any smaller meaningful units.

Free Morphemes. Some morphemes are called *free morphemes*, which are words themselves. The word **sun** is a free morpheme. It has a form consisting of three sounds: /s/ /ʌ/ /n/. It has a meaning that could be found in any dictionary. And finally, the form cannot be broken down into smaller meaningful units. The /s/ by itself is not meaningful; neither is the /ʌ/ or the /n /. Other free morphemes are **moon**, **Fresno**, **school**, and **Oklahoma**. The last word here may have more than one morpheme in the original Native American language from which it came, but in English, it has only one morpheme.

Bound Morphemes. Some morphemes are *bound morphemes*—that is, they must occur attached to another either free or bound morpheme. The prefix **un-** is such a bound morpheme: it has a minimal form associated with a meaning, but it cannot occur meaningfully by itself. It must be attached to another morpheme to be meaningful, as in the words **undo** or **untie**. Other examples of bound morphemes are: **de**code, **re**take, **pre**fix, judg**ment**, comic**al**, and san**ity**. All of the bound morphemes exemplified in this paragraph are *derivational morphemes*, and they are either prefixes or suffixes in English. (Other languages also use *infixes*, morphemes that are placed *within* the context of a word, not before it or after it.)

Derivational Morphemes. Derivation is a common *word formation process* in English in which a new word is created from a base word to which prefixes and suffixes are added. From the noun **care**, we form the adjective **careless**, which, through the addition of the suffix, has a different part of speech and a different meaning. Most would agree that **careless** is not at all the same word as **care**, but an entirely different but related word. We can continue to form new words almost indefinitely. For instance, to **careless**, we can add another suffix to form an abstract noun: **carelessness**.
Derivational morphemes have properties in common:

- They often (but not always) result in a ***change in the part of speech*** when the derived word is compared to the ***base*** they are added to.
- They can be either ***prefixes*** or ***suffixes*** in English.

- They vary in *productivity*. In other words, some derivational morphemes can be added to many words, and some can be added to few words.
- They make a *substantial and sometimes unpredictable change in the meaning* of the word.
- In fact, they are *creative*; they result in what we would think of as a *new and different word*.

Bound Roots.   Another kind of bound morpheme used in derivation is called a *bound root,* which is a root to which a prefix or suffix must be added in order to form a word, but the root itself never occurs alone. Many of the bound roots we have in English came from words of Greek and Latin origin that were borrowed as "learned vocabulary" or through French. Examples of bound roots are: pre**cept**, pro**vide**, super**vise**, and im**port**.

Inflectional Morphemes.   Another kind of bound morpheme, called *inflectional*, merely adds some additional grammatical information or inflections to a word, without creating a new word. An example of an inflectional morpheme is the **-ed** past tense ending or the **-s** that is added to form plural nouns. When the past tense ending **-ed** is added to the verb **play** the result is the word **played**, which we would all agree is not a newly created innovation but merely a different form of the original base word. This process, when grammatical suffixes are added to bases to cause a change in grammatical form, is called *inflection*. Inflectional processes are rule governed; that is, past-tense verbs, plural nouns, and so on are formed by means of grammatical and morphological rules which add a certain morpheme to the base word to encode grammatical information.

Inflectional morphemes have some common properties:

- They *do not usually change the part of speech* when the inflected word is compared to the base they are added to.
- In English, they are always *suffixes* and never prefixes.
- They are *very productive*; they can be added to almost any word of a certain part of speech.
- The *change in meaning* they cause is a quite predictable grammatical detail.
- They are *mechanical*; they do not result in a new and different word, just *a different form of the same word*.

Inflection is an important process in many languages of the world, but in English there are only eight inflectional morphemes:

Nouns	**s** (plural)	The students needed their books.
	s (possessive)	One student's book was on the table.

Verbs	**s** (third person singular present tense)	He speak**s** English.
	-ed (past tense for regular verbs)	He want**ed** to learn French.
	-ed (past participle for regular verbs)	He has liv**ed** in Canada for years.
	-en (past participle for some irregular verbs)	He has spok**en** French since then.
	-ing (present participle)	He is learn**ing** Japanese.
Adjectives and adverbs:	**-er** (comparative form)	He has bought a new**er** car.
	-est (superlative form)	He can't afford the new**est** car.

DERIVATION, PRONUNCIATION, AND SPELLING

You will already have noticed that English words can have quite complex morphological structures made up of many different kinds of morphemes: free, derivational, inflectional, or bound roots. In any word, however, if there is an inflectional morpheme, it will be the last one because it is the last part of speech that determines the type of inflectional morpheme that can be added. Examples are: progressives = pro + gress + ive + s, untied = un + tie + ed, preceptors = pre + cept + or + s.

Adding derivational morphemes to bases and roots can affect the derived words in several ways. Sometimes the pronunciation of the derived word changes when compared to the original base or root: **sane + ity = sanity; pro + gress + ion = *progression*.** Sometimes both the pronunciation and the spelling changes, as in **re + ceive + tion = reception.** Although these seem like random events, they can be explained by regular morphological and phonological processes. The apparent spelling anomalies that can result are reduced when you understand the underlying system.

Pronunciation Changes

English has many words that are derived from a simple base by adding prefixes and suffixes. Prefixes don't usually cause pronunciation changes except *assimilation* in place of articulation, as in **im**perfect versus **in**decisive. Assimilation refers to a phonological process where one sound becomes more similar to a sound that is adjacent to it. The final nasal phoneme of the prefix, presumed to be alveolar /n/, becomes bilabial /m/ when it is placed before a bilabial /p/ or /b/. This is why some people misspell **input** as **imput**. However, derivational suffixes often change the pronunciation of graphemes in the word. Changes occur to consonants, vowels, and stems, and to the stress pattern of a word. If the stress pattern changes, there may be some additional consequences to vowels. There are two types of consonant changes, palatalization and velar softening.

Palatalization.   When a stop or fricative consonant that is produced elsewhere in the mouth becomes palatalized, the process is referred to as palatalization. Usually the consonant becomes a palatal fricative or affricate. Typical examples are **suppress–suppression** or **native—national, nature**. In the first example, the final alveolar fricative /s/ sound of the base word **suppress** is pronounced like the palatal fricative /ʃ/ in the derived word **pressure**. In the second example, the same root word (a bound root that also occurs in the word **innate**) is pronounced with an (alveolar stop) /t/ in some words, but with a palatal fricative /ʃ/ in **national**. In the word **nature**, however, the **t** has become a palatal affricate, /tʃ/.

Velar Softening.   Another type of consonant change occurs when a velar stop, either /k/ or /g/, becomes "softened" to /s/ or /dʒ/, respectively. Examples are **electric—electricity** and **analog—analogy**. In the first example, the velar stop /k/ in **electric** is softened to /s/ in the derived word, **electricity**. In the second case, the final /g/ of **analog** is pronounced as /dʒ/ in the derived word **analogy**.

Vowel Laxing.   Some suffixes, when added to a base word, have the effect of changing the pronunciation of a vowel in the derived word. Examples are **deprave–depravity**, **divine–divinity**, and **extreme–extremity**. The base word **deprave** has the tense vowel /ey/ in the second syllable, whereas the derived word **depravity** has the lax vowel /æ/. Similarly, the base word **divine** has the diphthong /ɑy/, while the derived word **divinity** has the lax vowel /ɪ/ in the second syllable. **Extreme** has the tense vowel /iy/ in its second syllable but **extremity** has a lax /ɛ/ in that position. Because of the alternation between tense and lax vowels, *vowel laxing* is the name for this change. The tense vowel or diphthong alternates with its most similar lax vowel.

Stress Change With Vowel Reduction.   *Stress* means a louder or more forceful pronunciation of one syllable of a word than of other syllables in a word. The word **confessor**, for example, is stressed on the second syllable **fess**. The addition of suffixes can change the stress on a word, meaning that in the base word one syllable is stressed, but in the derived word, another syllable is stressed. Change of stress is complex, but it is not really a problem by itself. The difficulty is that, because of a phonological rule of English, a change in stress can result in a change in pronunciation. The phonological rule in question is that of *vowel reduction*. Vowel reduction refers the fact that when vowels have little or no stress on them, their pronunciation is reduced to /ə/. In fact, sometimes a vowel is reduced so much that it disappears from the pronunciation altogether. Thus, this phonological change can be described as a two-step process. First, stress shifts to another syllable, and second, the newly unstressed vowel reduces to schwa.

Examples are **grammar–grammatical** and **labor—laboratory**. In the first case, the word **grammar** is stressed on the first syllable, so its vowel has its full value of /æ/. The second syllable is unstressed, so the vowel is pronounced as /ə/. However, in the word **grammatical**, stress has shifted from the first syllable to the second syllable. The pronunciation of the second vowel is now its true value of /æ/, and the first vowel is reduced to /ə/. Thinking of the derived word **grammatical** is a good way to remember that the commonly misspelled word **grammar** is spelled with two *a*'s.

The example of **labor—laboratory** is more complex. In American English, **labor** is stressed on the first syllable and the second syllable receives a secondary stress. In **laboratory,** primary stress remains on the first syllable although vowel laxing takes place, /ey/⇒ / æ/, but the second syllable's stress is reduced to nothing because of the addition of **-atory**. The reduction in stress on the second syllable is so severe as to cause it to disappear. In British English, the primary stress shifts to the second syllable, so it doesn't disappear, but the vowel in the first syllable is reduced to /ə/.

Stem Change. Sometimes the pronunciation changes from a base word to a derived word, but it technically isn't explained by a phonological process. Instead, the cause is a change in the stem of the word itself. In other words, some words historically have two stems, one that serves as the basic word, and another one that serves as the base for derivation. Examples are: **receive—reception**, **permit—permissive**, and **divide—divisive**.

To sum up, we can say that English relies heavily on derivational morphemes to create new words, and because of certain phonological processes (vowel laxing, stress change with vowel reduction, velar softening, and palatalization), the derived words aren't always pronounced like the bases they come from. Sometimes a different stem is used to form the base of a derived word.

These processes involve only a segment of the English vocabulary, the Latinate vocabulary, or words and morphemes that have come from Latin and Greek origins. Native Germanic vocabulary, or words and morphemes that have come down through the history of English from its earliest days as a Germanic language, do not undergo the same word formation processes, phonological processes, and pronunciation changes. Still, Latinate vocabulary now comprises roughly half of the words and morphemes commonly used in English, so the pronunciation changes have caused a problem with the writing system, which does not reflect this variation.

Morphemes and Phonemes in Writing

These phonological changes from a base word to a related derived word are a big problem for writing. The problem resides in the fact that our writing system represents both phonemes and morphemes; it is *morphophonemic*. In other words, our writing system is phonemic in that it represents the sounds of our language, but it is also morphemic in that it also attempts to represent morphemes consistently. For instance, the same free morpheme occurs in all of these: **put, input, output**. This is not a problem because there is no phonological change in these words.

Now say this set of words: **physics, physicist, physician**. This set of related words shows evidence of velar softening and palatalization, yielding three pronunciations at the end of the base word: /k/, /s/, and /ʃ/. The question is: Would it be best to change the spelling to reflect the pronunciation accurately (as in, say, **fiziks, fizisist, fizishen**)? Or is it best to maintain the spelling to show clearly that the words have a morphemic relationship even though the words are not pronounced the same? In other words, which is more important for writing—the pronunciation or the morphological relationship? For our spelling system, the morphological relationship is more important. The different pronunciations are in fact ignored in spelling; the spelling shows that the same basic morpheme is involved in this set of words.

There are various pronunciations of a morpheme because of derivational changes, but the English writing system prefers to write morphemes consistently. But this presents a dilemma. In the word set just discussed, we have one morpheme with three alternative pronunciations for the final grapheme in the base word: **physic**s with a /k/, **physic**ist with an /s/, or **physic**ian with a /ʃ/. Which pronunciation is to be chosen as a basis for spelling the word consistently?

English writing is based on the following three rules of thumb that govern our morphophonemic system:

Tense Vowel or Diphthong.   To write a morpheme consistently in spite of variations in vowel pronunciation, the spelling that represents a *tense vowel or diphthong* is basic, as in prod**u**ce–prod**u**ction or extr**e**me–extr**e**mity. Similarly, always represent the original vowel even though it may be reduced to [ə] with a change of stress, as in d**e**fine–d**e**finition or gr**a**mmar–gr**a**mmatical. The phonological processes of vowel laxing and vowel reduction are disregarded for the most part in spelling.

Stop ⇒ *Fricative* ⇒ *Affricate.*   Where there are stops and fricatives, prefer a spelling that indicates the stop pronunciation, as in physi**c**s–physi**c**ist, physi**c**ian, where the **c** indicates the stop /k/. Where there are stops and affricates, as in inna**t**e, na**t**ure, prefer the stop spelling. In pre**ss**–pre**ss**ure, the **ss** indicates the alveolar fricative /s/ and not the palatal fricative, indicating that alveolar is written in preference to palatal even if both sounds are fricatives. The phonological processes of velar softening and palatalization are usually not shown in spelling.

Most Inclusive Spelling.   Finally, if there are graphemes that are pronounced in some cases and not pronounced in other cases, choose a spelling that shows the grapheme in question and keep the spelling consistent, as in si**g**n–si**g**nature, bom**b**–bom**b**ard.

This section has described some problems resulting from English derivational processes, namely, that the addition of suffixes (and prefixes to a lesser extent) brings about changes in the pronunciation of the base word. The English writing system, on the other hand, prefers to maintain the spelling of the original morpheme, before vowel laxing, reduction, palatalization, or velar softening occurs. This is one of the main reasons for the fact that graphemes and phonemes do not correspond in a one-to-one fashion in English writing and hence, that English writing is opaque.

For example, looking back to the charts in chapters 5 and 6 and Appendix A, one can see that many of the apparent problems in English grapheme-to-phoneme correspondences are explained. For example, a common spelling for /ʃ/ is **ti**. It is clear that this is caused by one extremely productive derivational suffix in which palatalization has occurred: **-tion**. The most efficient way to deal with this is to store the morpheme **-tion** as a graphemic/phonemic image in the mental lexicon, which is what expert readers mostly likely do. In this way, the reader can read **ti** as /ʃ/ unambiguously, easily, and effortlessly, if it occurs in the context __**on**. Other examples where morphology and phonology explain unexpected spellings listed on the charts are that a common spelling for /tʃ/ is **tu**, which is another example of palatalization, as in **culture** or **picture**, the specifications that **gn** and **mb** are pronounced as /n/ and /m/, respectively, and the tense vowel/lax vowel correspondences.

STORAGE OF MORPHOLOGICAL KNOWLEDGE IN MEMORY

If expert English readers store common morphemes with their phonological representations and can read them efficiently, then that explains certain observations we have made about reading. As we have seen elsewhere, problems with the English writing system are mainly problems in writing or spelling, not in reading. The expert reader can read **grammar**, **definite**, or **misspell** with no difficulty. These words do not present problems for expert readers because the graphemic/phonemic image is matched in its usual way with the visual stimuli. In spelling, the graphemic/phonemic image may not be as usable or productive except as a check after the fact.

The English writing system, as we see once again, is mainly problematic only for two groups of people learning to read English: native English-speaking children and ESL/EFL students, because they must build up a vast knowledge of graphemic/phonemic images encoding, for instance, that *c* is usually pronounced /k/, unless it occurs in the context **i_ity or i_ist**, as in **electricity**, **toxicity**, or **classicist**. This knowledge is stored in the mental lexicon, our extensive storage of English graphemic/phonemic images, each with a number of associations to *semantic memory*, or our memory for word meaning. Accessing the words and morphemes in the mental lexicon is called *word recognition*.

Knowledge of derivational morphemes must be contained in the mental lexicon because people can use them to make up new words if they need to. For instance, sometimes people forget or don't know a word. One strategy is to use morphemes to make up a word: **sensitiveness** instead of **sensitivity**, and so on. Also, sometimes people make a slip of the tongue in saying words, adding the wrong suffix. However, it is probably the case that many derived words are also included in our lexicon. That means that our mental lexicon lists **sane**, **sanity**, and **ity**. It lists **progress**, **progression**, and **ion**. It lists **receive**, **reception**, and **tion**.

The English mental lexicon is probably redundant, to allow flexibility in the processing of the inconsistent derivation in English. In decision-making systems, there is a trade-off between redundancy in knowledge or information storage and efficiency in processing. Sometimes it is more efficient in processing time to store information inefficiently and redundantly, rather than storing in the most efficient way, which can increase the complexity of the processing and therefore the processing time.

However, readers differ in what they know about morphology. Knowledge of derivationally suffxed English words facilitates accurate reading in the school years and even in high school for English readers (Fowler & Liberman, 1995; Tyler & Nagy, 1990). The ability to see the derivational morphemes in an English word is dependent on the knowledge that a reader has about the language, which is acquired mainly through schooling (Derwing, Smith, & Weibe, 1995). The greater the reader's knowledge about prefixes, roots, and suffixes, the greater is his or her ability to see structure when looking at words.

Word Recognition

In any case, in word recognition, the reader has unconsciously formed a graphemic–phonemic image of the word in question and matched it with a representation of a word contained in the mental lexicon. The word is recognized and the meaning in semantic memory can then be accessed. If the reader reads a new word, it won't be recognized because there is no match for the new word stored in that reader's mental lexicon. However, the new word then can be added to the reader's mental lexicon, and any meaning that can be gleaned from the text (or the dictionary) will be associated with it. If the new word is morphologically complex, containing a prefix, a free morpheme, and a suffix, the reader can use her or his knowledge of derivation and decision-making strategies to try to guess what the meaning of the new word is. This is not always easy because, as we have already seen, when prefixes and suffixes are added, the meaning changes can be unpredictable. Still, the meanings of the derivational morphemes stored in the mental lexicon are clues to the meaning of new words.

This discussion has been fairly abstract, so let us make it more concrete with an example or two. The reader's eyes take in the graphs **s u n n y** and associates them with the phonological representation /sʌniy/. The resulting image is matched with the word **sunny**, which is part of the lexicon of English, recognition of the word is achieved and the meaning is accessed. Suppose the reader's eyes take in the graphs **b e e r y** and the reader associates them with a phonological representation /biriy/. Suppose this reader has never encountered this word before (as in **The police officers thought the interior of the car smelled beery after the crash**). The reader can use a number of strategies to deal with it. The reader can recognize that this is a possible word in English, separate the two morphemes, access them, **beer** and **y**, and combine them to infer what the meaning of the whole word must be: **like beer. Beery** can also be understood using a straightforward analogical strategy to words like **sunny**.

Recognizing words depends on knowledge of words and morphemes in the mental lexicon and processing strategies like matching perceived words to stored words, or detecting something that could be an English word, separating its morphemes if possible, accessing meanings for morphemes, re-combining morphemes (beer + y = like beer), and/or analogy to morphologically similar (beer + y : sunny) (Figure 8.1).

English Morphology and English L2 Reading

Knowledge of derivational morphemes and the phonological changes that go with them may be helpful to the English learner. Although many of the patterns are somewhat inconsistent and do not allow automatic processing, they are still very productive and useful as patterns. Recall that there is evidence that some ESL and EFL students do not use a phonological strategy when they come across unknown and "unpronounceable" words in their reading. Instead, they use a meaning-based strategy of trying to associate a visual image with some kind of meaning association, whatever that might be. For English, a phonological strategy is more empowering. Knowing how derivation works can aid students in this because morphemes can be segmented and pronounced. Knowledge of the pronunciation changes that occur in derivation can result in more accurate pronunciations.

Further, derived words are not all listed in dictionaries, especially the abridged dictionaries that nonnative-speaking students carry around. To look up derived words, it is often necessary to look up the root word and then apply knowledge of the prefixes and suffixes. For nonnative-speaking students whose linguistic competence develops slowly and whose reading vocabulary is often meager, direct instruction in the derivational morphemes of English, although time-consuming, may be extremely helpful, especially for those who wish to pursue higher education in an English-speaking environment.

Do ESL and EFL readers use knowledge of English morphology and processing strategies to read unknown words? The main strategies that

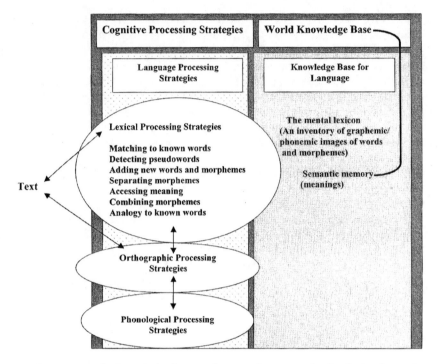

Figure 8.1 The knowledge base and processing strategies for derivation and word identification.

ESL/EFL learners can use in word recognition are cognate recognition (Carroll, 1992), context (Bensoussan & Laufer, 1984), graphemic similarity (Walker, 1983), and morphological processing. The cognate strategy is only available to ESL and EFL readers of languages that are Germanic or Latin-derived. The use of context is only available if there is sufficient surrounding information and it can be utilized by the reader. Graphemic similarity (similarity in the appearance of a word in L2 to L1) is of limited use.

However, Osbourne and Mulling (1998), in their survey of this literature, find that students prefer these strategies and rarely rely on a morphological strategy to help them identify unknown words. In another study, Osbourne and Mulling (2001) found that many Spanish-speaking ESL students could use a morphological strategy if necessary, but they preferred not to, presumably because of the *cognitive load* that morphological processing entails. Cognitive load refers to the amount of mental work involved in a task—the more work, the more reluctant the reader is to do it.

There are a number of reasons that might account for the large cognitive load involved in processing English morphology. First, processing derivational morphology involves disassembling the word into component morphemes (which could be ambiguous), matching them with sound representations (which are opaque, as discussed earlier), accessing them in the mental lexicon and semantic memory (where they might not occur), and re-assembling the pieces into the whole word. ESL/EFL students may not have the knowledge base or processing strategies to do that, or their processing strategies might not work with automaticity. A further contributing factor might be that the students' own knowledge of their L1 morphology and the processing strategies they have already developed may interfere with pro-cessing English morphology.

MORPHOLOGY IN OTHER LANGUAGES

Comrie (1981, pp. 43–49) offers a useful way to discuss morphology in the world's languages by introducing the concept of two morphological dimen-sions. One dimension concerns the number of morphemes per word and the other dimension concerns the extent to which the morphemes within a word can be segmented or separated from each other (Figure 8.2).

Languages at point A are called *isolating*; normally, each word is made up of one morpheme. For example, although Chinese has some compound words made up of two morphemes, the typical word has one segmentable morpheme. Languages at point B are called *fusional*; normally words will have more than one morpheme per word and the morphemes often cannot be easily broken down into components. Languages at point C are called *polysynthetic*; words can be made up of many morphemes, but the individual

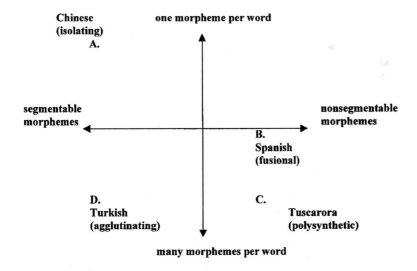

Figure 8.2 A continuum of morphological variation in the world's lan-guages. Adapted from Comrie, 1981, pp. 39–49, and used by permission of the University of Chicago Press.

morphemes may be hard to separate out. Languages at point D are called *agglutinating*: There are many morphemes and it is easy to segment the morphemes within a word. In general, languages can be characterized by how they fall within the quadrants formed by the lines on the chart in Figure 8.2. Keep in mind that any time a linguist sets up a neat dichotomy such as this one, he or she finds that it is sometimes difficult to wrestle the world's languages into the perfect position. Languages, the ultimate human creations, resist neat and tidy classifications.

Vietnamese, for instance, is an isolating language, in which each word usually has one morpheme. Comrie (1981) gives this example of a Vietnamese sentence (in which I have omitted some markings):

Khi toi den nha ban toi, chung toi bat dau lam bai

when I come house friend I PLURAL I begin do lessons

"When I came to my friend's house, we began to do lessons."

Note that there is no past-tense marking on the Vietnamese verb and that plural and first person (which would be "we") are also separate morphemes. Chinese languages, like Mandarin, are isolating.

An example of a fusional language is Spanish, in which the verb endings encode grammatical information that cannot be split into components of meaning:

To speak	hablar
I speak	hablo
you speak	hablas
he/she/it speaks	habla
we speak	hablamos
you plural speak	hablais
they speak	hablan

The ending on the Spanish verb encodes person, number, and tense grammatical meanings all rolled up into one morpheme. For example, **-o** in **hablo** captures these grammatical meanings (which could be separable morphemes but aren't): first-person singular present tense. Which part of the **-o** means first person singular? Which part means present tense? They are *fused* together into one form and cannot be pulled apart. Many European languages have fusional verb endings that indicate person, number, and tense. Some also have extensive fusional noun endings, which indicate number, gender, and grammatical relations like subject, object, possessive, and so on.

This example, from Napoli (1996), is a polysynthetic language, Tuscarora, a Native American language. The first word includes a number of different nonsegmentable (bound) morphemes.

Ae-hra-taskw-ahk-hwa?   ha? tsi:r

PREFIX-3rd Person Masculine-domestic animal-pickup-
                                        ASPECT MARKER   PARTICLE dog

"He regularly picks up dogs." [He is a dogcatcher.]

Many American Indian languages are polysynthetic; so are some Bantu languages and some Australian languages.

An agglutinating language is Turkish. In this partial example of a noun declension (*adam* means "man"), the morpheme boundaries are clear, so it is easy to segment the words into component morphemes:

	Singular	Plural
Nominative	adam	adam-lar
Accusative	adam-ı	adam-lar-ı
Genitive	adam-ın	adam-lar-ın

A casual look will indicate that *lar* means plural, ı means accusative (direct object), and ın means genitive (possessive). Another agglutinating language is Hungarian. In agglutinating languages, the words can be quite long, but they can be processed automatically because the morphology is transparent and consistent.

English has words that fall into all of the quadrants. Examples of isolating words (words made up of one free morpheme) are **sun**, **moon**, **carpet**. Fusional words, where the morphemes are fused together and inseparable are words like **were** (be + past tense + plural, although English verbs tend not to be fusional, as in **play** + **ed**, in which the **-ed** only indicates past tense) or **people** (human + plural). Examples of agglutinating words are compounds like **bookkeepers**, where each morpheme is easily pulled apart and the meaning of the whole is made from adding each part together. Polysynthetic words, made up of many inseparable morphemes, might be long derived words with Latin roots, like **antediluvian** and **antebellum**, or long chemical and medical terms. This variety in word types in English might cause increased cognitive load for ESL/EFL students whose languages contain predominately one type of word and who therefore might be unused to the other types. The problems might reside in their knowledge base (mental lexicon and semantic memory) or their processing strategies.

L1/L2 TRANSFER PROBLEMS IN MORPHOLOGY

In order to understand possible problems for the ESL/EFL reader in processing morphology, we need to consider two areas: the knowledge base and processing strategies. In each case, research is scanty but suggestive. First, the knowledge base, or mental lexicon, might be organized differently for different languages. (At present, it is unclear whether there is separate storage for L1 and L2, or whether there is one mental lexicon that serves more than one language, or whether there might be two interconnected lexicons for L1 and L2. See discussion in Singleton, 1997, and elsewhere.)

Mental Lexicon

Schreuder and Baayen (1995, p.132) propose that different language-specific characteristics of morphology may affect the way that the mental lexicon develops. Evidence from Caramazza et al (1988) and Jarvella et al (1987), which was reported in Schreuder et al. (1990), indicated that differences in the reading processes for Italians reading Italian (verbs with fusional endings) and Dutch can be attributed to the fact that Italian has a more complex (and fusional) verb system than Dutch does (which is more like English) and therefore knowledge of the verbs and verbal endings is stored in memory in different ways that are efficient for each language. Although still hypothetical, it is not unreasonable to think that isolating languages have separate words stored one by one as whole unchanging entities (and syntax operates to put them into the right order in that sentence.) An agglutinating language like Turkish might have all the morphemes listed and word formation processes (not syntax) operate to construct the predictable series of morphemes that make up the long words (and syntax operates to place these long words into their correct order).

Furthermore, words and morphemes in the mental lexicon might be stored in different relationships to each other. For example, Serbian has an extensive and complex fusional case marking system for noun phrases. There is a base noun form that adds inflections based on how the noun is used in the sentence: subject, direct object and so on. Lukatela, Gligorijevic, Kostic, and Turvey (1980) propose an organization of the mental lexicon in which the nominative case (for subjects) is the central one; the others "revolve" around it as satellites. This rather ornate organization for nouns is probably unnecessary for English, because nouns do not change their form according to their use except as singular or plural.

Bentin and Frost (1995, pp. 272–273) also argue for the influence of different morphology on word storage and identification. For example, they suggest that Lukatela's model of word identification based on the frequency of the nominative singular and not the frequency of other inflected versions of the noun is heavily dependent on the richly-inflected Serbo-Croatian language and has little plausibility for English, which has few nominal inflections. They argue, "The lexical presentation and parsing of morphologically complex words which are possible in language with an agglutinative word structure such as Turkish must be different than those in a language with a nonconcatenative morphology such as Hebrew, in which different inflections and derivatives are formed by infixing word-patterns within the consonantal string that forms the root morpheme."

They suggested that fusional languages like Serbian, agglutinating languages like Turkish, and infixing languages like Hebrew will have different word storage in the mental lexicon, and these, presumably, are also different from English. If ESL/EFL learners have a mental lexicon organized in a certain way for their L1s, do they use the same organizational principles and structure in acquiring an English mental lexicon or do the demands of learning English words necessarily create a mental lexicon appropriate for English? Alas, we do not know the answer to that.

Reading Strategies

Is there any evidence that readers of different L1s develop different low-level morphological processing strategies because of differences in the morphological structure of their words or mental lexicon? The answer here too is sketchy, but interesting. We saw earlier that patterns of derivational morphology do not seem to be very accessible to English speakers unless they have been schooled in them, but they can use morphology to read unknown words if they have the knowledge. We have also seen that words in English can be of any of the four morphological types. This leads to the hypothesis that native English readers do not rely much on consistent morphological processing strategies, but rather have a number of strategies that they can employ if necessary, depending on how transparent or segmentable the word is: matching the perceived word or morpheme to a word or morpheme stored in the mental lexicon or detecting pseudowords (i.e., words that could be English but aren't in the mental lexicon). If a word is identified as unknown, the reader can separate potential morphemes if necessary, accessing the meaning of the words and morphemes, and recombining the pieces. The reader can also use analogy to similar known words to get a hypothesis about what the word is and its meaning.

Schreuder and Baayen (1995, p. 132), who proposed that different language-specific characteristics of morphology may affect the way that the mental lexicon develops, also assume different "language-specific models of morphological processing." We might imagine that languages that have words made up consistently from one type of morphological pattern might encourage readers to use one strategy uniformly. For example, the matching strategy is useful for isolating languages. If the word is found to be an unknown pseudoword, the L1 strategy might be to add the new word without any further analysis because morphological analysis is not an option. Matching one-to-one may be less useful for agglutinating languages. Readers might have to do morphological analysis or analogy in order to process words in reading, so separating, accessing meaning, and recombining might be frequently used strategies. If students are used to applying one strategy to the exclusion of others, they may show signs of only partial positive transfer or negative transfer to English reading, which seems to require both.

For example, Chinese writing doesn't contain information about morphology because it is an isolating language not given to morphologically complex words, although compound words are common. In addition, the sinograms themselves do not lend themselves to indicating any changes in the words that they encode, because they are printed "as is", unlike alphabetic writing, which can print the words in present tense or past tense, singular or plural, through changes in spelling. Taft and Zhu (1995) discuss a number of questions concerning morphological processing in Chinese writing; they make some suggestions for morphological processing that are quite different from any ever proposed for English. It is quite possible that Chinese learners of English reading do not process the grammatical information from derivational and inflectional morphemes in English, or that they do not process it efficiently and automatically.

Garnham, Oakhill, Ehrlich, and Carreiras (1995) showed that gender marking in languages like French and Spanish is used to determine reference between a pronoun and a noun phrase. In French and Spanish, all nouns are either "masculine" or "feminine," and adjectives, determiners, and pronouns must match them. It seems like readers of Spanish and French have developed a strategy to process gender marking of nouns, but English does not have the same type of gender markings. In English, most nouns are neutral with respect to gender and are referred to with "it" unless there is some reason to assign them a gender (as in referring to boats as *she*). French and Spanish speakers will not be able to rely on their L1 strategy to process nouns and they may lack the strategies that English speakers develop.

Koda (1993) studied second-language learners of Japanese (21 Americans, 12 Chinese, and 13 Koreans). A sentence completion task measured knowledge of case-marking particles. The data confirm that sentence comprehension differs among second-language readers of Japanese with varying L1 backgrounds and suggest that reading skills transferred from native language interact with L2 linguistic features in shaping processing strategies. Besides the potential difference in reading strategies, English learners are affected by lack of knowledge of English inflectional and derivational morphology. The Japanese learners studied in Schmitt and Meara (1997, p. 26) show "a rather weak awareness of derivative suffixes and their use [and they] lack convincing mastery of even inflectional suffixes."

Implications for ESL Reading Instruction

As ESL and EFL students are learning words in English, they should be building up such a storage of morphemes, rimes, and syllables through direct instruction and through extensive reading practice. This morpheme store will help with reading and with effective use of English dictionaries. Students like Ho whose first languages are isolating may have difficulty with the complex morphological structure of some English words. Their mental lexicons may need restructuring to include knowledge of derivational morphemes and they must learn the inflectional morphemes of English. If the L1 writing system doesn't encode morphological changes in words, readers may not have efficient processing strategies like separation and recombination for morphological changes in English words, such as tense, possessive, or plural. They may be relying on a simple matching strategy, which is not effective unless they have a perfect match for each word in their mental lexicon.

Students who speak Hebrew or Arabic, like Mohammed, may have L1 processing strategies that focus more on infixed morphological changes rather than on the prefixed and suffixed morphology of English. This would be similar, say, to detecting the difference between **sit** and **sat**, which is not a very useful strategy to generalize for English. English has a small set of verbs that form their past tenses by "infixed" (in a way) vowel changes; although these words may be frequent, their number is small. Students like Mohammed may, like Ho, benefit from direct instruction in reading derivationally complex words and inflectional endings so that their lexical processor works optimally using matching, separating/recombining, and analogy to morphologically similar words.

Students like MariCarmen and Despina come from languages that are largely fusional with complex verbal systems of many inflectional endings and complex noun/adjective/pronoun agreement systems that use gender and case markings to show relationships and reference. This rich and informative inflectional morphology is probably processed with more attention than the meager inflectional morphology of English, which provides few cues to verb tense and noun agreement. Japanese uses a system of particles (not inflections, but separate words) to indicate the functions that nouns have in sentences (subject, object, indirect object, etc.). Readers who come from these languages need to learn that English uses strict word order more heavily to encode meaning relationships. They, like Mohammed and Ho, benefit from direct instruction in derivational and inflectional morphology, and strategies like separating and recombining. Students from Latin- or Greek-based languages have the benefit of shared derivational morphology with English (pre-, post-, -ment, -tion, etc.); they may focus more exclusively on Germanic morphology (-ness, -dom, -ly).

For some advanced English L2 readers, it may be useful to comment on the fairly consistent phonological rules of English that affect the pronunciation of derived words (press–pressure) and therefore complicate our spelling. This may enable students to sound out words more effectively to determine whether they know the word by sound and to discard a meaning-based reading strategy for words that are hard to pronounce. It may even be useful to tell students that English writing is not just phonemic but also morphemic in that the accurate representation of sound is sacrificed to maintain the semantic connection between words that can be perceived if the root morphemes are spelled consistently. Our system tries to strike a balance between representing phonemes (sound) and morphemes (small meaning units), and sometimes the need to represent morphemes overrides the need to represent sound accurately. This may help students form a lexical entry for a word and see meaning relationships between words, or at least connect words in the mental lexicon. The point of morphological instruction and practice with processing strategies must be to reduce the cognitive load associated with the task, so students must understand the system, practice the strategy overtly, and generalize the strategy to all of their reading. It is only then that they will make use of English morphological cues in reading.

SPOTLIGHT ON TEACHING

Gunning (1988) has a list of prefixes, suffixes, and Greek and Latin bound roots. He lists these common prefixes and suffixes with their level of difficulty for English speakers. Do you agree with this order of difficulty for the nonnative speaker of English? Is this order of difficulty related to the productivity of the morpheme? Which ones cause phonological changes in the base words to which they are attached?

	Prefixes	Suffixes
Primary:	dis-, pre-, re-, un-	-able, -er, -ible, -ful, -less, -ness, -y
Intermediate:	anti-, co-, de-, en-, fore-, il-, im-, in-, ir-, inter-, non-, over-, post-, semi-, sub-, super-	-age, -al, -an-, -ant, -ent, -ese, -est, ic, -ive, -like, -ment, -or, -some, -th, -ward

Advanced: ad-, circum-, contra-,   -ance, -hood, -ism, -ity,
              counter-, ex-, extra-,   -ize, -osis, -ship
              out-, sur-

The following inductive sequence can be used for teaching morphemes like **un-**.

Step 1. Show examples like **happy** and **unhappy**. Discuss the difference in meaning between the two words. Contrast other words that students know too: **kind/unkind**, and so on.

Step 2. Have students articulate what **un-** adds to the meaning of the base word, but if they can't, articulate it yourself for them. Have them write it down in a vocabulary notebook.

Step 3. If you are introducing a suffix, discuss how it changes the part of speech of the original word: **care/careful, help/helpful, use/useful**. Show these words in different grammatical contexts: *I care for my pets. I am careful to give them water.* Have students articulate the difference if they can.

Step 4. Controlled practice with typical activities on a group or individual worksheet:

    a. Rewrite "He was not happy⇒He was unhappy."
    b. Complete the sentence with the correct word or fill in the blank.
    c. Match the correct word with its definition.
    d. Provide the morpheme and a list of words it can be added to. Have students make up words, define them, and write sentences with them.
    e. Contrast the morpheme with others that are like it, if any: -less,/-ful, pre-/post-.

Step 5. Guided Practice:

    a. A structured Language Experience using words with the morpheme.
    b. Bring in examples of the morpheme from other books or readings. They should write these in their vocabulary notebook.
    c. Probably you selected this morpheme to do a mini-lesson on because it appears in something that your class is reading. Allow class members to identify the morpheme in the reading when they see it.

Now *you* choose one of the morphemes from Question 5 and write a lesson plan for teaching it.

DISCUSSION QUESTIONS

1. Have you figured out the **naked** and **baked** example? If not, look them up in the dictionary and try a little morphological analysis.
2. What is strange about the pronunciation of the word *beloved* with three syllables (be-lov-ed)? Where did this pronunciation come from?
3. In which "order" were the suffix and prefix added to the word **hurry** to make **unhurried**? That is, was the **-ed** added first and then the prefix **un-** or vice versa? What is your reasoning for your answer? Is this the same reasoning for **daunt⇒undaunted** or **unbridled** from **bridle**?
4. Besides derivation, one common word formation process in English is *compounding*. Noun compounds may be made up of N N combinations (tomato juice), Adj N combinations (blackbird), and even V Particle combinations (pick up). Say these sentences. What do you notice about the way that the compound is pronounced in (i), when compared to the other sentence in each pair? What is the difference in meaning?

   a.   i.   Please bring me some orange juice.
        ii. This is the red juice and that is the orange juice.
   b.   i.   The president lives in the White House.
        ii. The white house on the corner is new.
   c.   i.   She drives a pick-up truck.
        ii. Please pick up some eggs on your way home.

5. Is there any rule about when to write compound words as one word, with a hyphen, or as two (or more) words?
6. If you know another language, think about its morphology: isolating, polysynthetic, agglutinating, fusional, or a combination? What evidence do you have for your answer?

Chapter 9

Vocabulary Acquisition

Prereading Questions. Before you read, think about and discuss the following:

1. What is the structure of the word **unruly**? Why do we not say **ruly**? What might be the origin or derivation of the word **unruly**?
2. Are the words **park** (as in park the car) and **park** (city park) one word with two meanings or two words with separate meanings? What does the dictionary say?
3. How do you understand words that you've never seen before in print?

Study Guide Questions. Answer these while and after reading the chapter.

1. What are some top-down comprehension and word learning strategies teachers currently use? When you are reading, do you use these?
2. What is the idea of skipping words you don't know in reading and where did it come from? Do you do this?
3. What makes a reader a good word learner? What is the phonological loop? What is articulatory suppression?
4. What properties of words make them easier to learn?.
5. Can you think of additional examples of the word formation processes mentioned (borrowing, blending, acronym, abbreviation, back formation, clipping, coinage, conversion)?
6. How are compounds interpreted?
7. What special problems are caused by conversion?
8. How are metaphors interpreted? Give an original example of a metaphor.
9. Explain these terms: *polysemy, homophones, homographs, homonyms.* What is the keyword strategy?
10. What does the research tell us about gaps in ESL and EFL learners' vocabulary knowledge?
11. What implications are there for vocabulary instruction?

The goal of ESL and EFL reading classes is for learners to improve comprehension of the text; however, it is not always obvious how reading comprehension relates to vocabulary acquisition in the classroom. Teachers are not always sure how to balance vocabulary instruction and reading comprehension activities. To what extent is it possible to comprehend a text despite lack of vocabulary? Do readers acquire vocabulary while they are reading? Many teachers model and teach both top-down reading strategies and word-learning strategies, but there can be a conflict between the two. In this chapter we begin by looking at some top-down comprehension and vocabulary strategies, and we critique a common reading strategy because it offers only short-term benefits to students. Later, we study ways to supplement top-down vocabulary strategies with some word-analysis and phonological acquisition strategies.

TOP-DOWN VOCABULARY ACQUISITION STRATEGIES

Comprehension Strategies

Many reading textbooks for English learners suggest higher level cognitive reading strategies that can benefit students who are trying to comprehend a difficult text. For instance, a prereading examination of the text for organization, headings, summaries, and so on will help readers make predictions about the content and locate sources of help within the text. Learning to pick out the topic sentence in each paragraph will allow students to get most of the essential information in the text, taking full advantage of the predictable and formulaic nature of English written organization. Acquiring a repertory of reading skills like reading in depth, skimming for the gist, and scanning for specific information permits ESL and EFL readers to adjust their reading to the task that they need to perform.

Word-Learning Strategies

Lack of vocabulary remains one of the major obstacles for ESL or EFL readers. As a result, many textbooks offer valuable top-down word learning strategies for vocabulary. Teachers use prereading discussion and other activities to provide background knowledge so that new words have a context that increases comprehension. Background knowledge is stored in memory in data structures known as "schemas" that are built up from experiences in a cultural setting. For instance, we have schemas involved with shopping in a grocery store versus an open air market, or eating in a slow-food restaurant versus a fast-food restaurant. We have different expectations because of our different schemas. Prereading practice is thought to "activitate" the reader's background schemas to assist him or her in understanding the words and text.

In addition, students learn to distinguish and look up the words most essential to the meaning of the text, such as those that are repeated four or five times. Students may be encouraged to keep a vocabulary journal while reading, so that they can use their new words actively in speaking or writing. Students become adept at finding cues in the context of the sentence or paragraph to guess what the word means.

Students can also apply a cognate strategy; that is, they look for similarities between the English word and a word in their native language. Because cognates may be understood and acquired with support from the L1 lexical knowledge store, L2 readers seem to apply this strategy automatically. In the case where the student's L1 has many cognates with English, a valuable vocabulary strategy might be to "be wary of *false friends*," which are those words that are cognates but have very different meanings in L1 and L2. One type of word analysis strategy is for learners to look at the morphological cues within the word that might indicate something about its meaning or part of speech. Unfortunately, students seem to avoid this strategy because of the cognitive load involved in it (Osbourne & Mulling, 2001).

Skipping Unknown Words

Many teachers teach students to use these word identification and learning strategies in reading, but they do not consistently advocate vocabulary building during reading for comprehension. Instead, some teachers commonly advocate one reading comprehension strategy at the expense of vocabulary building, that is, to "skip the words you don't know and get the gist of the meaning." Although no reading textbook promotes this strategy outright, many teachers adopt it in the classroom, as I myself did at one time in my life. The idea seems to stem from conclusions drawn from a number of sources in the reading literature in the past 30 years, some of which have been discussed elsewhere in this book: "Readers are just guessing anyway," or "readers just sample the text and don't fixate on every word." In addition, some common assumptions inadvertently have led some teachers to accept the idea of skipping over unknown words in hot pursuit of comprehension.

Three Assumptions of Reading Instruction. One assumption seems to be that L2 readers can compensate for lack of specific language knowledge with background knowledge. For instance, Coady (1979) said the following:

> Since the various process strategies interact among themselves, the ESL student should take advantage of his strengths in order to overcome his weaknesses. For example, greater background knowledge of a particular subject could compensate somewhat for a lack of syntactic control over the language.... The proficient reader learns to utilize whatever cue systems render useful information and to put them together in a *creative* manner, always achieving *at least some comprehension*. Thus a weakness in one area can be overcome by a strength in another. (p. 11, emphasis added)

The second assumption is that readers do not need to understand everything in the text for adequate comprehension. Clarke and Silberstein, in a very influential article published in 1979, said the following:

> Students must be made aware of the number of language clues available to them when they are stopped by an unfamiliar word. They should realize that they can usually continue reading and obtain a general understanding of the item.... Most importantly, they must be taught to recognize situations in which the meaning of the word or phrase is *not essential for adequate comprehension* of the passage. (p. 57)

We find a similar point of view expressed in Been (1979):

> The readers should be given cues that lead him to ignore linearity, help him to exploit redundancies, and demonstrate *that meaning can be apprehended even though he does not understand every word.* (p. 98)

More recently, Day and Bamford (1998) reiterated the recommendation:

> Part of fluent and effective reading involves the reader *ignoring unknown words and phrases or, if understanding them is essential, guessing their approximate meaning.* (p. 93)

The third assumption is that vocabulary instruction takes up too much time in the reading class. For example, in Gaskill (1979), we find these practical suggestions for teachers:

> Many instructors ask their students to learn vocabulary items that are found in their reading selections. This can be helpful if the number of words is held to a reasonable ten to twenty words per selection and if the list of words is accompanied with contextualized examples and practice. Preparing lists of vocabulary items and contextualized practice requires *additional preparation* on the part of the instructor.... Discussion of and practice with such lists takes *a lot of class time.* (p. 148)

Clearly, it is impossible to argue against these commonsense assumptions for the reading comprehension classroom. I have quoted them at length because they have a lot of validity, but the conclusion that some teachers have drawn seems to be that, given that the goal of the reading class is improvement in the comprehension of a message, not word learning, and that background knowledge can make up for lack of vocabulary anyway, and that readers don't need to understand every word, and that vocabulary learning is not an efficient use of reading class time, a good strategy is for ESL and EFL readers to skip over words they don't know.

Again, there is some merit in the suggestion. Lack of vocabulary is a serious problem for English learners in reading independently. Many ESL and EFL students, especially those in higher education, are required to read stories, articles, or books that are too difficult for them to read because there are too many words they don't know. It is frustrating to read something incomprehensible, so the natural inclination for the reader is to stop reading and do something else. If readers don't read, they don't improve. It is equally frustrating for most people to consult the dictionary for every unknown word. Dictionaries are fallible, the definition may be unclear or incomplete, and by the time readers have found the definition, they have lost track of what the sentence was about anyway. Teachers don't want students to be frustrated; they want them to read extensively because that is the one sure way to improve reading.

It also seems to be a common impression among teachers I have talked to that students will learn words automatically while they are reading—that they will at least acquire some new vocabulary while reading, even if they skip over unknown words. And anyway, teachers are cognizant of the fact that the goal of reading is to get meaning, not to read and remember words. So it was probably inevitable that reading teachers at one point began to advise students to skip the words that they didn't know in order to focus on getting the overall meaning of the text.

Short-Term Gain.   The strategy was designed to keep reading interesting and fun so that readers would read and, as a short-term task-limited procedure, it probably accomplishes its goal. One problem, however, is that it can become a long-term task-unlimited procedure for students. Some students adopt this strategy for the long run because it is easier than learning new words. They get into the processing habit of disregarding words that they fixate on as soon as they decide that it is not a word in their L2 mental lexicon. Once this habit is formed, it is hard to break.

Students also apply this processing strategy to all of the reading that they must do, even the reading in which it is essential to get more than just the gist. Rather than a strategy they can apply to challenging but relatively unimportant reading, it becomes their exclusive reading policy. Rather than applying it to the preliminary reading of a text that they are going to read more carefully again, they use it as the one and only "careful" reading they do. The simple truth is that if readers skip the words they don't know, they don't learn them, and often, they don't understand the texts they need to. The conclusion is that the short-term reading comprehension strategy is very detrimental to long-term vocabulary building. Even Day and Bamford (1998) cannot report substantial and consistent vocabulary gains through extensive reading programs.

(I provide a more personal example: An ESL student of mine was once involved in volunteer work that required him to read a short training manual. He took it home overnight and read it, but the next day, when the volunteer coordinator asked him a few questions, he couldn't answer. She was peeved and expressed irritation to me. I was surprised, because he was a serious student. When I asked him about it, he told me that he had just skipped the words he didn't know. He didn't realize that he should have read any differently because this is what his teacher had advised him to do in order to cope with difficult reading. This is probably an extreme case but I think of it every time I hear employers, teachers, and professors complain that their nonnative-speaking students can't understand what they read.)

The purpose of the next part of this chapter is to suggest additional word learning strategies for ESL and EFL readers to use in order to read efficiently at the same time that they improve vocabulary. We have seen that reading familiar words depends on low-level processing strategies and specific linguistic knowledge of writing systems, spelling patterns, morphemes, and so on. It turns out that learning unfamiliar words depends on the same sorts of knowledge too. It follows that improving low-level processing strategies and linguistic knowledge might help students retain more vocabulary words from their reading and vocabulary exercises.

LEARNER VARIABLES IN VOCABULARY ACQUISITION

First of all, what makes a person a better word learner? Studies show that good word learners have certain characteristics. Ellis and Beaton (1993) tell us that for one thing they have an ability to store new words in long-term memory. If we can learn how they do that, we might teach their word learning strategy to those who are not as good at learning vocabulary.

Memory and Ability to Repeat

There is a lot of evidence that a better word learner can repeat new words easily, and repetition ability depends on the short-term memory (processing strategies) and the long-term memory (knowledge store) of the learner (Baddeley, Gathercole, & Papagno, 1998; Cheung, 1996; Service & Kohonen, 1995). In order to repeat audibly a new word (a sequence of graphs) that the learner has read, he or she must access (at least some of the) graphemic images stored in long-term memory and hold them in short-term memory while they are matched to a phonemic image from the inventory of phonemes stored in long-term memory. Then the graphemic/phonemic image is held or rehearsed in short-term memory while the motor commands to the mouth are formulated and executed. If the learner's short-term memory or long-term memory is not adequate to the task, the learner cannot repeat the unknown word and cannot store it as easily.

The storage of words in the mental lexicon in long-term memory is an important part of the knowledge base for reading in a number of ways. Repetition ability and the reader's existing vocabulary knowledge "bootstrap" on each other. Phonological skills influence the learning of new words, but also, the larger the existing storage of words in the mental lexicon, the easier it seems to be to come up with phonological analyses. From the point of view taken in this book, it is clear that this supports the idea that readers use probabilistic reasoning and analogy to known spelling patterns to read unknown words, and the better able readers are to do this, the better they can repeat and thus retain a new word too.

The Phonological Loop

The reader's ability to repeat new words is part of an interactive cycle, as noted by Gathercole, Willis, Emslie, and Baddeley (1991, and cited in Ellis & Beaton, 1993). Successful word learning appears to depend on what has come to be called the *phonological loop* in vocabulary acquisition (Baddeley et al., 1998, p. 158). The phonological loop comes into play in listening comprehension and in reading to allow the listener or reader to learn unknown words.

The phonological loop works in the following way. After the word is heard or read, a phonological image is formed. The loop allows for the retention of the phonological image for short periods of time in short-term memory. The loop actually consists of two parts, a knowledge base called a phonological store, which stores the image, and a rehearsal process, a strategy that serves to refresh decaying representations that might disappear from short-term memory. The function of the loop is to store unfamiliar forms in short-term memory while permanent memory structures can be constructed in the mental lexicon, thereby leading to word learning. Repetition ability is taken to be an indicator of the loop. People with poor short-term memory have a hard time repeating words. Likewise, vocabulary knowledge is also related to repetition ability. These findings are consistent for both L1 and l2 word learning (Figure 9.1).

An ingenious type of experiment shows the effect of the phonological loop in reading (at least the reading of single words). In reading, the graphs

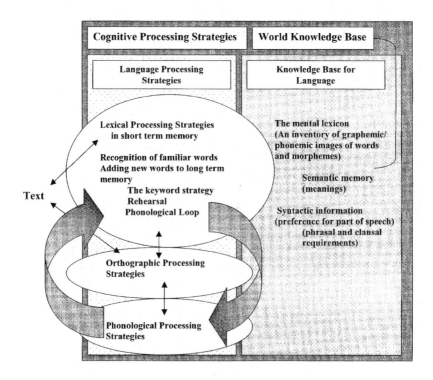

Figure 9.1　The human word processor.

on the page are matched to graphemes in our head and these, in turn, are matched with a phonological image of the phonemes associated with the graphemes. This is the phonological loop. The functioning of the loop can be disrupted in reading by having readers say a nonsense syllable (like bla bla bla) while they are reading. This method, called *articulatory suppression*, has a "clearly deleterious effect on the acquisition of foreign language vocabulary" (Baddeley et al., 1998, p.162). The idea is that if the reader does not, for some reason, form and retain a phonological image of an unknown word that is being read, he or she will not form an entry in the mental lexicon, and therefore will not recognize the word when it is read again.

Active Word Processors

Baddeley et al. (1998) offered a dynamic model of learners as active processors of new words through phonological storage in the knowledge base and a stratgegy of rehearsal to add to their knowledge base in the mental lexicon. Instead of skipping over new words, learners combine their top-down comprehension and word learning strategies with phonological and repetition strategies to focus briefly on new words as they encounter them in the text. That means that teachers should suggest that instead of treating unknown words, especially those that are difficult to pronounce, as "kanji," learners should attempt to pronounce them and store a visual and sound image along with some ideas of the meaning gleaned from the text.

These instructions will be easier for learners to implement if they are not overwhelmed by the sheer numbers of new words in their reading materials. Word learning is an active process and perhaps more class time needs to be devoted to it. However, it seems to be the case that some words are simply easier to remember and learn than others.

LEXICAL VARIABLES IN VOCABULARY ACQUISITION

Words are very diverse, and some characteristics make some words easier to learn than others. If teachers know which will be easier and which will be harder, they might be able to teach vocabulary more efficiently, spending just enough time on each type of word. Ellis and Beaton (1993) studied some lexical variables that relate to the appearance of the word: acoustic similarity, word length, pronounceability or other phonological factors, and orthography (script, direction of script, sequential letter probabilities, and familiarity with grapheme–phoneme mappings). Other lexical variables have to do with word class or part of speech, word formation, and word meaning.

Word Appearance

Acoustic Similarity. Papagno and Vallar (1992) found evidence that acoustically similar words confused the phonological loop in the L2 learner even in visual presentation. In the phonological loop, the phono-logical image in short-term memory may be confused with similar words al-ready learned, and the confusion may impede or prevent storage of the new item in long-term memory.

Word Length.   Word length affects storage and retention in the pho-nological loop. Cheung (1996) found this to be an important factor for Hong Kong seventh-graders whose vocabulary size was smaller than the median for all the students studied. The longer the word, the harder it is to store and retain in the loop so that it can become permanently stored in the mental lexicon.

Pronounceability.   The more pronounceable a word is, the more eas-ily it is learned. Ellis and Beaton (1993) made the point that the more a word conforms to the expected phonological forms of the language, the more pro-nounceable it is. In matching graphs to graphemes to phonemes, the more knowledge readers have about the typical phonological structures of the lan-guage, the better they can form a phonological image of the word. If the readers can form a phonological image and rehearse it sufficiently to store it in long-term memory, as in the phonological loop, they will retain the word.

In this book, we have already considered the problem of pronounceability elsewhere. We saw that there is a tendency for Japanese readers of English to use a visual strategy to remember words; that is, they try to match the visual appearance of the word with a meaning concept, as if the English word were a kanji or logographic symbol. I think this explains some unusual findings by Saito (1995), who was investigating the effects of pronounceability and articulatory suppression on phonological learning in Japanese learners of Japanese nonwords presented in katakana or syllabic writing. In this study, subjects were shown easy- and difficult-to-pronounce "nonwords" under a control condition and an articulatory suppression condition. Then they were asked to recall the words in a free recall task in which they were asked to write down the words they remembered. Then there was a cued recall task in which the subjects were given the first syllable of the word and had to complete the word. The prediction would be that pronounceability of nonwords would re-sult in better word learning, and it did. Articulatory suppression, however, was expected to inhibit word learning for the nonwords.

In contrast, Saito found that in both the free recall and the cued recall, the unpronounceable nonwords were learned better in articulatory sup-pression than in the control condition. I think that articulatory suppression inhibits phonological storage in short-term memory and favors visual or graphemic storage, which could be expected to be well remembered in re-call writing tasks. In other words, the Japanese subjects reacted to the articulatory suppression condition by treating the unpronounceable katakana nonwords as kanji, just as they seem to do with unpronounceable English words.

Orthography. In Ellis and Beaton's (1993) study of English learners who knew no German, the degree to which the German word conformed to the orthographic patterns of English affected the ability to translate words from English to German. It is obvious that these subjects who knew no German had no knowledge of German letter-to-sound patterns and could only learn words based on their similarity to English. This study does, however, reinforce the idea that L1 orthography can help in reading L2 to the extent that there is overlap between the two systems. Where there is little or no overlap, L1 interferes or does not facilitate. Problems with English orthography may be significant contributors to the lack of vocabulary acquisition in reading generally. If ESL and EFL learners cannot match graphs to graphemes to phonemes quickly and automatically, the phonological loop may not be able to function to store and retain the word in long-term memory. If the phonological loop is not able to function, students may fall back on visual strategies for reading, which we have argued are not the most efficient way to read English words.

Word Classes and Collocations

Ellis and Beaton (1993) found that nouns are easier to learn than verbs, and this finding is consistent with other psychological literature for first-language acquisition. It is unclear why nouns should be easier to learn than verbs, but one reason given is that their meaning tends to be more imageable or easy to visualize. In the case of English and German, probably the nouns and verbs correlate highly with each other because the two languages are closely related in syntax, so German L1 readers can probably transfer their knowledge to English.

For readers from other first languages, however, part-of-speech differences from L1 to L2 may be a cause for confusion in reading, because it is necessary for the reader to understand parts of speech in order to assign the correct syntactic structure to a sentence. Correct comprehension of syntactic structure is an important precursor to correct comprehension of meaning. The opinion from Coady cited earlier, that background knowledge can make up for a lack of syntactic knowledge, must be tempered with a consideration that, as one of my linguistics professors used to say, syntax was made so that we can talk about things that are contrary to our expectations about the world. How else could we understand the sentence "A man bit a dog" if it weren't for the dominance of syntax over background knowledge?

Opaque Parts of Speech. Part-of-speech information is opaque in English. A fusional language like Spanish marks part of speech clearly because it marks nouns with (generally) either an **-a** ending or an **-o**, and adjectives and pronouns carry corresponding markings with the nouns they match. The Spanish noun and adjective system of marking is different from the system that marks verbs, a three-way (-ar, -er, and -ir) series of conjugations in different tenses, persons, and numbers. Because of the noun, adjective, and verbal inflections, many words in Spanish, even in isolation, are unambiguous as to grammatical category.

There are many languages with even stricter marking of grammatical category information than Spanish; in these languages there is no ambiguity at all between different parts of speech. The nouns are often clearly marked as to their function in the sentence (subject, direct object, etc.) and verbs are clearly marked with their inflections of person, number, and tense. For students from these languages, the scarcity of overt marking in English and the tendency for words to switch categories (called *conversion*) causes uncertainty in attributing a part of speech to an English word, and therefore phrasal structure is hard to compute and accurate meanings are difficult to comprehend. Further, any factors that favor noun learning over verb learning will not operate if the student cannot identify a word as a noun.

On the opposite side of the spectrum, some isolating languages have even fewer consistent markings of part of speech than English does. Although spoken Chinese words have different categories, the written sinograms don't reflect grammatical parts of speech at all; they are invariant. Students whose L1 is like this may also have problems with English parts of speech because they may be unable to take advantage of the morphological information that is present in the English text.

Probabilistic Reasoning.   Most native English readers don't have conscious or learned knowledge of the part of speech of each word in each sentence as it is being read, but they have unconscious knowledge that allows them to compute phrasal and sentential structures quickly, then discard them as soon as the meaning is clear. Given the incomplete marking of English grammatical categories and given how common conversion is as a word formation process in English, perhaps it is more accurate to think of parts of speech as weighted probabilities or frequencies from which we form grammatical expectations. For example, from our experience with language, we form the expectation that **floor** will be a noun, say, 95% of the time and a verb 5% of the time, except in certain registers (such as the carpet installer).

Expert English readers use these lexical expectations, the cues from the text like word order and grammatical function words like **the**, **of**, or **to**, and their knowledge of typical English syntactic structures to determine the syntactic structure that they are reading. English speakers intuitively know that the subject of an English sentence is most typically a noun phrase, they know that **floor** is most likely going to be a noun, and they know that nouns are often preceded by **the**, so when they see the sentence **The floor the man swept was clean**, they will take the subject to be the first noun phrase **the floor**.

Collocations.   In addition, words themselves place requirements on the words that can or must go with them, and this is part of the knowledge that readers must have about words. It is often called *collocational knowledge,* the stored information in memory about the lexical, phrasal or clausal requirements that a word has. For example, the verb **put** might occur as the verb in the predicate of a sentence. If so, there are certain collocational requirements placed on the verb phrase that forms the predicate. **Put** requires two other types of phrases within the verb phrase: a direct object, and a location phrase, as in the sentence: **He put the car in the garage**. Taking away either the direct object **the car** or the location phrase **in the garage** would yield an ungrammatical sentence. The verb **remember** can take an infinitive or V + ing (**I remembered to go/going**), a that + sentence (**I remembered that he went**), or an object pronoun V + ing (**I remembered him going**). Each of these structures is associated with a certain semantic interpretation.

Word Formation

As we saw in the last chapter, languages can be isolating, agglutinating, polysynthetic, and/or fusional, so even the concept of "word" is different from language to language. People's knowledge of how to segment the words from an utterance varies according to the language and script learned. Words can be formed through different processes: prefixing, suffixing, infixing, concatenation of morphemes, compounding, and so on. The processes typical in a student's L1 may not prepare him/her for the variety of word formation processes in English: acronym, blending, coining, generalization, back formation, clipping, conversion, compounding. Earlier we saw that learners don't always take advantage of morphological cues in word analysis, possibly because of its cognitive difficulty. Therefore, ESL and EFL learners may benefit from direct assistance from teachers to learn additional processing strategies based on the way that words are formed in English.

Borrowing.   English has no problem borrowing words from other languages (**taco, patio, Wienerschnitzel, glasnost**), which has given English a very extensive, heterogeneous, and unruly vocabulary compared to languages that resist borrowing, whose lexicons are very homogeneous and rule governed. Because of borrowing in English, there can be more than one word to refer to similar objects (sausage, bratwurst, chorizo, pepperoni). In most borrowings in English, the written word is copied letter by letter closely, but it is pronounced more or less as an English word with perhaps some concern to authenticity, depending on the speaker. ESL and EFL readers can benefit if the borrowed word happens to be from their own language, but otherwise, recent or uncommon borrowings are probably all going to be new and unknown.

Compounding.   Besides derivation and borrowing, English frequently uses compounding to form new words. Compounding is also common in German, which allows long compounds of many free morphemes put together, and in Chinese, which prefers short compounds of two free morphemes. It is not as common in some other languages. For instance, many speakers of Romance languages like Spanish, French, or Italian prefer possessive structures with a prepositional phrase instead of the more typical compounds in English. For instance, they might say **the leg of the table** or even **the table's leg** instead of the more correct **the table leg**. When they read this compound they might wonder about the relationship between the two nouns. They might lack an interpretive strategy for these words because of their structure. The strategy is that the second noun is the object and the first noun is descriptive.

Long compound nouns made up of a number of words can be very confusing because the interpretive strategy must be applied over and over again; the compound "English Department Curriculum Committee Summer Retreat Planning Committee" requires quite a bit of mental gymnastics to understand. To understand what this compound means, first the student must realize that this is a compound and not a sentence or clause. The capital letters in this particular compound indicate that this is not a sentence, but if the compound is not capitalized, students may not understand that such a long group of words is a compound noun and not a sentence. Then the student must apply the interpretive strategy first to the individual two-word compounds and then to the four-word compounds and then to the eight-word compound: (((English Department) (Curriculum Committee)) ((Summer Retreat) (Planning Committee))).

There are other types of compounds also, among them, compound adjectives (red-hot, candy-apple red, etc.) and compound verbs made up of a verb and a particle (pick up, pick on, pick out, etc.) Compound verbs require an interpretive strategy that differentiates them from verbs with prepositional phrases. (This is often treated as a grammar issue but not necessarily a reading comprehension issue. However, syntax and reading comprehension are intimately connected.)

Acronyms and Abbreviations.   The words **radar**, **AIDS**, and **NATO** are formed by taking the first initial of each word or main part of a word in the originating phrase and pronouncing them together as one word; they are *acronyms*. This is distinguished from *abbreviations*, where the initials are pronounced as letters, as in **FBI** or **CIA**. (Another type of abbreviation is a shortened form of the original word that is written with a period at the end. This is not really a word formation process; that is, **Dept**. for **department** is not a different word.) It may be my imagination, but it seems like acronym and initial abbreviations are becoming more common in some other languages, possibly due to the influence of English. One strategy for dealing with these might work for students from Romance languages: Reverse the direction of the letters and translate them. In Spanish, for example, NATO is OTAN and the UN is La ONU. Other students should recognize them as acronyms or abbreviations and look in the text for a cue to what they stand for.

Back-Formation and Clipping.   These two superficially similar processes yield very different results in terms of word formation. **Edit** is a *back-formation* from the word **editor**. In back-formation, the original word (*editor*) is analyzed as having a derivational morpheme at the end, **-or**, which means "one who does X." The suffix is removed to form the new verb (**edit**) in analogy with pairs like **act–actor** and **bake–baker**. Thus, usually the word that is formed through back-formation has some kind of grammatical difference from the original word. Often, its part of speech is different, as with **enthuse** from **enthusiastic**. If students know the original word **enthusiastic**, they can use it as a cue to meaning, but they should also notice the change in part of speech. Back-formation explains the neologism **echolocate** from **echolocation** that was mentioned earlier.

On the other hand, **prof** is a *clipped* version of **professor**. Clipping means shortening a multisyllable word either from the end or from the beginning without much regard for the morphology of the word. Clipping doesn't really derive a new word with a different meaning and part of speech, but rather a different word that is just shorter than the original. **Prof** and **professor** mean the same thing, **math** and **mathematics** mean the same thing, and **golf pro** and **golf professional** mean the same thing. Clipped words differ from abbreviations (of the second type just shown) because clipped words can take on a life of their own. They are easier to pronounce and usually slangy or informal. The strategy for reading clipped words is to recognize them as such and relate them to the longer word if it is known. Alternatively, students may be more familiar with the clipped word; if so, they can relate the longer word to it when they see it.

Conversion.   We have already discussed the fact that in English parts of speech are opaque; that is, nouns are not marked unambiguously as nouns much of the time, verbs are not marked as verbs, and so on. One word formation process takes advantage of this because words are simply converted from one part of speech to another. It is possible to take a word like *egg*, a prototypical noun, and use it as a verb: **They egged him on to break the window.** A function word like *out* can become a content word: **They outed him on the Internet.** Conversion is inhibited if there is an existing verb already. For instance, we don't use *explosion* as a verb because we already have the verb **explode**. Something that also inhibits conversion is the existence of a very clear part of speech marking, such as the suffixes **-tion** and **-ence**, which are used to form nouns from verbs. However, there are a few examples of conversion even with these:

to confer⇒a conference⇒to conference (with students)

trans (bound root) or **transit→a transition→to transition** (from one activity to another)

Other Processes.   Other common word formation processes in English are blending, coining, and generalization. *Blending* is a process where two separate words are reduced and combined. For example, *brunch* is a *blend* of **breakfast** and **lunch**. In the case of **brunch**, it might be hard for ESL//EFL students to apply a strategy of breaking up the two parts to combine the meaning, because they might not recognize it as a blend. Other blends are more recognizable; **Reaganomics** and **chocoholic** come to mind. *Coined words*, or words "minted" out of thin air, are harder to detect. Many are trademark names like **Kleenex** or **Xerox**, so they might, in fact, be multinational. Sometimes trademark names or other proper names become common nouns or verbs through a process of *generalization*, as in **kleenex** or a **quizling**.

These word formation processes may cause the ESL/EFL student some difficulty in reading, especially authentic materials like academic texts or articles, magazines, and newspapers, because acronyms, new blends or coinages, back-formations, clipped forms, and abbreviations may not be in the dictionary and their meanings may not be self-evident.

Word Meaning

Even if readers recognize words, they may not have all of the necessary semantic information to understand the word and its meaning if they read it. They may lack knowledge of meanings other than the most common or the most literal denotation. They may lack knowledge of the social, political, or religious connotation that words have. They need to be able to process and understand metaphor, discard inappropriate meanings for polysemous words, and resolve lexical ambiguity problems. If semantic information about words is not automatically available to readers from their knowledge base as they process the text, comprehension of meaning is compromised.

Metaphor.   The use of metaphor to refer to an object creates challenges for readers. A *metaphor* is a figure of speech in which a word that denotes one thing is used in place of another to suggest a likeness or similarity between the two things. Using the word **ice** instead of **diamond** is a metaphor drawing on our awareness that diamonds and ice have similarities in appearance. If a waitress uses the term *ham sandwich* to refer to a customer in the sentence "The **ham sandwich** left without paying,' she is using a figure of speech drawing on the associated concepts of the individual customer and what he ate. This example of *metonymy*, where a word meaning an attribute or a part (the sandwich) is used in place of another that is the whole (the customer), is a specific type of metaphor.

Reasoning by Analogy.   Understanding a metaphor requires reasoning by analogy. To understand the use of **that old goat** in reference to an elderly character, students must first know that **goat** is being used to refer to the character and not some extraneous animal in the story. They must know what a goat is and what properties could be shared by a goat and an elderly man (which could potentially be bearded, smelly, shaggy, stubborn, reclusive, bossy, stringy, and thin) in order to successfully understand the analogy.

Native-speaking readers can usually understand figures of speech because the meaning associations stored in semantic memory are not self-contained and isolated one from another. Rather, they are widespread networks of interconnected concepts and associations that have been built up through the years as we have learned about words, culture, and the world. So when native-speaking readers come across a figure of speech, the associations evoked allow the readers to understand what the writer is trying to say. ESL/EFL readers may not have the stored cultural concepts and associations to understand common metaphors in English, or they may understand them in an unintended way. In addition, comprehension of metaphor is not universal. It is learned and developmental, and as such, it is reasonable to expect cultural variation in its use and interpretation.

Polysemy.   Metaphors can, through repetition, become so conventionalized that they lose their special status as a figure of speech and become merely cases of *polysemy*. Words that have more than one meaning are called polysemous. In some cases of polysemy, the meanings of the word are clearly related to each other and yet we are quite sure that the meanings are different. An example of this would be the use of the word **mouse**, which began as a metaphor to describe the computer part because if its resemblance to the animal in color, size, and shape, and possession of a tail. Now, many would probably say that the word **mouse** has two clearly different meanings equal in importance: the small animal and the computer part. It is ceasing to be a metaphor and becoming a case of polysemy; therefore, analogy is no longer necessary to understand the word.

In cases with a longer historical background, the meanings may seem more distant from each other, but we would agree, still, that they are related. An example is the word **point**:

He sharpened the point of the knife. (sharp end)

He wasn't sure of the point of the story. (purpose)

He made an interesting point. (an important detail in his argument)

He walked to a point ten feet from the outhouse. (specific location)

He made a point for his team. (a score)

The decimal point is in the wrong place. (a mathematical punctuation)

The problem with polysemous words for English L2 learners is that unfortunately for them, the commonest words they encounter tend to have the widest variety of meanings, and they only know one or possibly two of the main definitions for a word. And because the word is common, teachers may overlook the difficulty students have with polysemy because they assume that students must already know the word.

Homonymy. Polysemy, in which *a single word* has multiple meanings, must be distinguished from homonymy, in which *two separate words* happen to have the same sound and spelling. That is, homonyms are words that are both homophones and homographs at the same time. *Homophones* are different words that happen to have the same pronunciation. There are two types of homophones: those that have different spellings (through–threw, bear–bare, eight–ate, you–ewe) and those that have the same spellings (bear–bear, bank–bank, quail–quail). *Homographs* are different words that happen to be spelled the same. Again, there are two different types of homographs: those that are pronounced differently (bow–bow, lead–lead), and those that are pronounced the same way (bear–bear, bank–bank, quail–quail).

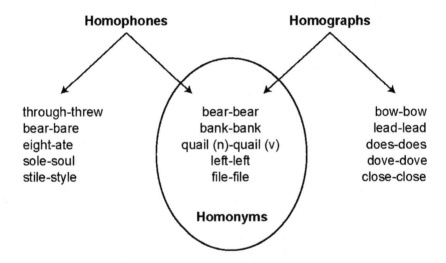

The words inside the circle, both homophones and homographs, are *homonyms*, two different words that just happen to have both the same form and the same pronunciation.

We can rule out metaphor in these cases because there is no similarity in meaning, and we can rule out polysemy in these cases because it seems quite clear that different words are involved, not different meanings of the same word. Homophones, homographs, and especially homonyms present some of the same decision-making dilemmas as polysemous words. Students may know only one word from a pair, so the meaning they assign is wrong and they won't detect it. If the readers know both words, they can still cause problem-solving nightmares for the reading processor that is developing in the ESL and EFL students because they create *lexical ambiguity*. If students are aware of two different homonyms, how do they know which word of the pair is intended for this context? If their comprehension of a text is already shaky, lexical ambiguity could sabotage it completely.

Top-down schema-activating prereading strategies mentioned earlier can help with polysemous words and homonyms because they will prime the reader to understand the text the right way. Other than that, one strategy is for students to acquire as extensive a mental lexicon and semantic memory as possible in their L2 and to use syntactic cues to narrow down the part of speech of the word in question.

WORD LEARNING STRATEGIES

I hope that I have made a strong case for discarding the strategy of skipping over unknown words as the main way to cope with vocabulary in favor of top-down and bottom-up word learning strategies. Some teachers are already using the top-down comprehension and word-learning strategies discussed earlier. Teachers may find also that reading about the origin of English words and instruction in their word formation might benefit ESL and EFL readers as well, so that they can apply cognate or morphological strategies. Awareness of the lexical variables that make words easier and harder to learn may assist teachers in selecting which words to highlight for learners. For instance, if nouns are easier for readers to learn on their own, teachers might focus more attention on verbs in the classroom. In addition, there is some research relevant to the effectiveness of two lower level or bottom-up word learning strategies: repetition and the keyword technique.

Repetition

As we have already discussed, repetition of the unknown word can be helpful. When the subjects in Ellis and Beaton's 1993 study repeated the unfamiliar L2 word, their ability to produce the unfamiliar word later was enhanced, presumably because the phonological loop was used and an entry in the mental lexicon was constructed. Learners should use their phonological skills to attempt to pronounce new words. The onset/rime strategy, probabilistic reasoning, and syllabification are helpful here.

The Keyword Strategy

This strategy also involves phonology. In this word learning strategy the learner associates the foreign word with the L1 word by means of a mediating word that is similar to the foreign word in sound. For example, the Spanish word for **bread** is **pan**; English-speaking learners of Spanish might visualize a loaf of bread in a pan. The Spanish equivalent (pan) for one word (bread) is learned by mediation of a similar sounding English word (pan). The keyword in this case is the English word *pan*.

When subjects used a keyword strategy, their ability to translate the L2 word to the L1 word was enhanced. Translation of the L2 word to L1 is considered to be a receptive skill, but probably appropriate to reading. The keyword strategy in some ways might be similar to a visual or "kanji" strategy for word identification, but there are some important differences. First of all, Ellis and Beaton found that acoustic similarity enhanced the association between the target unknown word and the native language keyword. This means that the target word *is* being processed phonologically, and a phonologically similar (but not orthographically similar) word is chosen as keyword. In the kanji strategy, the target word is not processed phonologically. The keyword strategy is also different in that the mediating image or sentence probably improves memory for meaning over a purely visual strategy in which an English word is associated by rote with a sinogram.

According sources cited in Ellis and Beaton (1993), the keyword method of learning vocabulary is superior to rote rehearsal or presenting vocabulary in context; however, they point out:

> However, theories of FL vocabulary learning and the role of phonological memory systems typically fail to make the important distinction concerning direction of translation. The present study's finds suggest that phonological factors are more implicated in productive learning when the student has a greater cognitive burden in terms of sensory and motor load. Ellis and Beaton (in press) demonstrate from individual differences analyses that *although keyword techniques are efficient means for receptive vocabulary learning; for productive learning they are less effective than repetition* (at least for learners naive to the pronunciation patterns of the foreign language). (p. 601, emphasis added)

It would seem that repetition is better (and simpler) than the keyword strategy overall, but the latter might be useful for learning certain words that may be especially salient or especially hard to remember.

ESL AND EFL READERS

Any teacher, even novice teachers, will agree that ESL and EFL readers face challenges with vocabulary acquisition, word recognition, word meanings, and collocational information. This is, of course, supported by research. For example, Schmitt and Meara (1997) found that L2 learners did not have extensive mastery of the word associations even for verbs they reported they "knew." They were only able to produce 50% of the word associations possible as compared to native speaker norms. This indicates that the meaning associations for the verbs they were tested on were only half as elaborated as they were for native speakers.

In an earlier paper, Meara (1983) found that L2 learners give more varied responses to test words than native speakers did and that their associations are often nonrelated words that sound similar instead of words that are related in meaning. This tells us that students' intuitions about words are not conventional. Their associations are simply from phonemic image to the similar phonemic image of other similar words. Their associations between words may not be through meaning at all.

Fragmentary knowledge of word meaning has an impact on comprehension. Ying (1996) found that adult English learners' incomplete knowledge of certain types of verbs (psychological verbs like **think** and perception verbs like **hear**) prevented them from processing sentences like the native speakers did.

English learners will also lack syntactic collocational information about the phrases and clauses that the word requires. Lennon (1996) found that advanced learners of English have a broad concept of verb meaning for simple verbs, but their knowledge of contextual and collocational restrictions is not precise. If this is the case, then even advanced ESL readers may have difficulty interpreting syntactic structures and this may influence their ability to comprehend what they are reading. Lennon concludes that even advanced learners may require classroom vocabulary work on simple verbs within their common lexical and syntactic contexts.

MariCarmen and Despina can supplement their natural tendency to use L1–L2 cognates to identify new words with other strategies described here. Mohammed and Ho especially need word learning and comprehension strategies to increase their productive and receptive vocabulary for reading and writing. They'll be a lot better off in the long run than if they just skip the words they don't know.

Certainly, at the early stages of English L2 reading, all new words should be learned productively through repetition, because the words common in early reading are likely to be common in listening, speaking and writing as well. Even in later advanced reading, most words should be learned productively so that they can transfer from reading to writing. However, there might be occasions, in very advanced stages of reading acquisition, when readers might wish to apply the keyword (visual receptive) strategy to remember some unfamiliar words that they will not be using in writing.

In summary, teachers should teach vocabulary in reading class in efficient ways in order to empower students to become active human word processors.

- To the extent that it is possible, choose readings that contain only a limited number of new words. Readings should be considered *comprehensible input*, that is, just slightly above the student's true reading level at present.

- Provide ample opportunities for students to read on their own for pleasure outside of class. They will be more motivated if they can select fiction or nonfiction on topics they are interested in. (Remember—Not everyone likes fiction.)
- Continue using the top-down, schema-activating, prereading comprehension and word learning strategies to prepare students to read effectively.
- Teach vocabulary and reading in the context of English phonology, orthography, morphology, word formation processes, and grammar to make more new words more pronounceable, repeatable, and comprehensible to the students.
- Teach vocabulary items with their part of speech and teach words, especially verbs, in collocations (Lewis, 1993, 1997).
- Teach students different word learning and recognition strategies to apply on their own while they are reading, in order to be proactive about increasing their overall vocabulary and comprehension and to decrease reliance on ineffective visual strategies.
- Teach students to distinguish between words to be learned productively (most words) and words to be learned receptively (a few words).

SPOTLIGHT ON TEACHING

These two strategies, repetition and keyword, can be modeled and practiced for learning new words, instead of skipping them. As we have seen, for words to be learned productively, the repetition strategy is best:

- Look at an unfamiliar word carefully using an onset/rime strategy and knowledge of English morphophonemic writing (to form a graphemic image), and try to pronounce it (to form a phonological image and to activate the phonological loop). Pronounce it several times (to store it in long-term memory). An incorrect pronunciation probably doesn't matter and is better than no pronunciation.
- Look at the syntactic and meaning context and try to determine something of the new word's part of speech and definition.

For words to be learned receptively in reading, model and practice the keyword approach:

- Look at the word carefully (to form a graphemic image). Try to pronounce it once.
- Try to determine something of the word's meaning and part of speech from the context.
- Associate the appearance of the L2 word with a similar L1 word and relate them through a visual image or a sentence; for example,

Spanish *jabon* (soap) can be remembered with the sentence "I jabbed him with the soap."

Select a reading passage from an ESL/EFL textbook. Identify five words to be learned productively and two words to be learned receptively. Design classroom activities around these words.

DISCUSSION QUESTIONS

1. Do you have any idea why ESL students made these mistakes in compositions they wrote while consulting small L1–L2 dictionaries?

   a. The ambulance went down the street with its mermaid on.

   b. Please cast the sugar into the coffee.

   c. That joke shamed me.

   d. We were expecting the bus for 45 minutes and then we left.

2. In this chapter, we discussed what information there might be within the lexical entries. Write lexical entries for the following verbs: **expect, hope, wait for.** Comment on similar aspects of the meanings of these words. Can this explain some of the ESL learner's difficulty with these words?

3. Lexical entries containing grammatical information are linked by association to meaning concepts (memories) in semantic memory, where we store the encyclopedic knowledge of the words of our language. Words have *denotations* (what they mean) and *connotations* (additional positive or negative associations in memory). What is the denotation of these words: *chair, art, density, happy*? What is the difference in the connotation of these words: *slim* versus *skinny*; *mother* versus *welfare mother*; *statesman* versus *politician*.

4. Try to identify the following words as homophones, homographs, or homonyms. Use a dictionary if necessary: tied–tide, do (verb)–do (musical note), pine–pine, row–row (a kind of fight), tea–tee, seal–seal, toe–tow, tic–tick, polish–Polish, colon–colon.

5. Go through the steps of what would happen in your reading processor if you came across these new words in the newspaper:
   When the congressman spoke to the women, his *Clintonism* was apparent.
   Stressed out? It's time to apply some *orlandotherapy*.

6. Is it possible to put all of your thoughts or experiences into words? What thoughts or experiences are resistant to "lexification"? (Can you understand that new word based on its morphology?)

Chapter 10

Getting to the Bottom of English L2 Reading Fluency

Prereading questions. Before you read, think about and discuss the following:

1. When do people need to read out loud, besides in the classroom?
2. How do you feel about reading out loud in public? What problems, if any, do you have?
3. How is oral reading similar to and different from silent reading?
4. What would you do if you wanted to speed up your silent reading?
5. What clues to meaning and intonation do punctuation marks provide for readers?

Study Guide Questions: Answer these questions while and after reading the chapter.

1. What is the "elephant in the living room"? Can reading instruction change brain activation in dyslexic children?
2. What additional questions does the brain activation evidence raise?
3. What is the balanced approach to reading instruction?
4. What are the first steps for most English L2 readers?
5. What changes might be necessary in reading curricula?
6. What is reading fluency? How are oral and silent fluency related?
7. What makes fluent oral reading difficult for the ESL or EFL reader? Should fluency tests be avoided?
8. What two additional areas of knowledge are crucial for fluency?
9. What reading strategies should be avoided? How should reading teachers respond to "mistakes"?
10. What is intensive practice? What is modeling? What should be modeled?
11. How can reading rate be improved?
12. How can readers stop "word-calling"?

This book has explored some of the exciting new research in the area of English L1 and L2 reading and offered a new concept of the proficient ESL and EFL reader. The proficient reader has an expert decision-making and problem-solving mind that uses extensive knowledge of language and the world, effective cognitive comprehension strategies, and quick automatic low-level processing strategies to interact with the text efficiently.

However, for most of the chapters, we have tiptoed around an "elephant in the living room." In an earlier chapter, we saw evidence from brain activation studies that different writing systems seem to cause human brains to acquire different patterns of activation based on the language that they learn to read. That means that knowledge and processing strategies are highly language dependent. To what extent can we even expect to be able to change, through instruction, the L1 patterns of activation that are hard-wired, so to speak, into the brain? Is native-like brain activation necessary for effective or fluent reading in L2? We do not know the answers to these important questions.

However, for L1 brain activation patterns to change, L2 readers may require direct instruction in English letter-to-sound conversion, onsets and rimes, and ample practice with easy readings and steadily increasing vocabulary to build up their facility with English reading strategies. To change the L1 knowledge and strategies, we must expect a more lengthy acquisition period; we must allow learners to acquire automaticity in reading English before requiring the comprehension of difficult texts. This chapter explores the acquisition of reading fluency in light of what we now know as the complexity of the reading process. Fluent readers are expert decision makers.

EFFECTS OF INSTRUCTION ON BRAIN ACTIVATION

Can learners in fact make a transition from L1 reading to L2? That is, is there any evidence that instruction changes brain activation? Unfortunately, the evidence from adult Chinese and Japanese L1 learners of English discussed in an earlier chapter is not very encouraging. The Chinese and Japanese students did not appear to use English strategies to read English. Instead, they seemed to continue using their L1 strategies because their brain activation was the same for both languages. However, there is some evidence for a positive effect from instruction on brain activation from a few studies of dyslexic children. Narayana and Xiong (2003) compared two groups of readers, a group of dyslexic boys and girls and a group of "normal" readers between the ages of 11 and 12. Their brains were scanned while they did a phoneme mapping task (**oa** in **ploat** sounded the same as **ow** as in **crow**) and a morpheme mapping task (**builder** and **build** vs. **corner** and **corn**).

First of all, the different tasks resulted in activation in different parts of the brain in both normal and dyslexic readers, and the amount of activation in each area was less in dyslexic readers than in normal readers. Then the dyslexic children received 28 hours of instructional treatment, at the end of which the activation patterns increased and were no different from normal readers. Aylward et al. (2003), in a similar experiment, had identical results; they concluded that comprehensive reading instruction leads to reading improvement and changes in brain function. Simos et al. (2002) also looked at the effects of intensive remediation on brain activation patterns in dyslexic children with severe difficulties in word recognition and phonological processing. After the remediation, the children showed significant improvement in reading skills, and brain activity was increased. The authors concluded that remedial instruction could reverse problems in brain activation that underlie dyslexia.

The studies report few details about the comprehensive or intensive reading instruction given to the children. The instruction involved activities to enhance linguistic awareness, knowledge of the alphabetic principle, fluency, and reading comprehension. It is not clear if the evidence from dyslexic readers is directly relevant to ESL and EFL readers, but it is at the very least encouraging. Nevertheless, these studies also raise a lot of crucial questions, which remain for neurologists to answer for reading teachers.

The first question is that, given that there are age-related factors in language acquisition and learning, was the activation change and improvement in reading found in the dyslexic children related to their younger age? Recall that the Chinese graduate students began learning English after the age of 12, so perhaps the Chinese graduate students were less able to acquire English reading strategies because they began learning as older students. This would argue strongly for beginning L2 literacy instruction as early as possible, certainly before puberty.

Second, would different instructional methods result in different activation patterns and improved reading scores, or would the patterns and improvement be independent of instructional method? In other words—would top-down methods yield the same result over time as phonics methods since readers end up reading the same writing system at the end? Are there different rates of acquisition related to different instructional methodologies? What are the effects of extensive or intensive practice of various types and amounts? We do not know very much about how the Chinese and Japanese students learned about the English writing system and acquired English reading skills.

The evidence from dyslexic children at least holds out the promise that reading instruction can affect brain activation at the same time that reading improves. The findings suggest that instruction and practice, especially at an early age, may improve the use of reading strategies that are appropriate to the second language. In the absence of more research that is more directly relevant to ESL and EFL readers, I would suggest that a balanced, integrated, but fully elaborated reading methodology, with sufficient instructional time and attention, will be most likely to lead to automaticity and fluency in English reading.

A BALANCED APPROACH TO READING

The discussion in this book has aimed specifically at getting to the bottom of the reading processor, specifically, reinforcing and strengthening our understanding and appreciation for the details of low-level knowledge and processing strategies our students need in order to read in English. This focus, however, doesn't mean that higher level knowledge of the world and top-down processing strategies are less important.

In fact, the bottom of the reading processor serves the top because the more efficiently and "quietly" the bottom functions, the more attention there will be for higher level processing of meaning, implications, outside references, and so on. Language processing skills are one subcomponent of more general cognitive processing; linguistic knowledge is just one area of the complete knowledge about the world, culture, or personal memories that the reader has. This is a more balanced and integrated view of reading, worthy of the name "whole language."

The balanced integrated perspective offers a different picture of what "guessing" involves: split-second decisions based on accurate perception, reasoning abilities, and stored knowledge. To make good guesses, an ESL and EFL reader must pass through the various stages of acquisition posited by Chall and Ehri. While they can be assisted through early to advanced reading by teachers who get them started and guide them with the right strategies and knowledge, the best way for readers themselves to acquire automaticity with bottom-level processing is by extensive active practice with reading material that is enjoyable and easy. Extensive practice means that students read inside the classroom to learn and apply strategies, and they read on their own outside the classroom to perfect their skills with interesting relevant fiction or nonfiction. If readers are motivated to read on their own (and this is where social factors such as peer pressure or cultural appreciation and ownership of literacy and literature also play a role), they will become expert unconscious decision makers and problem solvers.

From the First Step

They say that a long journey always begins with the first step. A lifelong rewarding journey of English reading also begins with the first tentative attempts of English learners like Mohammed, Ho, Despina, and MariCarmen to decode our morphophonemic writing. The earliest step (in fact, a prereading step) in learning to read is, of course, listening comprehension. Study after study has shown the importance of phonological awareness, especially segmentation skills, in early reading for native English readers. Phonological awareness is acquired through aural and oral activities, but total mastery of the sounds of English is not necessary before beginning to read. Often, learning the letter shapes and sounds together can bootstrap phonological awareness. Students need to learn the alphabetic principle anyway, so teachers should teach it explicitly.

For some learners, their L1 orthography, their true starting point, matters a lot. For them, the process must begin with slow and laborious acquisition and practice with English orthography. Teachers must not rush ESL and EFL students through this stage, but allow them to continue to read easy texts for as long as they need to. It is important to recall that native-speaking children learning to read English show great variety in how long it takes them to become good readers. Some are reading well at 4; others take until the age of 7 or 8 to become fluent readers. In our anxiety to show progress in English L2 reading, we often rush students into texts that are too difficult, without allowing them the time to acquire automaticity with English graphemes and common spelling patterns. We will rush our students if we overlook or minimize the complex task of switching from their L1 orthography to English.

Just as we have gained insight into the need for a "silent period" in speech production for some students, and have therefore tried to avoid pushing learners into speaking before they are ready, we also need to respect the need for students to have the time and opportunity to acquire automaticity in reading before moving on to challenging material. To build this time and opportunity into the reading curriculum may mean expanding our notion of the beginning and intermediate student. One or two courses at these levels may not be sufficient for everyone.

During this expanded curriculum, students may benefit from practice sounding out words without worrying about their pronunciation. They also need numerous ways of getting feedback on the connection between graphemes and phonemes: listening to stories while they follow along or reading out loud to someone else in a safe, nonjudgmental environment. They should not resort to the strategies that may have transferred from the L1 orthography, such as the visual strategy or the partial alphabetic strategy. The fully alphabetic strategy may be a good jumping off point for ESL/EFL students, because it helps them implicitly learn the probabilities that a grapheme will be pronounced a certain way, as long as they are getting accurate feedback. However, instead of using each syllable as a reading unit, teachers need to instruct students in the 100 or so common spelling-to-sound patterns that form the basis for reading by analogy in the consolidated alphabetic stage.

Only very advanced ESL and EFL readers can read by "sampling" the text, with few short fixations and few regressions. It often takes a lot of effort, practice, and learning to get to that point. All of the processing strategies must be working together so accurately and efficiently that they work at an unconscious level. All the knowledge of English graphemes, morphemes, and words must be readily accessible in long-term memory. English learners must be active, soaking up and storing new words, morphemes, and meaning in their knowledge base for receptive and productive use. For them to learn to do this, early reading must be carefully controlled to be at their comfortable but challenging level and they should not be pushed into reading texts that are too challenging too soon. They should be able to take to time to practice word learning strategies like the phonological loop or the keyword strategy (Figure 10.1).

The Destination: Advanced Fluency

Silent Reading Fluency. The term "reading fluency" is often applied indiscriminately to both silent and oral reading; however, that may be counterproductive. The aim of most English L2 reading instruction is automatic silent processing at a good rate with optimal comprehension; we'll

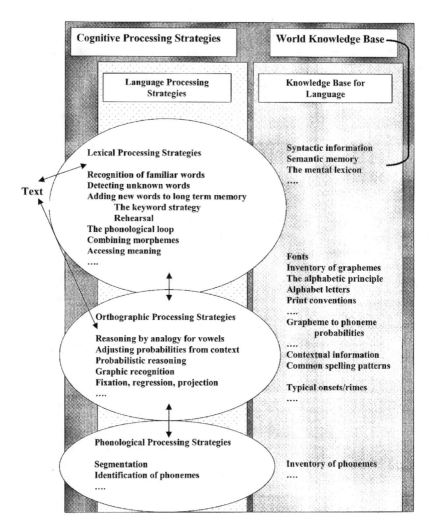

Figure 10.1 A hypothetical model of the bottom of the reading processor.

call that *automaticity*. Reading out loud with fluency (i.e., with proper speed, intonation, and comprehension) is of secondary importance for most students and their teachers. Automaticity should be the goal for reading instruction, and not oral fluency.

Fluency is sometimes used as a synonym for automaticity in the following sense. To read fluently in silence means that readers have a number of skills that work together. They can read at an appropriate rate or speed with sufficient comprehension. This means that they must have enough eye fixations without having too many fixations. Each fixation must allow the reader to scan several words. They must recognize the words they are reading without too many miscues, and be able to construct a correct phrasal and sentential structures. They must understand the punctuation and assign appropriate intonation. They must not have too many eye regressions caused by confusion or lack of understanding. To have optimal comprehension, readers need to accomplish all of these tasks automatically so that they can construct meanings in short-term memory and store them in long-term memory.

Fluent Oral Reading.   Fluency in oral reading is the same as fluent silent reading but with an added complex task, one that is especially challenging for ESL and EFL readers. Fluent oral reading entails pronouncing the author's words, phrases, and sentences with the right sounds, emphasis, rate of speed, phrasing, and intonation. For many native readers, fluent oral reading can be problematic if they are nervous, have a short eye span, or do not understand words, punctuation, and the overall meaning. For nonnative readers oral reading is even more problematic because, in addition to those problems, reader anxiety can be greater, vocabulary can be lacking, knowledge of punctuation may be incomplete, and background knowledge to understand the meaning may be absent.

Fluency Tests.   Most teachers agree that fluent silent reading is more important than fluent oral reading because the former is expected in our culture, but the latter is not. There are only a few occasions where older children or adults are expected to read aloud: in their place of worship, in drama class, in certain professions. However, in the classroom setting, fluent oral reading is sometimes taken as an indicator of automatic silent reading because if someone can read fluently out loud, the implication is that he or she can also read silently with automaticity. This is because if a reader can succeed in a more difficult task (oral reading), he or she probably succeeds at the easier task (silent reading). It is in this sense that oral reading is sometimes used as a measure of silent reading, and therefore oral fluency tests are often used to test for general reading ability.

Teachers and testers must recognize that oral fluency tests probably discriminate against the nonnative speaker because the task that is being tested is different and more complex for the nonnative reader than for the native reader. The task is different for the English learner, from the lowest level of reading strategies and knowledge to the highest. Therefore, the results of oral fluency tests on ESL and EFL readers must be evaluated on a different scale or in a different way from native readers. ESL and EFL readers should be compared with each other and not to native readers, unless they are already at the upper levels of fluency.

For instance, in the area of pronunciation, "errors" may mean different things for the different populations. Pronunciation errors in native speakers are speech disorders, and they are associated with reading difficulty because they may stem from intellectual development problems, neurological impairment, or inability to discriminate sounds in hearing (Bond et al., 1989). It is possible for ESL and EFL readers to have such speech disorders also, and these must be carefully distinguished from their "normal" accents, which are simply the result of nonnative motor commands or movements of the mouth, but do not indicate a problem with the mental phonemic inventory, development problems, or impairment. Teachers themselves may test for auditory discrimination problems, but other disorders may require more specialized testing.

In summary, the relationship between oral fluency and silent automaticity is not completely clear for ESL and EFL readers, but it is probably the case that oral fluency achieved by English learners in a relaxed and comfortable setting (i.e., not during testing) may indicate how well silent automatic processing takes place also. In addition, improvement in reading fluency and proficiency may transfer to improved silent automaticity, an idea that motivates many reading teachers to work on oral fluency in reading. It may also be the case that oral reading fluency contributes to general oral fluency in speaking; the better one can read out loud, the better one can use intonation, pronunciation, and proper rate in speech (and, of course, vice versa).

IMPROVING ORAL READING FLUENCY

To improve their learners' oral reading fluency, ESL and EFL teachers must focus on three things: increasing the readers' knowledge of English, improving the readers' automatic use of reading strategies, and providing reading tasks aimed at improving specific aspects of fluency.

Knowledge

Naturally, readers need as much knowledge as possible for fluent reading, from top-level background cultural and world knowledge, to mid-level syntax and words, to bottom-level letters and sounds. Many other books deal with the need for top-level knowledge and ways to meet this need, and this book has already dealt with vocabulary, morphemes, phonemes, and graphemes. However, there is a little more to say about two areas of knowledge: basic vocabulary and punctuation.

Function Words.   At the mid-level, one area that teachers can specifically focus on is knowledge of basic vocabulary, especially *function words* (prepositions, particles, pronouns, determiners, conjunctions, wh-words, auxiliaries) and very common content words like adverbs (very, so, then, enough, too, as) or irregular verbs. These words are essential for understanding the structure of phrases and collocations. Readers can read faster with better intonation and comprehension if they recognize these common words because knowing the part they play in English phrases and sentences helps readers construct syntactic structures and interpret them. These words are often sight words, which means that they must be learned as a whole item because the onset/rime strategy won't work well with them. Flash cards and a word wall with basic vocabulary will encourage knowledge of very common sight words.

Punctuation. Because punctuation operates at all levels of language from the level of morphemes (apostrophe) to the level of discourse (indenting), readers cannot read and comprehend without knowledge of it. Periods, commas, question marks, quotation marks and the like tell readers how to interpret the information or message they are reading and how to pronounce the sentences out loud. If learners know intonation patterns in English for statements, yes/no questions, wh- questions, and exclamations and the punctuation marks that signal them, their reading will be more fluent. After going over the uses of different punctuation marks, teachers might highlight them in the text or ask learners to highlight them, so that consciousness-raising takes place.

Strategies

Counterproductive Strategies. Certain reading strategies or behaviors need to be discouraged because they interfere with fluency in reading. For instance, some ESL and EFL readers read each word separately one by one; in native English readers, these are "word-callers." Instead, good readers read phrase by phrase, by actively using their knowledge of function words, collocations, and grammar. Good readers also refrain from pointing a finger at each word, although they can use their index finger to move quickly across and down the page to increase their speed. They need to minimize regressive eye movements and work on increasing fixation lengths. At the end of the line, readers need to be able to return to the next line down easily. Naturally, subvocalizing or whispering should be inhibited.

Instructional Strategies. Crawley and King (1991) have a lot of suggestions for reading remediation for English L1 readers that would also assist English L2 readers. They recommend some strategies for reading teachers to practice when listening to learners read out loud. First, teachers should let students figure out new words and not be too quick to supply them. (Naturally, the selection to be read out loud should be easy to begin with, with few new words.) This is called increasing the teacher's "wait time." Second, reading teachers should ignore omitted words or substituted words if the meaning of the sentence is intact. For instance, if a reader skips over the word *very* it is probably best to let it go. If a reader substitutes the word *cat* for *kitten*, it probably won't affect the meaning too much.

However, if the omission or substitution causes a problem with meaning, teachers may use their judgment about whether to stop the reader or not. If they decide to stop the reader, they might say, "Does that part make sense to you?" In this way teachers model how the reader needs to monitor comprehension of the text while reading. Teacher should also model top-level comprehension strategies as well, demonstrating out loud how to look for context cues in the entire sentence, the previous sentence, or the sentence after. They should model the various word analysis strategies. Overall, teachers will help learners increase their fluency in oral reading if they provide many opportunities for learners to succeed in reading out loud in a comfortable relaxing setting. For readers to succeed, teachers must carefully select readings that are at their comfortable or, better yet, very easy level of reading.

Reading Tasks

To improve fluency in oral reading, ESL and EFL learners should work intensively with a single reading passage, with repeated exposures in different ways. To start with, learners should have ample opportunities to read the material silently for comprehension and discuss any unknown words, ideas, and grammatical structures. They use appropriate word analysis strategies (onset/rime, morphology, syllable structure) efficiently to pronounce new words. Then, they might listen to the selection being read by another more proficient reader several times or to a tape-recording of the selection. Alternatively, they can listen to the selection first and read silently second. Third, they should practice reading the selection out loud several times by themselves or to an encouraging and helpful peer or reading buddy. They may tape-record their own reading of the selection and listen to it with careful attention to pronunciation, intonation, and reading rate. They might exchange tapes with another student and listen to each other. ESL and EFL learners often like to dramatize the reading as a play or dialogue. Only after intensive practice like this, should ESL and EFL learners be invited to read aloud in a more formal setting.

Reading Rate. The speed with which readers can process the words, phrases, and sentences with adequate comprehension is called the *reading rate*. Once ESL and EFL readers have some familiarity with a reading and have practiced it, they measure their reading rate by counting how many words they can read out loud per minute. Once they have measured their typical reading speed with an adequate level of comprehension, they have a *base rate* to improve. Still reading out loud, they push themselves to read more quickly than their base rate, while maintaining phrasing, intonation, pronunciation, and so on. They might set a timer for a half a second less and try to read the passage within that time frame. Over a period of time, the readings can become ever so slightly longer and less familiar, while the reader pushes himself or herself to read faster while maintaining comprehension. Silent reading rate can also be measured and increased using similar techniques.

Phrasing. Some learners benefit from having complex readings with complex sentence structures divided up into phrases at first. For instance, a reading can be presented visually in either of the two following ways. With some practice, the readers themselves can mark the phrases in the text physically. (This may be easier if learners are using computers.) The ultimate goal is for the learners to "chunk up" the sentences in normal texts by themselves. Learners may also need assistance with English phrasal stress. Each phrase receives one or two heavier "beats" on the main words, with other words given less emphasis.

> Most claims about improving reading speed / cannot be taken very seriously, / but English L2 readers / can learn to read faster. /To do so, / they need to practice/ with very easy reading material / that motivates them / and that they can understand readily, / either under the supervision of a teacher / or on their own. / / Once they have measured / their typical reading speed / with an adequate level of comprehension, / they have a base rate to improve.

Most claims about improving reading speed

cannot be taken very seriously,

but English L2 readers can learn to read faster.

To do so, they need to practice with very easy reading material

that motivates them and that they can understand readily,

either under the supervision of a teacher or on their own.

Once they have measured their typical reading speed

with an adequate level of comprehension,

they have a base rate to improve.

Modeling. There are various modeling techniques, some of which have already been mentioned. Using audiotapes, books on CD, downloaded books, speech synthesizers, and the like, ESL and EFL learners hear professional readers read. Teachers can model reading as learners follow along. Choral reading or responsive reading (teacher reads, learners repeat) can provide a good model for pronunciation or reading rate.

FINAL WORDS

The goal of every ESL and EFL reading teacher is for readers to be able to process and comprehend the author's message at the proper rate of speed silently. It means that the reader is an expert decision maker with knowledge and strategies that are appropriate for English. It might mean that a fluent reader has a pattern of brain activation similar to that found in native speakers. To the extent that oral reading fluency contributes to silent automaticity, it can be included as a goal for the ESL or EFL reading teacher. If oral reading is typically used as a test of reading skills in a school district, ESL or EFL readers should have opportunities to improve their fluency.

As our students take their first steps on the journey to advanced reading, let's give them the best provisions and tools we can. Let's make their first steps as confident and effective as possible so they can read more rapidly and more easily later. We can do this if we get to the bottom of English L2 reading.

Appendix A

ENGLISH GRAPHEMES

Venezky's 1970 book *The Structure of English* is still one of the most comprehensive treatments of English spelling conventions, and I summarize and update a significant portion here with permission of the publisher, Mouton de Gruyter. Most people can understand that consonant and vowel graphemes are used to correspond roughly to consonant and vowel phonemes, and that will be our first topic in this appendix. However, there is another use for graphemes also.

Graphemes are sometimes used merely to give hints to the reader about how to pronounce other graphemes in the word; if they serve this purpose, they are called **markers**. The most common marker is the so-called silent *e*, which clues the reader in to the pronunciation of the previous vowel, as in **pine** versus **pin**, or **vane** versus **van**. We will start our discussion with an exposition of the major and minor graphemes in English; later we will explore some of the uses of graphemes as markers.

As shown in Fig. 11.1, *simple graphemes* are composed of one written symbol (e.g., **b**, **d**, **f**, **q**) and *digraphs* are composed of two written symbols (e.g., **ch**, **gh**, **sh**). Simple graphemes and digraphs are similar in that they refer to *one sound*. Compound graphemes act as if they are doubled consonant sounds even though in English there is no difference in the pronunciation of these doubled consonants. For instance, the compound grapheme **bb** stands for /b/ and **pp** stands for /p/. These compound graphemes are called *geminated* (twinned). Other compound graphemes are not written as geminated, but they still stand for a doubled consonant: **ck** (instead of kk for /k/), **dg** (instead gg for /dʒ/, **tch** for chch for /tʃ/. There is also one grapheme that I have included as a compound grapheme but it is also a complex grapheme because it is written as one symbol but it refers to a real sequence of two separate sounds: x stands for /ks/.

The Consonant Grapheme to Phoneme Correspondences

Consonant Graphemes.

simple   compound

b	g	kh	q	t	wh	ck
c	gh	l	r	th	y	dg
ch	h	m	s	u	z	tch
d	j	n	sh	v		x
f	k	p	sch	w		all geminated consonants (pp, tt, ll, etc.)

Notes: a. **u** is a consonant unit when it corresponds to /w/, as in q**u**ack or lang**u**age.

b. **wh** is mainly used as a simple consonant corresponding to the voiced /w/ or or the voiceless /ʍ/. In some dialects, **wh** seems to have a compound usage /hw/ as in the "voiceless" pronunciations of the beginning consonants of **wh**at, **wh**ich, and **wh**en.

c. **sch** is a simple consonant grapheme when it is used as in **sch**ist or **sch**wa.

d. **gn** is a simple consonant grapheme when it is used as in **gn**ome, co**gn**ac or poi**gn**ant.

e. Geminated consonants are compound consonants that are simple consonants doubled: **bb, dd, ff, gg, ll, mm, nn, pp, rr, tt, zz**, as in e**bb**, e**dd**y, ga**ff**er, e**gg**, fe**ll**, di**mm**er, di**nn**er, a**pp**le, pu**rr**, be**tt**er, bu**zz**. In fact, **ck, dg**, and **tch** actually stand for two consonants as well: **ck = cc** and **kk, dg** = **gg** or **jj**, and **tch = chch**. For some reason, our writing system has resisted writing true geminates for these and has preferred to use **ck, dg**, and **tch**, as in ba**ck**, e**dg**e, and wa**tch**.

---

b   **b** in de**b**t, dou**b**t, su**b**tle = /0/ .

final **b** in bom**b**, com**b**, tom**b**, crum**b** = /0/

b and **bb** elsewhere = /b/

Note: 1. /0/ means that the grapheme is not pronounced.

2. When there are two bilabial consonants in the middle of a word, only the second is pronounced: cu**pb**oard, su**bp**oena, cla**pb**oard, ras**pb**erry.

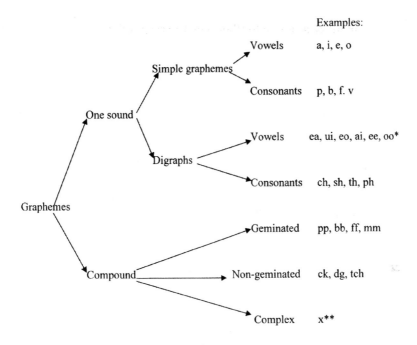

*Vowels with repeated symbols are called digraphs, not geminated.

**The symbol x is ONE symbol for two REAL sounds. It is compound and complex.

3. Note these **nonproductive** alternations. Nonproductive
   means that people do not make up new words following
   this pattern.

bombard	bomb
crumble	crumb
debit	debt
iambic	iamb
indubitable	doubt
number	numeric
rhombus	rhomb
thimble	thumb

c   *c* in **c**ello and con**c**erto = /tʃ/

    c in vi**c**tual, **c**zar, and indi**c**t =/0/

    c before i, y, e (and in fa**c**ade) = /s/

    c elsewhere = /k/

    Note: 1. Unproductive alternations: corpuscular, corpuscle; muscular, muscle

ch   **ch** in fu**ch**sia or ya**ch**t = /0/

    ch = /k/ before **l**, **n**, **r**, and in the following examples of words of Latin or Greek origin:

cache	chasm	hypochondria
alchemy	chemi-	lichen
anarchy	chiropodist	machination
anchor	choir	mechanic
archaeology	cholera	monarchy
archaic	choral	orchestra
archangel	chord	orchid
archetype	chorus	parochial
architecture	dichotomy	patriarch
archive	echo	pentateuch
catechism	epoch	psych-
chameleon	eucharist	stomach
chaos	eunuch	character
hierarchy		

ch = /ʃ/ in the following words of French origin:

cache	chassis	chivalry
chagrin	chateau	chute
chaise	chauffeur	cliché
chalet	chauvinism	crochet
challis	chef	echelon
chamois	chemise	machine
champagne	chiffon	mustache
chandlier	chevalier	parachute
chanty	ricochet	chaperon
charade	chic	charlatan

ch elsewhere = /tʃ/.

d   **d** = /0/ between /n/ and another consonant, as in han*d*kerchief or gran*d*mother

d elsewhere = /d/

Note these unproductive alternations: defend–defense, expend–expense, respond–response.

f   **f** in of = /v/

f elsewhere = /f/

Note that in the following words, **f** becomes **v** when the word is made plural: calf, elf, half, knife, leaf, life, loaf, self, sheaf, shelf, thief, wife, wolf.

In the following words, **f** becomes **v** when a noun becomes a verb: belief, grief, half, life, proof, relief, shelf.

Similarly, there are some other unproductive alternations: bereft–bereave, cleft–cleave, drift–drive, fifth–five, gift–give, left–leave, serf–serve, twelfth–twelve. The **f/v** alternations stems from a regular phonological process in the history of English. This phonological process is no longer productive.

g   **g** = /ʒ/ in the following words of French origin:

bourgeois	mirage
camouflage	prestige
corsage	protégé
garage	regime
lingerie	rouge
massage	sabotage

g = /g/before e, i, y in the following large number of "exceptions."

begin	gift	girth
eager	finger	gear
geese	get	gig
giggle	gild	gill
gird	girdle	girl
give	gynaecology	hunger
lager	linger	malinger
target	tiger	yogi

g = /dʒ / before e, i, and y generally

g = /g/ elsewhere

Notes: **ng** becomes /ŋ/ except in comparative and superlative forms
of adjectives, where it remains /ng/ as in stro**ng**–stro**ng**er.

gn in word initial position = /n/ as in **gn**ome

gm and **gn** at the end of words = /m/ and /n/, respectively.

gh   **gh** = /f/ in these: cough, rough, enough, tough, laughter

gh = /g/ at the beginning of words: ghost, ghetto, and in aghast,
spaghetti

gh elsewhere = /0/.

h **h** = /0/ in heir, honor, herb, hour, vehicle and other words of
French origin

h = /0/ preceded by a consonant: philharmonic

h = /h/ elsewhere.

j **j** = /dʒ/ except in words borrowed from Spanish: Juan, marijuana.

k **k** = /k/

Note: in **kn**, **k** = /0/ except in **acknowledge**, possible because of the **c**.

Nonproductive alternations: speak–speech, leak–leach,
wreak–wretch, wicca–witch

l **l** in the word colonel = /r/

l in would, could, should, half, calm, chalk = /0/.

l otherwise = /l/.

Note: **l** occurs in many consonant clusters: **pl, bl, cl, chl, gl, fl, sl,
spl** at the beginning of words, **lp, lt, ld, lk, lch, lm, rl, rld,
lb** at the ending of words.

le at the end of words is syllabic (is pronounced like a syllable /★ ●/)
as in simp**le**, kett**le**, nett**le**.

m **m** = /m/

Note: The initial cluster **mn** = /n/ mnemonic.

n **n** = /n/

Note: **n** before **k** and **g** becomes /ŋ/.

p **p** = /0/ in corps, coup, and receipt and the first p in sapphire.

p in clusters **pn, ps**, and **pt** = /0/, as in pneumonia, psychology,
ptomaine.

p elsewhere = /p/.

ph   ph = /f/.

q   q = /k/ and always appears before *u*.

r   **r** = /r/

   Note: r occurs in many clusters: **br, chr, cr, dr, fr, gr, phr, pr, scr, shr, spr, str, thr, wr** at the beginning of words, and **rb, rp, rd, rt, rg, rf, rth, rsh, rch, rm, rn, rl, rpt, rst, rld** at the end of words. **r** in the sequence **er** becomes a syllabic r as in butter, better, baker.

rh   rh = /r/, as in rhino, cirrhosis.

s   **s** = /s/ at the beginning of words and at the end of words, generally.

   s = /s/ in the middle of a word before or after a voiceless consonant

   s = /z/ after a voiced consonant and in as, has, his, is, and was.

   s = /z/ elsewhere, as in design, dissolve, the verbs: house, use and close

   Note: **s** occurs in many clusters: **ps, sc, sch, schw, scl, scr, sk, sl, sm, sn, sp, sph, spl, spr, squ, st, str, sv, sw** at the beginning of words, and **sp, st, sk, rst** at the end of words.

   Note: s = /0/ in aisle, corps, island, isle, bourgeois, chamois, Illinois, debris, rendezvous. Some of these words have an s inserted in the spelling for no good reason and some are of French origin.

sh   sh = /ʃ/.

t   t = /0/ in some clusters as in listen, often, soften, castle.

   t = /t/ elsewhere except when palatalized in derivational morphology.

   t = /0/ in depot, debut, mortgage and in words ending in et with the accent on the final syllable: valet, buffet, ballet. These words are of French origin.

Note: t occurs in many clusters: **pt, st, str, tr, tw** at the beginning of words and **ct, ft, ght, lt, mpt, nct, nt, pt, rpt, rst, rt, st, tz, xt** at the ending of words.

th   **th** in thyme and Thomas = /t/

th in clothes, isthmus and asthma = /0/.

th at the beginning of function words = /ð/ as in the, this, that, then

th in the middle of words and in -the, or -ther = /ð/, hither, clothe, brother.

th elsewhere = /θ/.

Note these nonproductive alternations: bath–bathe, breath–breathe, cloth–clothe, north–northern, south–southern, teeth–teethe, worth–worthy

u   **u** = /w/ after *q* and in some cases after *s*: suede, persuade.

Note: in forms ending in -que, -quet, quette, and in the words liquor, piquant, u = /0/.

v   **v** = /v/.

w   **w** = /0/ in answer, sword, two, and toward.

w = /w/ elsewhere

wh   **wh** in who, whore, and whole = /h/.

elsewhere, **wh** = /w/.

Note: Some people have /hw/ or /ʍ/ in what, where, which and so on, but this is becoming increasingly rare.

x   **x** = /z/ at the beginning of words

x = /gz/ in the middle of words, if the preceding vowel is unstressed: exaggerate.

x = /ks/ elsewhere

y   y = /y/ as in yes, yet

z   **z** in final *tz* = /s/ as in chintz or glitz

z = /z/ otherwise.

tch   **tch** = /tʃ/ as in kitchen, match.

ck   **ck** = /k/ in back or pick

dg   **dg** = /dʒ / in edge, midget

There has been a general tendency to replace geminate consonants in Latin words with the above English complex digraphs, but these are exceptions: exaggerate, account.

gn   **gn** = /n/ in champagne and /ny/ in mignon, poignant, and vignette.

kh   **kh** = /k/ in khan and khaki.

sch   **sch** = /ʃ/ in shist and schwa.

Note: All of these words are borrowed from other languages.

The Vowel Grapheme to Phoneme Correspondences

The grapheme to phoneme correspondences for consonants are fairly regular, in spite of what you might think after reading the preceding information, but the correspondences between vowel graphemes and vowel phonemes is more unpredictable. Spoken English has had a very unstable vowel system for a number of centuries. One change was the Great Vowel Shift, which influenced the pronunciation of many vowel graphemes, like **i**, **e**, and **a**. Although the change took place in speech, our writing system had been standardized by that time and the changes in pronunciation were not reflected in our writing system. This is why, in other languages, **i** = /i/, **e** = /e/, and **a** = /ɑ/, but in English, **i** tends to be /ɑy/, **e** = /iy/ and **a** = /ey/. Sociolinguists tell us that vowel changes are still occurring.

Vowel Graphemes.

primary	secondary		
a	ai/ay	ie	ue
e	au/aw	oa	ui
i	ea	oe	ae
o	ee	oi/oy	eau
u	ei/ey	oo	eo
y	eu/ew	ou/ow	uy

Major Patterns for Vowels

Spelling	Phoneme Correspondence	
	Tense V plus Glide	Lax
a	/ey/	/æ/
	sane	sanity
	mate	mat
	ration	rattle
e	/iy/	/ɛ/
	athlete	athletic
	mete	met
	penal	pennant
i	/ɑy/	/ɪ/
	rise	risen
	malign	malignant
	site	sit

Spelling	Phoneme Correspondence	
	Tense V plus Glide	
o	/ow/	/ʌ/
	cone	conic
	robe	rob
	posy	possible
u	/uw/	/ʌ/
	induce	induction
	rude	rudder
	lucre	luxury

Notes: 1. Generally, the tense vowel with a glide is pronounced when it is in the context of the following:

a. a single consonant grapheme followed by another vowel (penal, rise, cone, rude, etc.), or

b. a single consonant grapheme followed by a liquid (**l** or **r**) and then a vowel (ladle, zebra, noble, microbe).

2. Generally, the lax vowel is pronounced when it is in the context of

a. a compound grapheme or a cluster of consonants (ba**dg**e, sa**ddl**e, e**x**it, ante**nn**a, chi**ck**en, epi**st**le, po**ck**et, **cogn**ate, lu**x**ury, su**pp**er),

b. a consonant at the end of a word (sa**t**, e**bb**, hi**tch**, so**d**, ru**g**).

3. When a vowel is followed by /r/, the vowel is often distorted from its principal pronunciation. In the word **bird** or **girl**, we might expect [ɪ], yet the /r/ seems to overpower or even replace the vowel. We might expect [ʌ] in **fur**, **hurry**, or **urn**, yet again we see that the vowel has been replaced by a [ɹ̩]. When an [ɹ̩] replaces a vowel phone, it is called a syllabic r or [ɹ̩] pronounced like [ər].

o   When **o** (expected to be pronounced /ɑ/) is followed by a final **-ll** and a medial or final **l** plus a consonant, it is pronounced /o/: bold, polka, folk, jolt, molt, scold, told, yolk, troll. In the following words, we do find the expected pronunciation: pollen, trolley.

i before a final **-nd, -ld,** and **gn/gm** ⇒ /ɑy/, instead of /ɪ/: behind,
mind, child, mild, align, sign, paradigm.

i before **-gh-** ⇒ /ɑy/. The **-gh-** is not pronounced. Examples are:
light, bright, sigh, etc. Note these other correspondences that
hold before **-gh-** .

    ai before **-gh-** ⇒ /ey/ as in straight.

    au before **-gh-** ⇒ /æ/ as in laugh, draught. (gh ⇒ /f/.)

    au before **-gh-** ⇒ /ɔ/ as in caught, daughter, naughty, taught
etc.(gh ⇒ /0/.

    ei before **-gh-** ⇒ /ey/ as in sleigh, freight, neighbor

    ei before **-gh-** ⇒ /ɑy/ as in height

    ou before **-gh-** ⇒ /ʌ/ as in enough, rough, tough

    ou before **-gh-** ⇒ /o/ as in dough, furlough, thorough, though

    ou before **-gh-** ⇒ /u/ as in through

    ou before **-gh-** ⇒ /ɑw/ bough

    ou before **-gh-** ⇒ /ɔ/ or /ɑ/ as in bought, ought, cough, fought,
trough

ai/ay	⇒	/ey/ as in bait, day, player, wait
	OR	/ɑy/ in aisle, bayou, cayenne,
		/ɛ/ in again, said, against,
		/æ/ in plaid.

au/aw	=	/ɔ/ or /ɑ/ in audience, claw, cause
	OR	/e/ in gauge
		/æ/ in aunt, laugh
		/o/ in chauffer, chauvinist, mauve (from French)
		/ɑw/ in sauerkraut, umlaut (from German)

ea	⇒	/iy/ as in breach, reach, teach
	OR	/e/ in break, great

/ɛ/ before -l, in health, realm, wealth, before -sure, in measure, treasure, pleasure, and in the following frequent words:

bread	spread	endeavor	pheasant
breadth	thread	feather	sweat
dead	tread	weather	sweater
dread	treadle	heaven	threat
head	breast	heavy	treachery
instead	breath	leather	weapon
meadow	deaf	leaven	ready
death	peasant		

ee ⇒ / iy / as in bleed, eel, absentee

OR

/ɪ/ as in been, breeches, creek

/ey/ as in matinee, melee

ei/ey ⇒ /ey/ as in obey, reign, veil

OR

/ɑy/ as in eye, Fahrenheit, geyser, height, stein, walleye

/iy/ as in caffeine, ceiling, conceit, deceive, either, key, leisure, neither, seize

/ɛ/ as in heifer

eu/ew ⇒ /yu/ as in ewe, eucharist, pewter

/ow/ as in sew

ie ⇒ /ɑy/ (in final position in monosyllable words): die, lie, pie, tie

/iy/ in final position in polysyllabic words): calorie, collie, eerie, movie and in medial position: achieve, diesel, niece, yield

OR

/ey/ in lingerie

/ɪ/ in sieve

/ɛ/ in friend

Note: allied, applied, dried, etc. are ally + ed, apply + ed, dry + ed. bodied, candied, studied are body + ed, candy +ed, study + ed

oa ⇒ /ow/ as in approach, boast, goal, shoal or /ɔ/ or /ɑ/ as in broad

oi/oy ⇒ /oy/ as in boy, join, loiter, oyster or

/ɑy/ as in coyote

/iy/ as in chamois

/ə/ as mademoiselle, porpoise, tortoise

oo ⇒ /ɑw/ as in boot, broom, proof, tycoon, pooh

OR

/ʌ/ as blood, blood

/ow/ as in brooch

/ʊ/ as in book, foot, look, shook, wood, brook, forsook, mistook, soot, wool, cook, good, nook, stood, crook, hook, rook, took

ou/ow ⇒ /ɑw/ as in abound, crown, mountain, owl, allow, brow, cow, endow, how, now, plow, sow, prow, thou, vow.

/ow/ as in arrow, bow, glow, pillow, mow, sow

/ʌ/ as in double, trouble, country, enough, young, couple, touch, cousin, rough, tough, boulevard, could, should, would

/ɔ/ or /ɑ/ as in cough, trough

/ow/ as in boulder, bowl, cantaloupe, mould, owe, own, poultice, shoulder, soul, thorough

/uw/ as in bayou, cougar, group, caribou, routine, troubadour, rendezvous, soup, uncouth, boudoir, coupon, rouge, souvenir, vermouth, ghoul, route, toucan

ui   ⇒   /uw/ bruise, nuisance, pursuit, suitor

or /ɪ/ as in biscuit, build, circuit

The Use of Graphemes as Markers

So far the major and minor uses of consonant and vowel graphemes have more or less directly represented phonemes. We turn now to discuss the use of graphemes, not to represent phonemes, but rather to give information about other grapheme to phoneme correspondences elsewhere in the word. These *markers* give information about the way that other graphemes in the word are to be interpreted and pronounced.

1. The final **e** generally indicates the pronunciation of the previous vowel.

Tense vowel or diphthong:	Lax vowel
mate	mat
mete	met
site	sit
note	not
cute	cut

2. The final **e** sometimes indicates the pronunciation of the previous consonant as in the word peace. The final **e** in peace indicates both the pronunciation of the previous vowel as /iy/, and that the **c** corresponds to its "soft" alternative pronunciation: /s/ and not /k/. This principle is the same in words like bath and bathe, where the final **e** in the verb marks not only the vowel, but also the voiced pronunciation of the **th**, or /ð/. The final **e** in age or college indicates the "soft" or affricate pronunciation of **g**, /dʒ/.

3. The **u** in guest marks that the **g** is a "hard" (or stopped) /g/ and not its soft (or affricate) alternative: /dʒ/ guess, guide, guest, guise, catalogue, guilt, plague, guild. (Note that catalogue has an alternative catalog, because it is clear that the final **g** would be hard. This alternative is not available for plague (i.e., plag) because the vowel sound would be distorted. The final **e** maintains the tense pronunciation of the vowel as /ey/.)

4. Geminated consonants mark the preceding vowel as lax. Examples: anal/annals, fetal/ fetter, hypo/hippo, rotor/rotter, super/supper.

5. Suffixing. Final **e**, when it marks the preceding **c** or **g** as soft (fricative /s/ or affricate /dʒ/) or hard (stop /k/ or /g/) is dropped when followed by a suffix that achieves the same purpose. For example, where the final **e** marks the **c** as /s/, it can dropped when adding -ing, because the **i** in the suffix also marks the **c** as soft, but it must be retained in the word noticeable because the following **a** would make the pronunciation of the **c** "harden" to /k/ if the word were spelled "*noticable." (The asterisk marks a word that is incorrect.)

When a suffix like -ing is added to a word with a final "hard" **c** as in traffic, to make the work trafficking, note that a **k** must be inserted so that the hardness of the **c** is retained. Other words like this are: picnic/picnicking, panic/panicky, shellac/shellacked.

6. Graphemes inserted to make words consistent with English spelling patterns. Some of these spelling patterns appear to have arisen because of legibility problems when manuscripts were handwritten, so they are very old patterns.

   a. Final **u** is not allowed, so **e** is inserted in continue and blue, but note that this final **e** is dropped when suffixes are added because the **u** is no longer final: argue, arguing. Similar words: glue, plague

   b. Final **v** is not allowed generally, so an **e** is inserted at the end: love, glove, have. (Note that these appear to be counter-examples to the tense vowel and final **e** rule, but they are mandated by spelling patterns that do not allow a final **v**.

   c. Some common words would have consisted of two letters and in general, two-letter words are not allowed, so an extra **e** has been added: see, doe, toe, rye, axe, foe, hoe, sloe. (Note that many of these words have **o**, so the final **e** also serves to mark the vowel as tense.)

   d. Final **dg** is not allowed, so an **e** is inserted in words like edge, hedge, badge (Note that these appear to be counterexamples to the use of final **e** as a vowel marker; here it is only used to make the words consistent with spelling patterns.)

7. Some patterns are based on confusions with the addition of suffixes. In some words that would end in **s**, an **e** has been added to avoid the appearance of a plural word. The idea is that "moos" looks like a plural of "moo," so **e** is added to form moose. Similar cases are: goose, mouse, hearse, house, praise, raise, noise, poise. There are some adjectives and verbs that also avoid a final **s**: collapse, eclipse, dense, sense, else, false, coarse.

Exceptions are: summons, lens, and words ending in ous. (Note that many people misspell the singular lens as lense, so it is in the process possibly of becoming a regular spelling.) Other exceptions are hydraulics, mathematics, mumps, and billiards, which can be either singular or plural. When **s** is preceded by a simple vowel, **e** is not added because the resulting pronunciation might be distorted: us/use, his/rise, locus/recluse, tennis/improvise.

Common Graphemic Alternations

Sometimes there is a fairly regular pattern of alternative graphemes used in particular positions in the word.

1. **i** and **y**: Generally **i** occurs in initial or medial position; **y** in final position. However, there are many exceptions; for instance, **y** occurs in medial position in Greek and Latin borrowed words like embryo, asylum, and rhythm. Some exceptions, like rye and bye, have come about because a final **e** was added to avoid a two-letter word. Sometimes earlier scribes substituted a medial **y** to make words seem more learned: rhyme instead of the older form rime on a mistaken analogy with rhythm. Final **i** occurs in a few patterns of borrowed words like plurals of Latin words: alumni, fungi, cacti, and stimuli. Other examples are plurals of Italian borrowings: broccoli, confetti, ravioli, macaroni, and spaghetti, and other borrowed words: alkali, potpourri (French), anti (Greek), ski (Norwegian), chili (Mexican Spanish) khaki (Urdu), mufti (Arabic), yogi (Hindustani). These words apparently kept the spelling with *i* to maintain their appearance as foreign. Taxi is an American clipped word from taximeter.

   In suffixes: When words end in **ie**, **e** is dropped and the **i** changes to **y** to add the suffix –ing, presumably to avoid the two **ii**s that would result: die/dying (not diing), tie/tying (not tiing).

   When a suffix is added to a base word ending in **y**: In icy, the **y** is changed to **i**, iciest, or mercy and merciless. These then follow the consistent pattern where **i** occurs medially. Similarly, day/daily and say/said or lay/laid.

2. **u** and **w**: **u** appears instead of **w** in **gu**, **su**, **qu**, **nu**, **pu**, and **cu**. **w** occurs elsewhere. Examples are:

gu: anguish, distinguish, extinguish, jaguar, language, languid, linguistics
su: persuade, assuage, suede, suite, suave
pu: pueblo
nu: ennui
cu: cuisine

Another pattern (but with many exceptions) is that with **a**, **e**, and **o**, the **w** variant occurs before another vowel and in morpheme final position, when the **u** occurs elsewhere:

au: auction, audit, applaud, fault, trauma
aw: awe, draw, gnaw, saw, straw, thaw
eu: eulogy, eucharist, feud, neuter, pneumatic, rheumatism
ew: ewe, brewer, flew, threw
ou: ounce, oust, out, compound, trousers
ow: coward, however, power, allow, cow, vow

Exceptions:

aw before a consonant: awkward, awl, awning, dawn, scrawl, spawn
ew in medial position before a consonant: newt, pewter, lewd, shrewd
ow in initial and medial position before a consonant: owl, own, crowd, drowse, fowl, town
ou in final position bayou, caribou, bijou (French) and you, thou
u in final position is generally avoided (see earlier discussion), but in these words borrowed mainly from French: beau, bureau, chateau, plateau, trousseau, adieu, lieu, menu, tabu. Flu is a clipped form of influenza; presumably the *e* was not added to maintain the connection with influenza and avoid confusion with "flue."
ous becomes **os** before **ity**: viscous/viscosity, curious/curiosity, generous/generosity, monstrous/monstrosity.

APPENDIX B

ENGLISH PHONEMES
AND THEIR PRINCIPAL SPELLINGS

This information is adapted from *Word Recognition: The Why and How* (pp. 20–28), by P. Groff and D. Seymour (1987, Springfield, IL: Thomas), and is used by permission of the author.

Chart of English Consonant Phonemes
and Their Principal Spellings

In this table, we find the consonant phonemes in English, their most common graphemic representations, and the percentage of occurrence of the major relationships associating a particular phoneme with a grapheme.

Phonemic Symbol	Most Frequent Spellings:	Frequency:	Other Spellings:
b	**b**at	97	e**bb**
p	**p**at	96	ha**pp**y
d	**d**ot	98	a**dd**
t	**t**ap	**98**	pu**tt**
g	**g**ot	88	e**gg**, e**x**act, ro**gu**e
k	**c**at	73	ba**ck**, s**ch**ool, e**x**it, o**cc**upy
	keep	13	

Phonemic Symbol	Most Frequent Spellings:	Frequency:	Other Spellings:
tʃ	chap	55	watch
	culture	31	
dʒ	gem	66	budget, educate
	jet	22	
v	vat	99.5	
f	fat	78	phone, off
ð	the	100	
θ	thin	100	
z	as	64	buzz, dessert
	zap	23	
s	sat	73	pass, scent
	cent	17	
ʒ	fusion	82	regime
ʃ	action	53	social, mission, pension, ocean, chef
	shut	26	
h	hit	98	who
m	man	94	mummy
n	not	97	inn
ŋ	sing	59	
	bank	41	
l	lap	91	all, able
r	run	97	purr
y	senior	55	
	yet	44	
w	wet	92	liquid

Chart of Simple English Vowel Phonemes
and Their Principal Spellings

Phonemic Symbol	Most Frequent Spellings:	Frequency:	Other Spellings:
ɪ	*it*	66	giv*e*, senat*e*, and before r, her*o*, hear,
	myth	23	deer, here, pier, souvenir, fierce, weird
æ	at	96	bad*e*
ʊ	put	54	could, woman, sure
	foot	31	
ʌ	up	86	ov*e*n, touch, com*e*, budge
ε	bed	91	head, edg*e*, millionaire
	vary	29	
	hair	23	
	there	15	
i	be	70	ev*e*, elit*e*, ski, chief, baby
	eat	10	
	feel	10	
e	angel	45	aid, way
		35	
u	boot	38	you, threw, true, choose, lose, fruit
	truth	21	
	who	8	
	rud*e*	8	
o	both	38	oak, own
	cod*e*	14	
ɑ	odd	79	dodge, are, heart,

Phonemic Symbol	Most Frequent Spellings:	Frequency:	Other Spellings:
ɔ	all	n.a.	faucet, dawn, **ou**ght, caught, br**oa**d

Chart of English Diphthongs and Their Principal Spellings

Phonemic Symbol	Most Frequent Spellings:	Frequency:	Other Spellings:
ɑy	find	37	night, pie, dye
	ice	37	
	by	14	
oy	boil	62	
	boy	32	
ɑw	out	56	
	how	29	

Workbook Supplement

EXERCISE 1. PHONETIC DESCRIPTIONS AND SYMBOLS

A. Match the term with the definition or example that best fits it. Careful! Some answers may be used more than once and some not at all.

a. voiceless   c. interdental   e. phoneme

b. voiced   d. bilabial

1. when the vocal cords vibrate during speech
2. a sound produced by putting the tip of the tongue between the two teeth.
3. a meaning-distinguishing sound in a language
4. when the air passes through the vocal tract without making the vocal cords vibrate
5. a sound produced with the two lips pursed together

a. minimal pair   c. liquids   e. labiodental

b. allophones   d. nasals

6. math–match
7. phonetic variants used to realize a single phoneme
8. /l, r/

9. a sound produced with the lower lip pressed against the upper teeth

10. a sound produced when some of the air escapes through the nose

a. alveolar	c. fricative	e. glide
b. phone	d. affricate	

11. when the air flow is constricted by two articulators, causing friction

12. /f, s, v, z/ are examples of this type of sound

13. /y, w/ are examples of this type of sound

14. /t, d, s/ are examples of this type of sound

15. a sound produced when the air flow is stopped and then released with a puff of friction.

B. Say each of these words. Isolate the *final* sound. Then write the phonetic symbol and the full description for the final sound in each word:

16. wax	18. pressed	20. dear	22. allow
17. swish	19. edge	21. candy	23. laugh

C. Write the following words in phonetic transcription to indicate the way you say them. Compare your answers to other students' answers. Are there any differences in the transcriptions?

24. penny	27. orange	30. fish	33. think
25. petty	28. cot	31. jungle	34. pleasure
26. wash	29. caught	32. raisin	35. other

EXERCISE 2. SIMPLE VOWELS

A. Get a lollipop and put it in your mouth. Go over the chart of English vowels and say each cue word. Notice how the lollipop moves as your tongue moves.

B. Say the following sets of words. Are the vowels the same or different the way you say them? Write your answer in the middle column. Select the phonetic symbol that represents the sound of the vowels as you say them.

	Words	Same/Diff		Phonetic Symbols
#1	#2			
tan	ton	different		æ ʌ
tin	ten			
teen	tune			
Dane	tone			
dune	done			
Tom	tome			
Don	Dawn			
cut	cat			
cot	caught			
coot	coat			
cane	can			

C. Compare your answers with your classmates. Do you find any variation in the pronunciation of some words?

EXERCISE 3. PHONOLOGICAL PROCESSES
IN ENGLISH (PART 1)

A. There are three *true* diphthongs that occur in English: /oy/, /aw/,
and /ay/. Identify the diphthongs in the following words: house,
fight, kite, white, poison, toy, flounce, about. Write each word in
phonetic transcription? Is the phonemic transcription similar?

B. The glides /y/ and /w/ usually occur with some of the simple vowel
phonemes in English (the tense vowels) when they are pronounced.
This variation is allophonic, not phonemic.

   a. Transcribe the vowels in the following words using a diphthong
   (a tense vowel plus [y] or [w]) : bead, bade, leap, lay, booed, bode,
   school, poll. Write these vowels in the middle of [ ], because they
   are phones and not phonemes. Which vowels take [y]? What
   property do they have in common? Which vowels take [w]? What
   property do they have in common?

   b. Spanish does not have these diphthongized vowels. Speakers of
   English who learn Spanish often have trouble removing the diph-

thongs from their speech, so they can get rid of their accent. Say these words in Spanish. If there is a Spanish speaker in the class, compare the way you say the words. amigo, taco, tomo, que.

c. Here is another characteristic of English phonology that transfers to Spanish and results in a typical accent. Consider the fact that voiceless consonants are aspirated when they are syllable initial in English. The English speaker says "taco" with an aspirated /t/ and /k/, but the Spanish speaker doesn't. (Also, the /t/ in Spanish is dental, not alveolar.)

English speaker [tʰahkow]; Spanish speaker /tako/.

How might the English speaker pronounce the following words in learning Spanish? Write the transcriptions between [ ] because they are phonetic and not phonemic:

pato   patio   Que tal?   tengo

d. What difficulties might the Spanish speaker have in learning to pronounce English?

EXERCISE 4. PHONETIC AND PHONEMIC TRANSCRIPTION

I. Transcribe the following words using phonetic symbols. Use the following procedure:

1. Say the word as naturally as possible. Don't distort your pronunciation.

2. Find the phonetic symbol that represents your pronunciation of each phone in the word.

3. Don't forget to put them in [ ].

4. Indicate diphthongization of tense vowels, aspiration of syllable initial voiceless stops, and any other allophonic variation you are aware of.

A. breath, breathe, egg, edge, ache, axe, cloth, clothe, clothes, khaki, bureau, buy, trace, traceable, guest, write, ride, writer, rider. (Note: You may use [D] to indicate the "flapped t" sound that occurs between two vowels in *writer*.)

B. champagne, canyon, weave, web, deceive, deception, worth, worthy, through, throw, birth, thyme, then, these, those, aisle, chrome.

C. fifth, twelfth, north, northern, thief, thieves, cats, dogs, houses, louse, lousy, sugar, creature, create, simmer, singer, sinner, thing, thin.

D. lingerie, matinee, heaven, ghoul, kaleidoscope, plait, again, behind, consign, waggle, wander, sergeant, delirium, irrigate, beware, spur, cure.

II. Select A, B, C, or D and write the phonemic transcription (between / /).

EXERCISE 5. PHONEMES AND ALLOPHONES

Phonemes are symbols that stand for abstract mental images of sounds, like /t/, /l/, and /o/. Phones are symbols that represent concrete sounds as we might hear them or say them. There are more phones needed to represent speech than phonemes. All the phones that have a relationship to a certain phoneme are called allophones. For example, all voiceless stops have at least two allophones, the "regular" pronunciation as in [p] and [k], and the aspirated pronunciation that occurs at the beginning of syllables: [pʰ], and [kʰ]. When the occurrence of one allophone is predictable when compared to the other, as in this case, we call this *complementary distribution*.

Complementary distribution means that the allophones are "distributed" as complements (in the mathematical sense of the word) to each other. In one context, one will occur and in the rest, another will occur. We can write this like this: *At the beginning of syllables, the aspirated allophone will occur. Elsewhere, the unaspirated allophone will occur. They are in complementary distribution.*

A. In the case of /t/, which has several allophones, [t], [tʰ], [D],[ʔ], which of these are in complementary distribution?

Write the distribution for [t], [tʰ]:
Is this a case of complementary distribution?
Write the distribution for [t] and [D]:
Is this a case of complementary distribution?
Examine these data to see of the distribution of [t] and [ʔ] is predictable:

[k ɪ t]   [k ɪ ʔ]   [b æ t]   [b æ ʔ]

Is this a case of complementary distribution?

If two allophones occur in the same environments in words unpredictably, they are in random distribution or *free variation*. Are [t] and [ʔ] in free variation?

B. Are these vowels in complementary distribution or free variation? (: indicates extra lengthening of the vowel.) Explain why or why not.

bead   [biy:d]   beat   [biyt]

mowed	[mow:d]	moat	[mowt]
snag	[snæ:g]	snack	[snæk]
lube	[luw:b]	loop	[luwp]

EXERCISE 6. PHONEMIC TRANSCRIPTION

A. Using what you have learned about phonemes and allophones, identify which of these are phonemic transcriptions by putting / / around them and which are phonetic transcriptions by putting [ ] around them:. Identify what the word is. There may be some ambiguity in some answers; if so, point it out.

t^{h}iy:m	tim			
ret	red	rey:Dər	redər	retər
mid	mit	miy:d	miyt^h	miy?

B. Write these words in phonetic and phonemic transcription. Note that aspiration can occur in syllable-initial consonant clusters with voiceless stops, such as pl, pr, kr, kl, and tr,

bleed
bleat
clothe
crude
clad
clatter
critter

C. How does knowledge of phonemes and allophones assist reading teachers of ESL/EFL learners?

EXERCISE 7. PHONOLOGICAL PROCESSES (PART 2)

So far we have talked about several phonological processes that occur in English and in this exercise we learn about a few more. One very common and general process is called *assimilation*. We say that assimilation has taken place when two sounds that are near each other become more similar to each other in terms of voicing, place, or manner of articulation.

A. Here are some examples of assimilation. Identify if they seem to be assimilating in voicing or place of articulation.

a. in**p**ut   [impʊt]

b. in**c**ome   [iŋkʌm]

c. escape**d**   [ɛskeypt]

d. Cho**m**sky [tʃɑmpskiy]

B. A special type of assimilation is called *palatalization*, in which a stop or fricative become palatalized, (e.g. [ʃ, ʒ, tʃ]) in some environments. Say each word in each set and listen careful to what you say. Underline where you hear palatalization in each word set. Do you see some generalizations in this process?

a.   innate   native   nature

b.   press   depression   depressive

c.   definition   define   definite

d.   cult   culture   cultural

e.   permit   permissive   permission

f.   rate   ratio   ration

g.   provide   proviso   provision

h.   act   actual   action

C. Another phonological process is called *velar softening*, in which /k/ and /g/ become "softened" to /s/ or /dʒ/. Pick out where the velar softening has occurred in these word sets. (Careful! There are also some examples of palatalization.) Then make any generalizations you can about the process.

a.   analog   analogy

b.   electric   electrician   electricity

c.   colleague   collegial   college

d.   mag- (bound root)   magic

e.   log- (bound roo)   logic   (socio)logy

   f.   automatic   automation   automacity

D. *Vowel reduction* occurs when vowels are so lacking in stress that they are pronounced as a schwa [ə]. Where has vowel reduction occurred?

a.	parade	[pəreyd]
b.	laboratory	[læbrətɔriy]
c.	telegraph	[tɛləgræf]
d.	telegraphy	[tɛlɛgrəfiy]
e.	police	[pəliys]

EXERCISE 8. MORPHOPHONOLOGICAL PROCESSES AND SPELLING PATTERNS

If English writing were truly alphabetic, the changes that occur in the pronunciation of word derived by adding suffixes, as shown in the last exercise, would mean that words like **native**, **nation**, and **national** would not look the same. In a consistent alphabetic writing system, where one symbol would represent one sound, it is possible that native would be written naitiv, nation would be written naishun, and national would be written nashunl. However, English has taken another course. English writing has another principle that governs these cases: the morphemic principle. This principle states that morphemes will maintain their visual appearance no matter how their pronunciations change because of phonological processes like assimilation, palatalization, vowel reduction, and so on. Although this principle doesn't always hold, it has a strong consistency.

Given the morphemic principle, we are still faced with a quandary. Which of the pronunciations of a morpheme is basic? Which is the one to represent consistently, if there are alternatives? Certain procedures have evolved in answer to this question. We try to maintain the spelling of the tense vowel or diphthong, the "hardest" consonant, and include graphemes that are pronounced in some words but are silent in other words.

1. To write a morpheme consistently in spite of variations in pronunciation, the spelling that represents a *tense vowel or diphthong* is basic. Similarly, always represent the original vowel even though it may be "reduced" to [ə] with a change of stress.

    Examples: **protest–protestant**
                [protɛst] [pratəstənt]

because /o/ is tense and /a/ is lax.
sacrifice –sacrificial
[sækrɪfays] [sækrɪfɪʃl̩]

2. We assume that stops are "harder" than fricatives and fricatives are harder than affricates. Choose the *stop* rather than the *fricative*, and the *fricative* rather than the *affricate* to represent in the spelling.

Examples: **analog –analogy**
[ænəlɔg] [ænælədʒiy]
because /g/ is a stop and /dʒ/ is an affricate.
physic –physicist –physician
[fɪzɪks] [fɪzɪsɪst] [fɪzɪʃʌn]
because the letter *c* represents the stop /k/ and the other alternatives are fricative [s] or affricate [ʃ].
refrigerate–refrigeration
[rəfrɪdʒəreyt] [rəfrɪdʒəreyʃʌn]
because /t/ is a stop and /ʃ/ is an affricate.
depress–depression
[dəprɛs] [dəprɛʃʌn]
because /s/ is a fricative and /ʃ/ is an affricate.

3. Choose the most complete spelling, that is, the spelling that includes all sounds although they may be silent in some words.

Examples: **paradigm –paradigmatic**
Because the /g/ is pronounced in **paradigmatic,** it must be written in the word **paradigm** in order to preserve the most complete representation of the morpheme.
iamb —iambic
Because the /b/ is pronounced in **iambic,** it must be written in **iamb.**
Exercises:

A. Match the justification (tense vowel or diphthong, stop > fricative > affricate, or most complete spelling) with the pronunciation and spelling difficulty in the following word sets. Some words may have more than one justification.

   a.   domestic–domesticity

   b.   phlegm–phlegmatic

   c.   severe–severity

   d.   define–definite

    e.   electric–electricity

    f.   confess –confession

    g.   bomb –bombard

    h.   signature –sign

B. Find two original examples for each of the morphemic spelling principles.
C. English writing has been called *morphophonemic*. What does this mean?
D. These are counterexamples to the morphemic principle. Explain how they are exceptions.

    a.   goose–gosling

    b.   maintain–maintenance

    c.   pronounce–pronunciation

EXERCISE 9. GRAPHEMES: PROBABILITIES AND RIMES

In teaching reading, teachers sometimes distinguish between words that follow spelling patterns and those that don't. Words that have irregular spellings are called *sight words* and they are commonly taught as whole words that must be memorized. Most function words are sight words.

    Here are some words from common sight word lists. Divide them into categories of (a) words that are best taught as sight words, (b) words that are probably not sight words based on the probabilities, (c) words that could be taught as a common rime pattern, or (d) words that could be taught as compound words. Sometimes there may be more than one good answer for a word.

above	dead	head	neighbor	soldier	wolf
across	deaf	heart	neither	some	woman
again	debt	heaven	night	someone	women
aisle	desire	heavy	none	something	won
answer	do	here	ocean	sometime	would
anxious	does	high	of	son	wrong
any	done	idea	office	soul	you
bear	don't	Indian	often	special	young

beautiful	double	instead	oh	spread	your
because	doubt	isle	once	square	
been	dove	key	one	steak	
behind	dozen	kind	onion	straight	
believe	early	knee	only	sure	
bind	earn	knew	other	sword	
both	eight	knife	ought	their	
bough	enough	know	patient	there	
bread	eye	language	piece	they	
break	father	laugh	pretty	though	
bright	fence	laughed	pull	thought	
brought	field	leather	purpose	to	
build	fight	library	push	together	
built	find	light	put	ton	
bury	folks	lion	quiet	tongue	
busy	four	live	ranger	too	
buy	freight	lived	ready	touch	
calf	friend	love	really	two	
captain	front	machine	right	use	
caught	garage	many	rough	usual	
chief	get	measure	said	vein	
child	ghost	might	says	very	
clothes	give	mild	school	view	
colt	gloves	million	science	was	
coming	gone	mind	scissors	wash	
cough	great	minute	sew	weather	
could	guard	mischief	shoe	were	
cousin	guest	move	sign	who	
cruel	guide	Mr.	snow	wild	
curve	have	Mrs.	soften	wind	

EXERCISE 10. ONSETS AND RIMES

ESL/EFL readers can use a strategy of reasoning by analogy to try to pronounce a new word found in reading. If learners can pronounce a new word, even imperfectly, it helps them decide whether they know the word in their productive oral vocabulary or whether they have heard the word in their receptive vocabulary. If so, they may already have a lexical entry for the word in their mental lexicon to which they can attach additional information about the visual image of the word or about the meaning as encountered in the reading. If, after trying to figure out the pronunciation, ESL/EFL readers still don't know what the word is, they can begin to form a new lexical entry with the visual/auditory image they have formed in response to the unknown word and start making connections to meaning from the information in the passage. An additional strategy then is to guess the meaning from context.

a. Use analogy to known spelling patterns to sound out these "new" words.

b. What clues from the context help you define the "new" word?

c. Write any additional information that you might tell students to help them with this word and with other words in general.

d. If the onset/rime strategy does not seem to help, is the word best taught as a sight word? The first one is done as an example.

---

1. (From label) Apply *deodorant* topically under arms for all day protection.

   a. deodorant. Syllables: de - o - dor- ant

Onsets and rimes:	Analogies:
d / e	me
/ o	no
d / or	for
/ ant	plant

   b. Context clues: something you can apply; you apply it under your arms; it protects you.

   c. -ant as a suffix is usually unstressed and pronounced [ənt]

   d. No

---

2. Before 1965, no financial *transactions* were possible for women without their husband's consent.

3. Newspapers used to carry *sex-segregated* help-wanted ads.
4. Few women held *prominent* positions in medicine, law, or politics.
5. No women *anchored* the news programs on television.

EXERCISE 11. INFLECTIONAL MORPHEMES AND ASSIMILATION

English does not use inflectional morphology very much. These are the inflectional morphemes:

Nouns: -s marks the regular plural: He needed two book**s**.
   -s marks the possessive form (especially of animate things) The dog**'s** dish is empty.
Verbs: -s marks the third person singular present tense He want**s** the newspaper.
   -ed marks the past tense for regular verbs: He want**ed** the newspaper.
   -ed marks the past participle for regular verbs: He has stud**ied** in Canada for years.
   -en marks the past participle for many irregular verbs: He has spok**en** French since then.
   -ing marks the present participle for all verbs: He is learn**ing** Japanese.
Adjectives and adverbs: -er marks the comparative form: He has bought the new**er** car.

   -est marks the superlative form: He can't afford the new**est** car.

a. Examine the following data about the plural -s suffix (morpheme) and answer the questions that follow:

decks	maps	boxes	cats	dogs
ditches	fads	tabs	hills	rivers
dishes	buses	cuffs	coves	combs

1. How many spellings are there for this morpheme?

2. What three pronunciations are there for this morpheme? (These are called *allomorphs*.)

3. List the words in three columns based on the pronunciation of the suffix. List both the singular and plural words.

4. Can you identify the phonetic property shared by the final sounds of each of the singular words in each columns?

5. If I said there was a phonological process called *voicing assimilation*, would that help explain what is going on here?

6. If I said there was a phonological process called *dissimilation,* would that help explain some of what is going on there?

7. Does this example follow the morphemic principle of English writing that morphemes are written the same no matter how they change in pronunciation?

Using these sets of data, answer the same set of questions:

b.

Dave's	Bill's	Fred's	Ross's	Jack's
Max's	Matt's	Jeff's	Doug's	Mr. Birch's
Jeb's	Rap's	Mary's	Jennifer's	Maria's

c.

leaves	dents	relaxes	spends	traps
confesses	clutches	robs	sniffs	speaks
logs	spills	plays	draws	naps

d.

waited	needed	learned	saved	sniffed
snored	mapped	cracked	noted	rubbed
fogged	spilled	played	wanted	excused

How much of this is useful to teach your typical ESL/EFL student?

EXERCISE 12. DERIVATIONAL MORPHEMES AND WORD FORMATION

A. Identify the following as a derivational prefix or suffix, or as a bound root: comment*ary,* re*ceive,* *pro*-war, pro*gress,* *non*standard, *sub*processor, process*or,* pro*cess,* *pro*cess. What does each morpheme mean?

B. Divide these words into their component morphemes: moccasin, money, monoxide, morpheme, mortgaged, mousetrap, muffler, multiple, multivariable, mustache, mythology. You may need a dictionary or use dictionary.com.

C. Look back at the definitions of inflectional morphemes and derivational morphemes and try to classify each of the following examples as one or the other. Note the context the word appears in. Make a note of the difficulties you have.

a. Jennifer is tall**er** than Jane. Jennifer is a basketball play**er**.

b. She is play**ing** basketball right now. Play**ing** is her main activity.

c. She expect**ed** to win the game. Her expect**ed** win did not happen.

D. How can you explain these different forms of the morpheme "-in"?

a. illegal   c. improbable   e. inconceivable (in rapid speech)

b. irrelevant   d. inefficient   f. intangible

References

Abu-Rabia, S. (1997). Verbal and working memory skills of bilingual Hebrew–English speaking children. *International Journal of Psycholinguistics, 1*, 25–40.

Adams, M. (1990). *Beginning to read: Thinking and learning about print.* Cambridge, MA: MIT Press.

Aebersold, J., & Field, M. L. (1997). *From reader to reading teacher: Issues and strategies for second language classrooms.* Cambridge, England: Cambridge University Press.

Aidinis, A., & Nunes, T. (1998). The role of different levels of phonological awareness in the development of reading and spelling in Greek. *Reading and Writing, 14*(1–2), 145–177.

Alderson, J. C., & Urquhart, A. H. (1984). *Reading in a foreign language.* London: Longman.

Aylward, E., Richards, T., Berninger, V., Nagy, W., Field, K., Grimme, A., Richards, A., Thomson, J., & Cramer, S. (2003) Instructional treatment associated with changes in brain activation in children with dyslexia. *Neurology, 61*(2), 212–219.

Baddeley, A., Gathercole, S., & Papagno, C. (1998). The phonological loop as a language learning device. *Psychological Review, 105*, 1158–1173.

Bauer, T. (1996). Arabic writing. In P. Daniels & W. Bright (Eds.), *The world's writing systems* (pp. 559–564). New York: Oxford University Press.

Been, S. (1979). Reading in the foreign language teaching program. In R. Mackay, B. Barkman, & R. Jordan (Eds.), *Reading in a second language: Hypotheses, organization, and practice* (pp. 91–102). Rowley, MA: Newbury House.

Ben-Dror, I., Frost, R., & Bentin, S. (1995). Orthographic representation and phonemic segmentation in skilled readers: A cross-language comparison. *Psychological Science, 6*, 176–181.

Bensoussan, M., & Laufer, B. (1984). Lexical Guessing in context in EFL reading comprehension. *Journal of Research in Reading, 7*, 15–31.

219

Bentin, S., & Frost, R. (1995). Morphological factors in visual word identification in Hebrew. In L. Feldman (Ed.), *Morphological aspects of language processing* (pp. 271–292). Hillsdale, NJ: Lawrence Erlbaum Associates.

Berndt, R. S., Reggia, J. A., & Mitchum, C. C. (1987). Empirically derived probabilities for grapheme-to-phoneme correspondences in English. *Behavior Research Methods, Instruments, & Computers, 19*, 1–9.

Bernhardt, E. (1991). *Reading development in a second language: Theoretical, empirical, and classroom perspectives.* Norwood, NJ: Ablex.

Bond, G., Tinker, M., Wasson, B., & Wasson, J. (1989) *Reading difficulties: Their diagnosis and correction.* Englewood Cliffs, NJ: Prentice Hall.

Booth, J., & Burman, D. (2005) Using neuroimaging to test developmental models of reading acquisition. In H. Catts & A. Kamhi (Eds), *The connections between language and reading disabilities* (pp. 131–153).Mahwah, NJ: Lawrence Erlbaum Associates.

Bradley, L., & Bryant, P. E. (1983). Categorizing sounds and learning to read—A causal connection. *Nature, 303*, 3.

Braten, I., Lie, A., & Andreassen, R. (1998). Explaining individual differences in reading: On the orthographic component of word recognition. *Scandinavian Journal of Educational Research, 42*, 389–399.

Bryant, P., Nunes, T., & Bindman, M. (1999). Morphemes and spelling. In T. Nunes (Ed.), *Learning to read: An integrated view from research and practice* (pp. 15–42). Dordrecht, The Netherlands: Kluwer.

Byrne, B. (1998). *The foundation of literacy: The child's acquisition of the alphabetic principle.* East Sussex, England: Psychology Press.

Caramazza, A., Laudanna, A., & Romani, C. (1988). Lexical access and inflectional morphology. *Cognition, 28*, 297–322.

Carney, E. (1994). *A survey of English spelling.* London: Routledge & Kegan Paul.

Carrell, P. (1993). Introduction: Interactive approaches to second language reading. In P. Carrell, J. Devine, & D. Eskey (Eds.), *Interactive approaches to second language reading* (pp. 1–7). Cambridge, England: Cambridge University Press.

Carroll, S. (1992). On cognates. *Second Language Research, 8*, 93–119.

Castro-Caldas, A. (2004). Targeting regions of interest for the study of the illiterate brain. *International Journal of Psychology, 39*(1), 5–17.

Chall, J. (1983). *Stages of reading development.* New York: McGraw-Hill.

Cheung, H. (1996). Nonword span as a unique predictor of second language vocabulary learning. *Developmental Psychology, 32*, 867–873.

Chikamatsu, N. (1996). The effects of L1 orthography on L2 word recognition. *Studies in Second Language Acquisition, 18*, 403–432.

Chitiri, H., & Willows, D. (1994). Word recognition in two languages and orthographies: English and Greek. *Memory and Cognition, 22*, 313–325.

Clarke, M., & Silberstein, S. (1979). Toward a realization of psycho-linguistic principles in the ESL reading class. In R. Mackay, B. Barkman, & R. Jordan (Eds.), *Reading in a second language: Hypotheses, organization, and practice* (pp. 48–65). Rowley, MA: Newbury House.

Clymer, T. (1963). The utility of phonic generalizations in the primary grades. *Reading Teacher, 16*, 252–258.

Coady, J. (1979). A psycholinguistic model of the ESL reader. In R. Mackay, B. Barkman, & R. Jordan (Eds.), *Reading in a second language: Hypotheses, organization, and practice* (pp. 5–12). Rowley, MA: Newbury House.

Comrie, B. (1981). *Language universals and linguistic typology.* Chicago: University of Chicago Press.

Crawley, S. & King, M. (1991). *Remediating reading difficulties.* Dubuque, IA: Wm C. Brown.

Crowder, R., & Wagner, R. (1992). *The psychology of reading.* Oxford, England: Oxford University Press.

Day, R. R., & Bamford, J. (1998). *Extensive reading in the second language classroom.* Cambridge, England: Cambridge University Press.

Derwing, B., Smith, M., & Weibe, G., (1995). On the role of spelling in morpheme recognition: Experimental studies with children and adults. In L. Feldman (Ed.), *Morphological aspects of language processing* (pp. 3–27). Hillsdale, NJ: Lawrence Erlbaum Associates.

Dewey, D. (1970). *Relative frequency of English spellings.* New York: Teachers College Press.

Downer, M. (1991). *Viewer's guide teaching word identification.* Video in the series *Teaching reading: Strategies from successful classrooms.* Produced by the Center for the Study of Reading. Champaign, IL. P. 11.

Edwards, W., & von Winterfeldt, D. (1986). On cognitive illusions and their implications. In H. R. Arkes & K. R. Hammond (Eds.), *Judgment and decision making: An interdisciplinary reader* (pp. 642–679). New York: Cambridge University Press.

Ehri, L. (1998). Grapheme-phoneme knowledge is essential for learning to read words in English. In J. Metsala & L. Ehri (Eds.), *Word recognition in beginning literacy* (pp. 3–40). Mahwah, NJ: Lawrence Erlbaum Associates.

Ellis, N., & Beaton, A. (1993). Psycholinguistic determinants of foreign language vocabulary learning. *Language Learning, 43*, 559–617.

Eskey, D. (1979). A model program for teaching advanced reading to students of English as a foreign language. In R. Mackay, B. Barkman, & R. Jordan (Eds.), *Reading in a second language: Hypotheses, organization, and practice* (pp. 66–78). Rowley, MA: Newbury House.

Eskey, D. (1988). Holding in the bottom: An interactive approach to the language problems of second language readers. In P. Carrell, J. Devine, & D. Eskey (Eds.), *Interactive approaches to second language reading* (pp. 93–100). Cambridge, England: Cambridge University Press.

Fowler, A. E., & Liberman, I. Y. (1995). The role of phonology and orthography in morphological awareness. In L. Feldman (Ed.), *Morphological aspects of language processing* (pp. 157–188). Hillsdale, NJ: Lawrence Erlbaum Associates.

Freeman, D., & Freeman, Y. (1999). The California Reading Initiative: A formula for failure for bilingual students. *Language Arts, 76*(3), 241–248.

Garnham, A., Oakhill, J., Ehrlich, M., & Carreiras, M. (1995). Representations and processes in the interpretation of pronouns: New evidence from Spanish and French. *Journal of Memory and Language, 34,* 41–62.

Gaskill, W. (1979). The teaching of intermediate reading in the ESL classroom. In M. Celce-Murcia & L. McIntosh (Eds.), *Teaching English as a second or foreign language* (pp. 144–154). Rowley, MA: Newbury House.

Gaskins, I. (1997). Teaching the delayed reader: The Benchmark School model. In J. Flood, S. B. Heath, & D. Lapp (Eds.), *Handbook of research on teaching literacy through the communicative and visual arts* (pp. 657–677). A project of the International Reading Association. New York: Macmillan.

Gathercole, S. E., Willis, C., Emslie, H., & Baddeley, A. D. (1991). The influences of number of syllables and wordlikeness on children's repetition of nonwords. *Applied Psycholinguistics, 12,* 349–367.

Geva, E. (1999). Issues in the development of second language reading: Implications for instruction and assessment. In T. Nunes (Ed.), *Learning to read: An integrated view from research and practice* (pp. 343–367). Dordrecht, The Netherlands: Kluwer.

Goerwitz, R. (1996). The Jewish scripts. In P. Daniels & W. Bright (Eds.), *The world's writing systems* (pp. 487–498). New York: Oxford University Press.

Goodman, K. S. (1967). Reading: A psycholinguistic guessing game. *Journal of the Reading Specialist, 6,* 126–35.

Goodman, K. (Ed.). (1968). *The psycholinguistic nature of the reading process.* Detroit, MI: Wayne State University Press.

Goodman, K. (1973). On the psycholinguistic method of teaching reading. In F. Smith (Ed.), *Psycholinguistics and reading* (pp. 158–176). New York: Holt, Rinehart, and Winston.

Goswami, U. (1998). The role of analogies in the development of word recognition. In J. Metsala & L. Ehri, (Eds.), *Word recognition in beginning literacy* (pp. 41–63). Mahwah, NJ: Lawrence Erlbaum Associates.

Groff, P., & Seymour, D. (1987). *Word recognition: The why and how.* Springfield, IL: Thomas.

Gunning, T. (1988). *Teaching phonics and other word attack skills.* Springfield, IL: Thomas.

Hatch, E. (1979). Reading a second language. In M. Celce-Murcia, & L. McIntosh (Eds.), *Teaching English as a second or foreign language* (pp. 129–134). Rowley, MA: Newbury House.

Henderson, L. (1982). *Orthography and word recognition in reading.* London: Academic.

Henderson, L. (1984). Writing systems and reading processes. In L. Henderson (Ed.), *Orthographies and reading: Perspectives from cognitive psychology, neuropsychology and linguistics* (pp.11–24). Hillsdale, NJ: Lawrence Erlbaum Associates.

Jarvella, R. J., Job, R., Sandstrom, G., & Schreuder, R. (1987). Morphological constraints on word recognition. In A. Allport, D. G. Mackay, W. Prinz, & E. Scheerer (Eds.), *Language perception and production: Relationships between listening, speaking, reading, and writing* (pp. 245–265). London: Academic Press.

Kanda, Shunho. (2000, September 24). "Universities." *The Yomiuri Weekly, 59*(41), 37.

Kang, H., & Simpson. G. (1996). Development of semantic and phonological priming in a shallow orthography. *Developmental Psychology, 32,* 860–866.

King, R. (1996). Korean writing. In P. Daniels & W. Bright (Eds.), *The world's writing systems* (pp. 218–227). New York: Oxford University Press.

Koda, K. (1993). Transferred L1 strategies and L2 syntactic structure in L2 sentence comprehension. *Modern Language Journal, 77,* 490–500.

Koda, K. (1995). Cognitive consequences of L1 and L2 orthographies. In I. Taylor & D. Olson (Eds.), *Scripts and literacy* (pp. 311–326). Dordrecht, The Netherlands: Kluwer.

Lennon, P. (1996). Getting "easy" verbs wrong at the advanced level. *IRAL, 34,* 23–36.

Leong, C., & Tamaoka, K. (1995). Use of phonological information in processing kanji and katakana by skilled and less skilled Japanese readers. *Reading and Writing, 7,* 377–393.

Levin, I., Ravid, D., & Rapaport, S. (1999). Developing morphological awareness. In T. Nunes (Ed.), *Learning to read: An integrated view from research and practice* (pp. 77–105). Dordrecht, The Netherlands: Kluwer.

Lewis, M. (1993). *The lexical approach: The state of ELT and a way forward.* Hove, UK: Language Teaching Publications.

Lewis, M. (1997). *Implementing the lexical approach: Putting theory into practice.* Hove, UK: Language Teaching Publications.

Logan, R. K. (1986). *The alphabet effect: The impact of the phonetic alphabet on the evelopment of western civilization.* New York: William Morrow.

Lukatela, G., Gligorijevic, B., Kostic, A., & Turvey, M. (1980). Representation of inflected nouns in the internal lexicon. *Memory and Language, 8,* 415–423.

Mair, V. (1996) Modern Chinese writing. In P. Daniels & W. Bright (Eds.), *The world's writing systems* (pp. 200–208). New York: Oxford University Press.

Meara, P. (1983). Word associations in a foreign language. *Nottingham Linguistic Circular, 11,* 29–38.

Medsker, L., & Liebowitz, J. (1994). *Design and development of expert systems and neural networks.* New York: Macmillan.

Merritt, R. (1999). Technology: Introduction. *Encarta 99 Encyclopedia,* CD-ROM.

Millward, C. M. (1996). *A biography of the English language.* Fort Worth, TX: Harcourt Brace.

Moats, L. (1995). The missing foundation in teacher education. *American Educator, 19*(2), 43–51.

Morais, J., Cary, L., Alegria, J., & Bertelson, P. (1979). Does awareness of speech as a sequence of phonemes arise spontaneously? *Cognition, 7,* 323–331.

Morton, J., & Sasanuma, S. (1984). Lexical access in Japanese. In L. Henderson (Ed.), *Orthographies and reading: Perspectives from cognitive psychology, neuropsychology and linguistics* (pp. 25–42). Hillsdale, NJ: Lawrence Erlbaum Associates.

Muljani, D., Koda, K., & Moates, D. (1998). The development of word recognition in a second language. *Applied Psycholinguistics, 19,* 99–113.

Naeslund, J. C., & Schneider, W. (1996). Kindergarten letter knowledge, phonological skills, and memory processes: Relative effects on early literacy. *Journal of Experimental Child Psychology, 62,* 30–59.

Nakada, T., Fujii, Y., & Kwee, I. (2001) Brain strategies for reading in the second language are determined by the first language. *Neuroscience Research, 40*(4), 351–358.

Napoli, D. (1996). *Linguistics: An introduction.* New York: Oxford University Press.

Narayana, S. and Xiong, J. (2003) Reading treatment helps children with dyslexia and changes activity in language areas of the brain. *Neurology, 61,* E5–E6.

Nunes, T. (1999). *Learning to read: An integrated view from research and practice.* Dordrecht, The Netherlands: Kluwer.

Oney, B., Peters, M., & Katz, L. (1997). Phonological processing in printed word recognition: Effects of age and writing system. *Scientific Studies of Reading, 1,* 65–83.

Osburne, A., & Mulling, S. (1998). Vocabulary recognition in Spanish-speaking learners of English as a second language. In A. Osburne & S. Mulling (Eds.), *Writing together: A project for team research* (pp. 12–28). Ann Arbor: University of Michigan Press.

Osburne, A., & Mulling, S. (2001). Use of morphological analysis by Spanish L1 ESOL learners. *International Review of Applied Linguistics, 39,* 153–159.

Oz, A. (1989). *Knowing a woman* (in Hebrew). Jerusalem: Keter.

Papagno, C., & Vallar, G. (1992). Phonological short-term memory and the learninbg of novel words: The effects of phonological similarity and item length. *Quarterly Journal of Experimental Psychology, 44,* 47–67.

Park, K. (1998). *Kwangsoo's thoughts* (in Korean, p. 94). Seoul, Korea: Sodam.

Paulesu, E., McCrory, E., Fazio, F., Menoncello, L., Brunswick, N., Cappa, S., Cotelli, M., Cossu, G., Corte, F., Lorusso, M., Pesenti, S., Gallagher, A, Perani, D., Price, C., Frith, C., & Frith, U. (2000) A cultural effect on brain function. *Nature Neuroscience, 3*(1), 91–96.

Perfetti, C. Liu, Y., & Tan. L. (2002) How the mind can meet the brain in reading: A comparative writing systems approach. In H. S. R. Kao, C.-K.

Leong, & D.-G. Gao (Eds.), *Cognitive neuroscience studies of the Chinese language* (pp. 36–60). Hong Kong: University Press.

Rachlin, H. (1989). *Judgment, decision, and choice: A cognitive/behavioral synthesis.* New York: Freeman.

Ryan, A., & Meara, P. (1991). The case of the invisible vowels: Arabic speakers reading English words. *Reading in a Foreign Language, 7,* 531–540.

Saito, S. (1995). Effects of pronounceability and articulatory suppression on phonological learning. *Perceptual and Motor Skills, 81,* 651–657.

Sakuma, N., Sasanuma, S., Tatsumi, I., & Masaki, S. (1998). Orthography and phonology in reading Japanese kanji words. *Memory and Cognition, 26,* 75–87.

Sasanuma, S. (1984). Can surface dyslexia occur in Japanese? In L. Henderson (Ed.), *Orthographies and reading: Perspectives from cognitive psychology, neuropsychology, and linguistics* (pp. 43–56). Hillsdale, NJ: Lawrence Erlbaum Associates.

Schmitt, N., & Meara, P. (1997). Researching vocabulary through a word knowledge framework. *Studies in Second Language Acquisition, 19,* 17–36.

Schreuder, R., & Baayen, R. (1995). Modeling morphological processing. In L. Feldman (Ed.), *Morphological aspects of language processing* (pp. 131–154). Hillsdale, NJ: Lawrence Erlbaum Associates.

Schreuder, R., Grendel, M., Poulisse, N., Roelofs, A., & van de Voort, M. (1990). Lexical processing, morphological complexity and reading. In D. A. Balota, B. Flores d'Arcais, & K. Rayner (Eds.), *Comprehension processes in reading* (pp. 125–142). Hillsdale, NJ: Lawrence Erlbaum Associates.

Seidenberg, M. (1990). Lexical access: Another theoretical soupstone? In D. Balota, G. Flores D'Arcais, & K. Rayner (Eds.), *Comprehension processes in reading* (pp. 33–71). Hillsdale, NJ: Lawrence Erlbaum Associates.

Service, E., & Kohonen, V. (1995). Is the relation between phonological memory and foreign language learning accounted for by vocabulary acquisition? *Applied Psycholinguistics, 16,* 155–172.

Seymour, P. (1997). Foundations of orthographic development. In C. Perfetti, L. Reiben, & M. Fayol (Eds.), *Learning to spell: Research, theory, and practice across languages* (pp. 319–337). Mahwah, NJ: Lawrence Erlbaum Associates.

Shimron, J., & Sivan, T. (1994). Reading proficiency and orthography: Evidence from Hebrew and English. *Language Learning, 44,* 5–27.

Simos, P., Fletcher, J., Bergman, E, Breier, J, Foorman, B., Castillo, E., Davis, R., Fitzgerald, M., Papanicolaou, A. (2002). Dyslexia-specific brain activation profile becomes normal following successful remedial training. *Neurology, 58*(8), 1203–1213.

Singleton, D. (1997). Learning and processing L2 vocabulary. *Language Teaching, 30,* 213–225.

Siok, T., Zhen, J., Fletcher, P. and Tan, L., (2003) Distinct brain regions associated with syllable and phoneme. *Human Brain Mapping, 18,* 201–207.

Smith, F. (1971). *Understanding reading: A psycholinguistic analysis of reading and learning to read.* New York: Holt, Rinehart & Winston.

Smith, J. (1996). Japanese writing. In P. Daniels & W. Bright (Eds.), *The world's writing systems* (pp. 209–217). New York: Oxford University Press.

Stanovich, K. (1991). Changing models of reading and reading acquisition. In L. Reiben & C. A. Perfetti (Eds.), *Learning to read: Basic research and its implications* (pp. 19–31). Hillsdale, NJ: Lawrence Erlbaum Associates.

Taft, M., & Zhu, X. (1995). The representation of bound morphemes in the lexicon: A Chinese study. In L. Feldman (Ed.), *Morphological aspects of language processing* (pp. 293–316). Hillsdale, NJ: Lawrence Erlbaum Associates.

Tan, L., Liu, H., Perfetti, C., Spinks, J. Fox, P. Gao, J., (2001) The neural system underlying Chinese logograph reading. *NeuroImage, 13,* 836–846.

Tan, L., Spinks, J., Feng, C., Siok, W., Perfetti, C., Xiong, J., Fox, P., Gao, J., (2003) Neural Systems of second language reading are shaped by native language. *Human Brain Mapping, 3,* 158–166.

Taylor, I., & Olson, D. (1995). An introduction to reading the world's scripts. In I. Taylor & D. Olson (Eds.), *Scripts and literacy* (pp.). Dordrecht, The Netherlands: Kluwer.

Taylor, I., & Taylor, M. M. (1983). *The psychology of reading.* New York: Academic.

Tierney, R. J., & Readence, J. (2000). *Reading strategies and practices.* Boston: Allyn & Bacon.

Treiman, R. (1992). The role of intrasyllabic units in learning to read and spell. In P. B. Gough, L. C. Ehri, & R. Treiman (Eds.), *Reading acquisition* (pp. 65–106). Hillsdale, NJ: Lawrence Erlbaum Associates.

Tseng, O., & Hung, D. (1981). Linguistic determinism: A written language perspective. In O. Tseng & H. Singer (Eds.), *Perception of print: Reading research in experimental psychology* (pp. 237–255). Hillsdale, NJ: Lawrence Erlbaum Associates.

Tyler, A., & Nagy, W. (1990). Use of derivational morphology during reading. *Cognition, 36,* 17–34.

Underwood, G., & Batt, V. (1996). *Reading and understanding.* Cambridge, MA: Blackwell.

Urquhart, S., & Weir, C. (1998). *Reading in a second language.* London: Longman.

Venezky, R. (1970). *The structure of English orthography.* The Hague, Netherlands: Mouton.

Walker, L. J. (1983). Word identification strategies in reading in a foreign language. *Foreign Language Annals, 16,* 293–229.

Wallace, C. (1992). *Reading.* Oxford, England: Oxford University Press.

Wang, W. (1973). The Chinese language. *Scientific American, 228,* 55–56.

Weaver, C. (1994). *Reading process and practice.* Portsmouth, NH: Heinemann.

Ying, H. (1996). Multiple constraints on processing ambiguous sentences: Evidence from adult L2 learners. *Language Learning, 46*, 681–711.

Author Index

229

Subject Index